# India's Tryst with Democracy

## About the Editor

Dr. Shashikant Pandey is Associate Professor in the Department of Political Science, Babasaheb Bhimrao Ambedkar University, Lucknow. Having obtained, B.A., M.A. (Gold Medal) Ph.D. degree from Banaras Hindu University, Dr. Pandey has. taught at various institutions. He has published book and several research articles in various reputed journals.

He has participated in various national and International conferences and presented papers. He has actively participate in public discussions and given inputs to reputed international newspaper such as Wall Street Journal. Besides that, he is life- time member of All India Political Science Association, Mid-West Political Science Association, USA.

Currently, he is working on a joint collaborative project with Stockholm University, Sweden. His area of interest is Indian Politics, Democracy and Human Rights etc.

# India's Tryst with Democracy
## Changing Contours of Politics, Economy and Society

*Edited by*
**Shashikant Pandey**

CONCEPT PUBLISHING COMPANY PVT. LTD.
NEW DELHI-110059

**ISBN-13: 978-93-5125-268-9**

First Published 2017

*Published and Printed by*

Concept
Since 1974

**Concept Publishing Company Pvt. Ltd.**
**Regd. Office:**
A/15-16, Commercial Block, Mohan Garden,
New Delhi-110059 (INDIA)
*Phones* : 25351460, 25351794, *Fax* : 091-11-25357109
*Email* : publishing@conceptpub.com
*Website*: www.conceptpub.com

**Editorial Office:** H-13, Bali Nagar, New Delhi-110 015, India.

Cataloging in Publication Data--DK Courtesy: D.K. Agencies (P) Ltd. <docinfo@dkagencies.com>

**India's tryst with democracy** : changing contours of politics, economy and society / edited by Shashikant Pandey.
pages cm
Includes bibliographical references and index.
ISBN 9789351252689

1. India--Politics and government. 2. India--Economic conditions. 3. India--Social conditions. 4. Democracy--India. I. Pandey, Shashikant, editor.

DS445.I53 2017 DDC 320.954 23

Dedicated to my Late Grandfather
Shri J.P. Pandey

# Preface

There are legions of work available on Indian democracy. However, the vast canvas and complexities of Indian democracy provides scope to revisit it from various perspectives. This work tends to understand and explain Indian democracy from different dimensions and perspectives.

The purpose of writing this book is to explore the new challenges that have cropped up before Indian Polity especially in the post-liberalized period. It has dealt with the period when the most tectonic shifts have taken place in Indian politics. It has tried to look into Indian democracy through different perspectives and dealt with some less explored subject. Along with this, the reason for writing this edited volume was my familiarity with the subject as I have been teaching Indian Politics for the last 16 years. My close interaction with students, scholars who have contributed in this area tempted me to take up this project.

The book is divided into four parts and has been presented thematically. I hope, it would make a small contribution in exploring more about Indian democracy.

#### Acknowledgements

The idea to bring out this volume was conceived while teaching Indian Politics to Post-Graduate students at B.B. Ambedkar University. Indian politics as well as Indian democracy is one such subject on which some great scholarly works are available, and a lot is being written. Nevertheless, there is plenty of scope for others to contribute. In the present volume, an effort has been made to peep into some less explored and contemporary issues along with some old and debatable issues of Indian democracy. In this pursuit, I have been immensely benefitted by cooperation extended by various institutions, organizations as well as friends and relatives. First of all, I would like to thank the Vice-Chancellor of my University Professor R.C. Sobti for extending financial help to conduct a seminar on the theme of the proposed volume. I would also like to thank the ICSSR, New Delhi for being generous enough to help financially in conducting the seminar. Even though, the book was planned much earlier but some of the contributions are from the participants of the seminar. At the BBAU, I was immensely benefitted by the comments and suggestions of my colleagues Professor Sartik Bagh and Dr. Siddhartha Mukerji who not only contributed articles for this volume but also constantly motivated me to go ahead with this project. Dr. Siddhartha Mukerji needs special mention as he helped me in this endeavour right from conceptualizing to giving it final shape. I am also thankful to Dr. Sudhir Kumar from Jawaharlal Nehru University for extending support in giving nice shape to this book. I would also like to extend my gratitude to my friends, relatives and colleagues for their support and guidance such as Ashwani Upadhyay, Umesh Upadhyay, Ashish Dutt Pandey, Anupama Kaushik, Chandramohan

Upadhyay, Vishwanath Mishra, Santwana Pandey, Dr. S.K. Pandey, Sanjeev Joshi, Dr. Viveka Pandey etc. Many senior faculties such as Professor R.R. Jha, Professor R.K. Mishra, Professor I.D. Mishra, Professor Jagpal Singh, and Professor Pampa Mukherjee extended cooperation in different capacities. I would also like to thank my students who opted for a course on Indian politics and engaged with productive discussion both inside and outside the classroom. My students especially Ranjana Upadhyay and Rambachan Kumar also helped me in this endeavour without whose cooperation this project would not have seen the light of the day.

Finally, the support of my family has been indispensable. I would like to take this opportunity to dedicate this work to my mother and father for making me what I am today. I thank my sisters, brother and the extended family for their moral support and words of encouragement. I will be failing in my responsibility if I do not acknowledge the unflinching and loving support of my wife Dr. Tripti Pandey and children—Priyanshu and Srijan for being a constant source of support and strength.

I also feel honoured and privileged that this work was accepted by Concept Publishing Company Pvt. Ltd. They also extended superb editorial guidance and comments and helped in giving this volume a beautiful shape.

**Dr. Shashikant Pandey**
Associate Professor
Department of Political Science
B.B. Ambedkar University
Lucknow, U.P.

# Contents

## SECTION II
## Question of Rights and Conflicts

## SECTION III
## Politics and Civil Society

## SECTION IV
## Current Economic Pathways and Its Socio-Political Implications

# List of Tables and Figure

## LIST OF TABLES



## LIST OF FIGURE

# Contributor's List

**Dr. Amit Kumar Singh**, Assistant Professor, Department of Political Science, R.S.M. College, Dhampur.

**Dr. Henrik Berglund,** Associate Professor, Department of Political Science, University of Stockholm, (Uppsala University), Swedan.

**Prof. Madhurendra Kumar**, Professor, Department of Political Science, Kumaun University, Nainital.

**Prof. Ravindra K.S. Choudhary**, Assistant Professor, University Department of Philosophy, Vinoba Bhave University, Hazaribag-825301, Jharkhand, India.

**Dr. Roshni Sengupta**, Assistant Professor, Department of Political Science, Amity School of Performing Arts, Amity University, Maneshar, Gurgaon; Post-Doctoral Fellow, Leiden, Netherland.

**Prof. Sanjay Gupta**, Professor, Department of Political Science, Lucknow University, Lucknow.

**Dr. Sarabjeet Kaur,** Associate Professor, University Institute of Legal Studies, Punjab University, Chandigarh.

**Prof. Shashikant Pandey,** Associate Professor, Department of Political Science, B.B. Ambedkar (Central) University, Lucknow.

**Dr. Siddhartha Mukerji,** Assistant Professor, Department of Political Science, B.B. Ambedkar (Central) University, Lucknow.

**Sophia Helander,** Research Scholar, Department of Political Science, University of Stockholm, (Uppsala University) Sweden.

**Dr. Sudhir Kumar**, Assistant Professor, Centre for Political Studies, Jawaharlal Nehru University (JNU), New Delhi.

**Prof. Surendra Meher**, Assistant Professor, Department of Economics, B.B. Ambedkar (Central) University, Lucknow.

**Prof. Swarnamayee Tripathy,** Professor and Head, Department of Political Science, Utkal University, Orissa.

# 1
# Introduction

Democracy is globally accepted as an ideal form of government. It entails freedom and provides channels of dissent that makes it people-centric as compared to other forms of government. However, the present contour of democracy is the by-product of the long evolutionary process. Initially, it was Greek—probably the Athenians—who coined the term democracy, or demokratia, from the Greek words demos, the people, and Kratos, to rule. It signified "Rule of the People" (Dahl 2001:1) where ultimate authority rests with the people and Athens was considered as the cradle of democracy. However, many Greek philosophers were highly critical of Athenian democracy particularly from the humanist perspective as it excluded women, foreigners and slaves from the decision-making process that goes against the very fundamentals of democracy. Even Plato and Aristotle were highly critical of democracy. Plato believed that people in a democracy are not qualified enough to select rulers, and, therefore, they may elect incompetent leaders who may ruin the state. Similarly, Aristotle identified democracy with the rule of the many especially the rule of the mediocre who are guided more by their selfish interest than the interest of the state.

Therefore, initially, democracy was not interpreted in a positive sense, and it was considered more as a mobocracy. The protest, demonstration throughout the world paved the way for democracy. Prior to that, it was restricted democracy in the sense that voting rights as well as rights to get elected were confined to wealthy propertied and educated class only. Liberal intellectuals who endorsed this view were of the opinion that power cannot be transferred to the illiterate masses, and they have to be trained first in democracy before being given the right to vote. Therefore, right to vote to women, working class was given after long, protracted struggle. Democracy witnessed an unprecedented upsurge in last half of the twentieth century as other alternatives faded into oblivion. The reason for its popularity lies in the fact that it allows dissent and opposition that is suppressed in authoritarian regimes. Unlike authoritarian regimes, it accepts opposition as reasonable and legitimate which makes it quite attractive and helps in its expansion and acceptance across the globe.

In recent years, particularly after the collapse of the Soviet Union, the world is witnessing globalization of democracy. The reason for growing acceptance of democracy across the globe is the fact that it is the only form of government which believes in involving ordinary citizenry in governance process, at least theoretically, and treats them as stakeholders in the process of governance. It also provides them a platform to raise their voice in case of non-fulfilment of their demands by the state. It can also be credited for raising people's expectations by constitutionally mandating them to express their dissent peacefully. In other forms of government, leaders feel accountable to either select group of individuals or may not feel so. In a democracy, leaders have to communicate with the electorate on a routine basis to remain in contestation. These factors are primarily responsible for universalizing democracy as a form of government.

However, despite its growing acceptability, the gap between theory and practice puts a question mark on the success of democracy as a form of government. Therefore, the countries that are called successful democracies are those who have bridged this gap. In many democracies, it has been observed that democracy and democratic institutions are not allowed to function effectively by the elite and dominant caste/class and subaltern groups still feel alienated and marginalized. Therefore, the pace of social transformation is quite slow, and marginalized groups within these societies find it difficult to have a decisive presence in the governance process. If the working of democracy across the globe is summarized, one thing is obvious that marginalized groups (Caste, Class, and Race) across the world still feel excluded.

Nevertheless, there is a ray of hope in democracy. It provides them scope to unite and struggle against tyrannical practices and bring about social transformation. Unlike authoritarian regimes, their voices are not ruthlessly suppressed which opens the window of opportunity to marginalized groups to exert pressure on the ruling dispensation to pay heed to their genuine grievances. In case, they fail to deliver they are voted out of power by them. However, it has been observed that when ordinary citizens agitate, unite and confront the state, some of them are either co-opted or given political space. Those who do not find space resort to non-democratic practices as they challenge the might of the state as it was witnessed in Singur, Nandigram, Naxal violence, etc. It has been observed that when popular resistance defies the co-option-concession model, the state resorts to violent means, and people make a call for rebellion that is their fundamental democratic right. Rebellion is not against democracy *per se*; rather it is aimed at the state that has usurped power and has become unjust (Mukherjee 2009).

Paradoxically, the countries that opted for democracy after a long colonial past have on the one hand raised the expectations of their citizens and, on the other hand, failed to fulfil the burgeoning demands of their citizens. Several reasons may be associated with this: their inexperience with democracy, corrupt and irresponsive bureaucracy, military intervention in civil affairs, and vested interest of groups who held sway during colonial regimes along with mass illiteracy, economic underdevelopment, rampant poverty, ethnic conflict and so on.

The newly decolonized states may also be categorized as those who opted for democracy in post-colonized phase and remained democratic and others who opted for democracy but still struggling to become full-fledged democracies. One important reason for the failure of democracy in these countries had been that they had no time to prepare their societies for modern democratic institutions. The sudden introduction of democracies and modern state and its associated institutions did not augur well for these societies and countries as they were not trained to handle democracies. It gave birth to a conflicting situation of traditional society and modern state. The states that failed to cope up with this situation slipped into the authoritarian mode.

## Different Pathways to Democracy

Western Scholars have had a different interpretation of democracy as the path of modernization and development differs between West and post-colonial societies. Western countries that are considered the paragon of democracy have established democracy in a phased manner. Initially, their focus was not on democratization but industrialization. They completed the industrialization process by forcefully evicting farmers from their land. Their focus was more upon bringing about economic development first, and political freedom was granted much later especially the voting rights to women, uneducated and labour class. In India, unlike western countries, industrialization was not possible to bring about with violent means as representative institutions albeit on a limited scale were already there. The dominant and powerful class has not been able to dictate its terms so far as bringing about industrialization is concerned, and protest against land acquisition was common.[1] Therefore, industrialization, as well as democracy, has had different contours in India.

Apart from that, western societies were homogenous, and level of poverty and inequality was not as rampant as it is prevalent in many third world countries. They neither experienced colonization that ruined the economy of third world countries. Then, they have also not experienced problems associated with the diverse and plural character of these societies. Therefore, many scholars argue that Western interpretation of democracy cannot be applied to newly decolonized states, and they have to devise their mechanism that is best suited to address the problems associated with their societies. Explaining Indian position, Bardhan writes that in India, unlike much of the western world, democracy is reconciled with multiple layers of nationality, where a pan-Indian nationalism coexists with assertive regional nationalism in the same citizenry (Bardhan, 2010). Therefore, their pathways to democracy are bound to differ.

Therefore, if we compare western and post-colonial countries, their pathways to democratization is different. For example, when India attained Independence, the primary challenge was its nature of diversity as multiple identities were at play, and its diversity was also of a different kind, ridden with conflict. Therefore, different yardsticks have to be applied while comparing western and non-western democracies.

Contemporary period is witnessing a phenomenal growth in academic writings on Indian democracy. India, from the very beginning, has been an enigma for those who held a stereotypical view of democracy. It is partly because the concept of democracy has its origin in the West and, therefore, Western scholars tried to interpret it through western perspective. They hurriedly drew a conclusion that India is a deviant democracy as it has not lived up to the scripted

Western version of democracy (McMillan, Alistair, 2008:733-749). In the last few decades, many Indian scholars either based in India or abroad have written extensively on various facets of Indian democracy. They have also made efforts to convincingly argue that despite its demerits, Indian democracy is a model in itself and not a replica of the Western variant of democracy. Without going into merits and demerits of two contrasting positions, it can be argued that despite its inherent contradictions and weaknesses, India is successfully operating as a democracy and democracy has got institutionalized in this country.

Being a newly born democracy, it is still at a nascent stage and therefore passing through a transitory phase. Parallel forces are also working simultaneously to disrupt the democratization process in the form of communalism, casteism, secessionism, terrorism, etc. It has somewhat slackened the pace of democratization but has not dampened the spirit and faith of ordinary people in the democracy. Over a period, progress is visible in some critical areas, and economic growth has also taken place. However, simultaneously a contrast between India's economic growth and poverty is also apparent where limited broad-based social progress can be observed along with the fast-growing economy. It clearly reflects a lack of coherent and well-thought out policies. For example, the welfare programmes for poverty alleviation like redistributing land to the landless, providing good education and health to the poor and creating employment opportunities have largely been ineffective. It has happened despite massive financial allocation to address rural unemployment, primary education, and health. It has largely occurred due to the absence of a real commitment among state elites, poor implementation of welfare policies, weak monitoring, poor quality peripheral bureaucracy, and powerful vested interests who have often opposed or subverted such efforts (Kohli 2007: 1-44). What adds to the woes is the casual and lackluster attitude of political parties as well as political leadership in addressing issues that are related to governance. Therefore, the primary challenge being confronted by the state like poverty, inequality, uneven and lopsided development, corruption gets sidelined and hardly becomes an all-India issue. In other words, governance rarely becomes a national issue, and political parties deliberately play emotional card and never try to mobilize public opinion on developmental issues. However, the situation has changed in recent years. Development and governance that never had a decisive presence in electoral politics in India has occupied the preeminent position. In many States, State Chief Ministers had completed three consecutive terms such as Delhi, Gujarat, Chhattisgarh and Madhya Pradesh. It happened largely because they governed well and lived up to the people's expectation. The recent Delhi Assembly election can be defined as an eye opener as it was fought and won on issues that were concerned with ordinary people and people voted on the ground of governance. The similar trend can be observed during 14th Lok Sabha election as well where leaders deliberately focussed on the governance issues. William Dalrymple, an eminent historian while referring to Narendra Modi pointed it out.

> "On the campaign trail, whether from pragmatism or otherwise, Modi has largely kept his Hindu nationalism hidden and presented himself throughout as an able, technocratic administrator who can turn the country's economy around and stimulate much-needed development."[2]

Therefore, we are witnessing that discourse of democracy is changing in India. It no longer remains the pocket-borough of tiny elites who used to mobilize people around sentimental subjects without acknowledging and addressing their genuine grievances.

Even during 60s and 70s, political leaders like Mrs. Indira Gandhi made tall promises and had developmental agenda. However, most of them had populist agenda behind it and hardly had any blueprint as to how to bring about development. People during that phase of Indian politics were less politically mature and they were misled by rhetorical politics. However, at present, we have politically conscious electorate that cannot be deceived by mere rhetoric's unless they find concretization of such policies at the ground level. People have voted for Modi during 14th Lok Sabha election because he had delivered and produced concrete results in Gujarat. Although, it would be premature to arrive at any hasty conclusion, but development and governance is fast occupying centre stage that is a good sign for Indian democracy.

It does not mean however that mobilization and movement to root out socio-political ills have not erupted in the past or at present. However, barring few big movements like J.P. movement, V.P. Singh's anti-corruption crusade and recently Anna Hazare's fast to introduce Jan Lokpal, none other movement, and civil society activism has had a lasting impact as to change the course of the Indian polity. It is simply because barring few, most of the civil society groups have not been able to establish their credibility among masses. Civil society can bring about transformation in democracy if their energy is channelized properly, and political class develops trust on them which may lead to state-civil society partnership. However, in case of India, it remains a dream. It makes the job of political parties and politician's lot easier as people do not get united around fundamental issues of development as there is no agency to mobilize them which is aloof from power politics. It adversely affects the poorer class as they do not have the wherewithal to survive on their own in the absence of state assistance. Due to this despite having strong Constitutional as well as the legal support system, we have not been able to bring those on the periphery like Dalits, Adivasis, Women and minorities to the centre stage. They still constitute the most vulnerable segment of our population as they lag behind others in terms of reaping the fruits of development. Affirmative action policies have restored a certain sense of pride and dignity among the deprived groups, especially Dalits. It has worked like a propelling factor for them, but that is not enough to call Indian society an equal society (Varshney 2013: 64-95).

Similarly, in case of women, though legal as well as Constitutional mechanisms are there but they are either not stringent, or they are not implemented properly which has led to increasing crime against women. Recent data released by National Crime Record Bureau suggest that crime against women has increased between 2008-2012.[3] It raises the question of women safety in Indian democracy. For example, how much Indian democracy is successful in protecting the rights and dignity of women if they face the brunt of sexual abuse and patriarchal prejudices in everyday life? Nowadays, many movements are led by women like Medha Patkar, Aruna Roy, Arundhati Roy, Irom Sharmila and Vandana Shiva, however; it has not brought about a substantial change at the ground level. 73rd Amendment of the Constitution has reserved one-third seat for women in Panchayats. However, studies on the ground have made the startling revelation about their silence. It was found that most of them hardly exercise their independent judgement as they act like rubber stamps. Similarly, there is no agreement among political parties regarding reservation of one-third seat for women in Parliament which may have far-reaching consequences and may change the course of Indian democracy. Similarly, Muslims too are lagging far behind others as highlighted by Justice Sacchar committee and nothing concrete has been done so far to bring them into the mainstream. The insurgency in the north-east and Maoist violence is another such issue that requires a revisiting of government policies and programmes. It also puts a question mark on the ability of Indian state to deal with home-grown extremist groups as it has not been able to devise a long-term strategy to address them. For example, the naxal problem is chronic in many states as they are getting the support of the poorer section that is mostly due to the reckless mining by corporate groups without suitably compensating the tribal population. It has been going on with the active connivance of the state.

Similarly, our land acquisition policy, forest policy, rehabilitation policy have been such that they have turned the tribal people hostile to the State. Continuous and long neglect of their genuine grievances by the state has brought the situation to an extent where it is posing a threat to the unity and integrity of the country. The above-narrated stories are somewhat interlinked to each other like utter neglect, callous, indifferent and hostile attitude of state machinery, rampant corruption, and irresponsive bureaucracy, especially at the local level. An earnest and sincere effort to co-opt them and bring them to the mainstream from the periphery is lacking.

It leads to the question whether is it because those who are at the decision-making level deliberately avoid reaching out to the common masses as they do not want to share the power and resources at their disposal with them or is it because of the multiple challenges associated with hierarchical societal set-up which inhibits the growth of democratic culture? Regarding the first contention, it can be said that even during post-independence period, key institutions such as Parliament, Bureaucracy were occupied by the upper caste/upper strata of the society. People belonging to deprived groups were poorly represented in representative bodies and even those who found space within these bodies were numerically under-represented and neither had any stronghold within their groups/communities nor the government. As political development in India suggests, initially, our Parliament was elitist in character, and it was transformed after a long-sustained effort by the marginalized groups like backward castes and *Dalits*. They organized protests and demonstrations, floated various political parties, contested and won elections and formed governments in various states that brought about a sea-change in the pattern of their representation in Parliament.

Regarding the second contention, it is well-established that Indian society has been an intensely hierarchical society and therefore even after having Democratic Constitution, society, as well as societal practices, remain firmly entrenched in primordial modes. Therefore, it reflects that even after the anvil of democracy, those who were at the helm of affairs were not willing to share power. It is to a certain extent responsible for slackening the process of democratization in India. Along with these factors, the other factors that retarded the growth of democracy were the absence of strong opposition politics in India. It may have helped Congress initially as there were no challenges to its power that helped it in strengthening democracy during Nehru period but proved disastrous later on during the regime of Mrs. Indira Gandhi. Though, opposition began to surface in the late 1960s but could not sustain itself. Therefore, in the absence of a viable and active opposition front, the ruling dispensation ruled without strong and effective opposition. Media and civil society activism was also not as much visible as it is today. So, in the absence of any check and balance, the unrestrained exercise of authority by the ruling party weakened the democratic institution.

## Indian Democracy and its Historic Trajectory

Right from the very beginning, there was a near consensus among Indian leaders about the suitability of democracy to India even though; they had a varying opinion regarding the form of democracy. They looked at anti-colonial struggle as a democratic struggle and visualized post-colonial future in terms of democratic polity. Given the circumstances, democracy was an obvious choice as its foundation was laid down during freedom struggle itself. Under the leadership of Gandhi, groups were formed to fight the external enemy that required consensus building through co-opting dissent. It was visible in the functioning of the Congress as well as it operated on consensual principles (Bardhan: 2010). In other words, seeds of democracy were shown during freedom struggle itself.

In India, if we trace the historical journey of democracy during the freedom struggle, there were divergent views amongst nationalist leadership regarding efficacy and relevance of Parliamentary democracy for India. Leaders like Mahatma Gandhi, M.N. Roy, Vinoba Bhave, Ram Manohar Lohia and Jaiprakash Narayan, despite having different ideological orientations raised apprehension regarding suitability as well as the feasibility of Parliamentary democracy for India. They were mostly concerned about the hapless and impoverished people of this country. For them, under Parliamentary democracy, political parties compete for power and power remains in the hands of the few. Ordinary people hardly have any say in the formulation as well as an execution of policies meant to them. Therefore, the fundamental objective of democracy that weakest should have the same opportunity as the strongest remains a dream. Therefore, they were in favour of decentralization of authority to empower the downtrodden at the grass root level. In fact, that was the reason that both Gandhi and Jaiprakash Narayan had an aversion to party politics. They were of the opinion that it leads to unhealthy competition among parties to win popular support, and they may indulge in unethical practices to gain the support of the people. On the contrary, people like Ambedkar and Lohia were admirers of party politics. Ambedkar was of the view that it is only through party system, the voice of the under-represented class can be represented. Finally, it was left to the Constituent Assembly to chart the future course of action, and it unanimously decided to introduce parliamentary democracy in India.

The way our freedom struggle was conceived and organized, democracy was the obvious choice. People like Tilak, Gandhi, Ambedkar mobilized people on a massive scale as they believed in the democratic technique of mass mobilization (Palshikar and Vora 2004:23-24). Various associations, organizations were formed during freedom struggle based on different ideological orientations and allowed to flourish including subaltern voices. As India attained Independence from the foreign yoke, it had a daunting task before it to manage and build the Indian nation- state. Even though, India under the stewardship of Gandhi declared that non-violence would be its guiding philosophy, violence could not be averted. Even before Independence, while meeting of Constituent Assembly was going on to work out the Constitution of Independent India, large-scale violence erupted in many parts of the country. However, it failed to deter the firm resolve of our leaders, and they never deviated from their core objective of formulating a document based on democratic values. In other words, democracy and democratic values remained the essential guiding force.

For them, national interest remained paramount as they thought that India's destiny will be best protected by engaging people with a decision-making process that is possible only in a democratic set-up. In this regard, India's freedom struggle had already set the tone, as it was by and large; a mass movement and people had shown tremendous faith in the leadership. Hence, there was a little choice before the leadership to decide the form of government as democracy was the only available option to accommodate vast diversity. For this, credit may be given to Indian leaders for their visionary outlook in the sense that instead of interpreting diversity as a handicap, they succeeded in making it as a source of strength. Again, opting for a federal form of government was also a bold decision on their part under given circumstances. Many of our neighbouring countries such as Pakistan, Sri Lanka avoided opting for a federal model that ultimately proved disastrous for them.

While discussing the historical journey of Indian democracy, it is also equally significant to explore the role played by Constitutional principles that established democratic values such as Secularism, Freedom, and Equality. For instance, Article 24-28 of the Constitution of India deals with freedom of religion in a manner that accommodate the feelings of all religious communities without being discriminatory and paved the way for a secular democracy. What makes Indian secularism distinct from Western secularism is that it emphasizes upon maintaining peace between communities that was badly required under the given circumstances. It also interpreted liberty and equality both individualistically and non-individualistically which means that it recognizes not only rights of individuals to practice and profess their religious belief but also the rights of communities to establish and administer educational institutions (Bhargava 2010:95-96). In other words, federalism, secularism and other liberal values such as liberty and equality were introduced in the Constitution of India and suitably modified as per Indian requirement.

There was skepticism both in India and in the West regarding India's democratic project. There was a lot of apprehension within the country among the tiny elite/literate class as they had doubt about the success of the democratic project as it was enfranchising the illiterates. For many, it appeared that democracy came to India prematurely and in the prevailing circumstances the modern and pre-modern would collide headlong, and the multiple identities would tear the country apart (Suri 2008). Similarly, Western scholars were also apprehensive about the success of democracy in India because of widespread poverty, illiteracy, and ethnic heterogeneity. However, all these predictions and assumptions were belied, and democracy has not only survived but has got further consolidated.

These assumptions had certain logic into it as India had neither undergone modernization process nor had a break from its traditional past. Similarly, it neither had dominant bourgeoisie nor a strong working class. It has had a strong feudal legacy, a disorganized peasantry, a rigid hierarchical societal structure, widespread poverty and illiteracy and a numerically insignificant middle class that made the success of democratic project doubtful.[4] In other words, it remained an outlier in the light of most theories of democracy. It was a *sui generis* phenomenon, a case of Indian exceptionalism (Jayal and Mehta 2010: XV). Guided by their liberal-universal values, some Western Scholars were looking for a uniform formula for the success of democracy and Indian example, for them was defying the conventional wisdom. The precondition required for the introduction of democracy like social homogeneity, literacy, and economic development were absent which are the barometer to judge whether a country is democratic or not?

India's experiment with democracy was interpreted by them in the same light. Scholars like Selig Harrison were quite apprehensive about India's chances to succeed as a democracy and warned that India's "fissiparous tendencies" particularly its linguistic differences, would soon lead to balkanization or dictatorship. While making such assessment, they were more guided by their conventional wisdom. However, India's federal system has beautifully addressed this problem and guided it as to how to accommodate diversity (Rudolph and Rudolph 2002: 52-66). It is correct to argue that India has shown the ability and courage to accommodate diversity without seriously compromising with the democratic norms; nevertheless there are many grey areas which need serious introspection.

There are several criterions to judge whether a country is democratic or undemocratic. Voter's participation in the electoral process is considered one such important parameter to evaluate democracy. Without citizen's active involvement in the electoral process, democracy will prove to be a futile exercise. Therefore, independent exercise of judgement by the voters is a must as it gives sanctity to the entire democratic process. However, the way voters are mobilized in India along identity-based issues such as caste, religion, region etc.; it puts a question mark on the sanctity of this entire exercise. Similarly, Women vote in large numbers in India but do not have independent thinking under patriarchal setup. It has also been observed that poor voters participate in the electoral process in large number, but the bulk of the benefit is cornered by the rich and the affluent class. Does that indicate democracy? These are valid questions that have emerged in recent years and needs serious introspection. Nowadays, after enactment of the 73rd Constitutional Amendment, one-third seats are reserved in panchayats for marginalized groups including women and many women have become Sarpanch also. However, it has been observed that they hardly exercise their independent choice in decision making, and most of the decisions are taken by their husbands at their behest thereby making a mockery of democracy. It has also been observed that Dalit and tribal sarpanches are not allowed to work by the dominant caste/class groups, particularly in villages. It goes against the basic principles of democracy that believe in granting free choice whereas this is a constraint on free choice.

## Institutional Response to Democracy

India has had an excellent record in institutionalizing democracy through Constitutionalism, rule of law, a free press, a vibrant civil society and through regularly held election (Hasan 2009:127), but political institutions as a whole have not performed uniformly. On the one hand, there are many institutions that have earned respect and credibility like Election Commission, Judiciary, and President but same cannot be said about Police and Political Parties (Yadav: 2011, YouTube).

For the smooth functioning of democracy, it is essential that all democratic institutions must possess a certain degree of autonomy and be allowed to function without political interference and encroachment of social forces in their respective domain. In India, it has been observed that political class has interfered in the working of political institutions to the extent of discrediting them as an independent institution that has led to institutional decay. For instance, Parliament which is democratically constituted and a well-established body for public deliberation have suffered a dramatic decline. It is not discharging its duties such as lawmaking, representing the interests of the people and exercising control over the executive. It meets for very few days, and when it meets, it is marred by disruption and bills are passed hurriedly without discussion due to the paucity of times

(Carole 2010: 238-51). Post-Independence Parliament had great debates on issues of national significance such as the Hindu Code Bills, the linguistic reorganization of the states and about the role of planning and the mixed economy (Parekh 2011). In other words, Parliament as a deliberative body has suffered a considerable decline despite having more educated parliamentarians than we used to have previously. Similarly, our policing system that is still guided by nineteenth-century norms and based on colonial pattern has lost its credibility due to political interference, lack of accountability and responsibility, etc. Reform in the policing system is a must that is nowhere visible. It still rests on archaic and colonial police laws dating back to 1861. In Prakash Singh *versus* Union of India case, Supreme Court instructed Central and State Government to lay down practical mechanism to kick-start reform.[5] Therefore, what we witness in the case of India is that even though, democracy has survived and got further deepened, it has not been able to yield the desired result.

India conducted its first general election in 1952, and as it was expected, Congress won a landslide victory and Jawaharlal Nehru was sworn-in as Prime Minister of Independent India. As initial phase in any newly independent country is very crucial and for India, which had undergone the trauma of partition, it had a daunting task ahead as to how to keep the country united amidst ever-growing challenges. Nehru played a significant role in keeping the country united. He was responsible for building modern institutions. Therefore, he is rightly bestowed with the epithet of institution builder. During his tenure as Prime Minister democratic institutions along with democratic practices found considerable space. He had this uncanny ability to accommodate regional elites by making the best use of the federal process. Along with that the relatively low level of political mobilization among masses also helped him to run the government in a desired and smooth manner. However, institutional decay began to surface in the 1970s and it has been as widespread as it became part of the political process. The previously existing code of commitments to ethics and conventions of Parliamentary democracy had given way to arbitrariness, arrogance, corruption and violence at all levels of the polity (Sharma 1994). Mrs. Indira Gandhi style of functioning discredited democracy as well as democratic institutions such as the cabinet, the Parliament, the Judiciary and the Civil Service. It is said that if institutions are made subservient to the personal ambition or ideological predilections of political leaders, democracy cannot function effectively. For the successful working of democracy, leaders must accept institutional constraints in their decision making (Varshney *op. cit.*: 59). However, during Mrs. Indira Gandhi tenure many important institutions like bureaucracy were politicized as she believed in committed bureaucracy. Over centralization of authority became a norm, and federal structure suffered a severe jolt. She crushed every opposition to her authority, and its ultimate culmination was witnessed in the form of emergency in 1975. In this process, democratic institutions suffered a severe jolt and since then many institutions have not yet recovered and their credibility remains doubtful. Police, Bureaucracy, federal arrangements felt the strain of growing politicization (Rudolph and Rudolph, 1987). During this period, the executive became all powerful and power got centralized and personalized in the hands of Prime Minister Indira Gandhi which constituted a move from a hegemonic to a dictatorial mode of governance (Pai and Kumar 2014: 11) and for the first time, one could feel that India despite having sound democratic institutions can sleep into the authoritarian mode. Mrs. Gandhi failure to accommodate burgeoning demands of the disadvantaged sections created problems of governability. Instead of institutional accommodation of rising demands, she adopted a recalcitrant stance and established a pattern of personal rule, writes Atul Kohli (1988:4).

Therefore, India witnessed a period of fractured and polarized political and institutional structures in the 1980s. The personalization and centralization of power not only diluted the political autonomy, but also reduced Congress as a shell of its former self.. Under the circumstances, while Mrs. Gandhi returned to power in the 80s, she relied heavily on populist appeals and demagogic manipulation to strengthen her support base (Sharma 1994). India witnessed a democratic upsurge in the decade of late 1970s and early 1980s that transformed the political landscape of the country. All those groups that suffered some form of social deprivation like Other Backward Classes (OBCs), Scheduled Castes, *Dalits*, tribals and minorities became part of the expanded participatory base of the Indian Politics (Yadav 2000:121-34). All this led to plebianization of the composition of the Lok Sabha during the 1990s (Shankar and Rodrigues 2011:101). As the state has failed to fulfil the promises it has made to ordinary people, the marginalized groups turned to political activism to make their presence felt. Similarly, in the last three decades, the new social movement that has emerged also influenced Indian democracy in a bigger way. The Janata party experiment proved to be disastrous as it also compromised with Democratic principles and sacked Congress—led governments in states despite having a majority in the Legislature. Although, it was not in power for a longer duration and in the 80s Congress returned to power with thumping majority. During her second stint in 1980, Mrs. Gandhi, put socialism on the backburner and focused on economic growth. Therefore, what we witnessed during 1991, its beginning was made during Indira-Rajiv era itself.

**India in the 90s**

Since, the major focus of this book is the developments in the 90s, it would be befitting to discuss the trends that merged in the 90s. The period since the start of the 90s saw a tremendous change in Indian polity. Congress suffered defeat in 1989 election that heralded an end of an era of a single party dominance and the emergence of the fragmented multiparty system. This period also marked the emergence of coalition era in Indian polity where identities based on region, caste, class and community became significant (Pai and Kumar *op. cit.* 2014 : 11).

During nineties, two interesting trends were visible. On the one hand, India witnessed liberalization and opening of the economy that led to the expansion of middle class and during the same period 73rd and 74th Amendments were introduced which can also be termed as bottom up approach which led to the decentralization of authority and empowerment of the marginalized groups. Prior to this, India also witnessed ethnic conflict at a massive level in Punjab, Assam, which is also somehow linked to the democratization process. Therefore, the decade of the 80s and 90s is a significant period as the government has to deal with many odds and it witnessed a convergence between democracy and liberalization with the rise in middle class and also empowerment of the people at the grass root level. The democratization of institutions in one way justifies the liberalization agenda so that the poor do not resist and middle class become the beneficiary.

The decade of the 1990s is also significant in more than one way as it heralded a new era in Indian politics. India witnessed a significant liberalizing trend when it began effort to integrate itself with the global economy. During this period, a centralized interventionist state was challenged by an increasingly decentralized regulatory state and market economy. On the one hand, it consolidated the state-capital alliance whereas on the other further marginalized the marginalized groups. It was also a period when one-party dominance became thing of the past, and an era of coalition politics began. The common apprehension was that India will once again enter into a period of instability, poor governance, inordinate delay in decision-making, and it will lead to further weakening of democratic institutions. Of course, some of the ills with which coalition governments are associated with were present, but it also brought about some desirable changes in the Indian polity. For the first time, states that used to be the puppet in the hands of the ruling party at the centre particularly during Congress regime began to assert themselves. The federal arrangement was at its best when regional parties became part of the national level politics. It also brought about substantial change in the position of the Governor as well. They were no longer in the position to dislodge the opposition-ruled State Governments because of the weak status of the Union Government and also because many regional parties were extending support to the coalition government. The period of the 90s also witnessed mushrooming of local parties based on caste, ethno-linguistic and other identities which led to fragmentation of party system.

Another new trend was also observed during coalition period. Institutions that were supposed to play the assigned job were failing in their responsibilities such as executive and legislature. The inaction on their part laid to activism by other institutions such as Judiciary, President, and Election Commission. Judiciary entered into the policy-making domain because of executive inaction. Therefore, a new power dynamics has emerged, and power has started shifting from representative institutions to non-representative bodies. This shift is not a good sign for democracy as in Parliamentary democracy; Parliament is the sovereign body, and ultimate authority must rest with it.

The late 1990s also witnessed the active intervention by courts, civil society groups and brought about a qualitatively different set of campaigns which appeared on the political scene of India. The demand for the right to food, the right to education, the right to health, the right to work, and the right to information brought about issues of pressing concern into the limelight. These campaigns have fetched notable results in the form of Right to Education, the Employment Guarantee Scheme, and the Right to Information Act (Chandoke 2009: 280). Now, the realization has set in that to realize the twin objectives of democracy, i.e. freedom and equality along with civil-political rights, social as well as economic rights also has to be given equal status.

## Changing Contours of Indian Democracy

Democratic institutions in India have undergone sea change over a period of time. For instance, it could be argued that extra-parliamentary institutions like the President, Judiciary, and Election Commission have become more assertive due to a decline in the responsiveness of legislature and executive. Similarly, the process of regionalization has also brought about change in centre-state relation. India's federal process has also witnessed change particularly after the Bommai case.[6] It is difficult to dislodge any State Government now. Similarly, the liberalization process has also strengthened the position of states as they are nowadays directly negotiating with foreign counties and negotiating business proposals with local and foreign investors which are a new trend. It was beyond imagination few decades ago. In a way, top-down approach is gradually getting replaced by bottom-up approach. Under the impact of liberalization, technology that was initially the preserve of elite segment has also got democratized and under pressure, it is being used more and more for the benefit of rural as well as marginalized groups. Services like e-governance have been introduced. Ministry of IT has been constituted. All this has brought about institutional changes. Along with these structural changes India also witnessed change in institutional approach towards the marginalized groups. Marginalized groups such as women, SCs and STs asserted on a massive scale that resulted into Constitution of various commissions to address their long-pending grievances. Although, by merely having such arrangements, their problems will not be over however, it may help in allowing them opportunity to seek justice through these mechanisms. Therefore, these changes are the by-products of demands by various groups that have helped in strengthening democracy.

Over a period, the shape of Indian democracy has changed drastically. It is no longer a pocket borough of a tiny elite group, but people from the marginalized groups are also making their way up to the top echelons of power (Yadav 2000:121-34). Institutions like Parliament, State legislatures are fast becoming more and more representative because of the upsurge among marginalized groups. It has also substantially changed the social composition of the political parties. Change in social composition of voters, MPs, and MLAs, as well as the government, has made the system more representative. However, the question is how far it has made the democracy representative in terms of making ordinary people a stakeholder in the decision-making process. It is a good sign that marginalized groups are getting mobilized and entering the representative system through the reservation system. On the one hand, it reflects revolutionary makeover of a polity and on the contrary plight of women, Dalits and Adivasis continue to remain dismal. For Example, Dalits and Adivasis constitute the largest number of displaced people, and they suffer multiple development induced displacement on account of mega projects, Hydro Projects, steel plants and so on. Therefore, mere mobilization and representation *per se* is not sufficient enough for sustaining democracy. It needs to reflect in policy formulation as well as policy execution. This social churning is going on for quite some time in either manifest or latent form across the country, but its effect on the ground level is yet to be seen as social development indicators suggest upward mobility among the marginalized groups, but pace is very slow. At times, it also leads to conflict as those who have been in the advantageous position are not ready to relinquish their claim as they feel they are the sole custodian of Indian democracy. It is being challenged now by the mobilized and well-informed citizenry, resurgent civil society groups, new social movements, etc. The new social movement has brought in vibrant energy that may change the course of Indian democracy. Along with that, over a period, Indian democracy has also experienced a definite change in patron-client relationship dominated by the wealthy propertied class that used to be the hallmark of Indian society.

It has also been made possible because, Indian democracy provided sufficient space to those who are on the margin to form their political outfit and contest and win the election and form their government. However, it has only partially addressed their problem as elites have emerged within the marginalized groups as well, and they are cornering bulk of the benefits meant for the poor and impoverished among them. Therefore, the concept of creamy layer emerged. However, it has not dampened the spirit and resolve of the poor people as they participate in the electoral process in large number (Jayal 2001: 33). Statistics reveals that marginalized groups vote in large number as they want to occupy political space through the democratic process that is a good sign for Indian democracy. Ashutosh Varshney in his article has also argued that India's plebeian orders have participated greater than its upper and middle classes. While further substantiating his argument, he says that so far as voting in India is concerned, it has been observed that the lower the caste, income and education of an Indian, the greater the odds that he will vote.[7] It has brought about socio-political transformation. For example, if we look at the composition of parliament it has altered considerably as it is no longer the preserve of wealthy elite class.

Politics in India has undergone a complete metamorphosis in the 1990s as many developments took place in the social, economic and political field that has had a bearing on the polity. For instance, OBC reservation, unlocking and dismantling of Babri Mosque, liberalization of economy and arrival of coalition politics, civil society activism etc. brought about a sea change in the nature and character of Indian polity. New alignments and realignments emerged both at social and political level. India has witnessed tremendous change over a period that reflects certain trends. For example, democracy has gained salience and has been able to strike a cord with the masses and provided those sufficient space that is indicative of participatory democracy.

With the onset of a coalition government and mushrooming of regional parties, states have occupied a pivotal position in India's federal polity. The trend which used to prevail that policies were framed at the top level and were being implemented at the state level are being questioned particularly by regional parties which puts a break on the centralizing tendency of the Union. After the anvil of coalition-era, the interventionist institution such as Cabinet and Parliament have waned in significance whereas regulatory institutions such as Supreme Court, President and Election Commission have occupied the pre-eminent position.

The next change that is being observed is in the economic field particularly after the opening of the economy wherein gradual retreat of the social welfare state, decrease in subsidies, increasing shrinkage on public expenditure and opening up the social and economic space for the market forces is being witnessed. However, as Rudolphs (2002) argue, despite all the changes after economic liberalization, the Central Government still acts as a regulator and is not fading away. The only thing is that its role has reversed from intervener to the regulator (*ibid.,* : 52-66). It means India has charted its course and never thought of withdrawing from its social-welfare responsibility.

There are some other marked changes as well as we witness the flow of power and authority from the upper castes to lower castes that have completely changed the social base of political parties. Many new regional parties emerged along identity-based issues and made a significant dent in the traditional vote bank of the Congress Party especially in North India. It has also heralded an era of identity politics in India which were exploited primarily by regional parties that were formed along such identity-based issues. Meanwhile, those who have been historically disadvantaged have made their presence felt as they are also participating in the electoral process in large number and are trying to alter the discourse of democracy. Even though, they do not have the united voice, but they are bringing change in the course of Indian democracy. It apparently goes to the fundamentals of democracy that believes in ensuring representation of each and every segment of the population. In other words, democracy has penetrated the Indian political imagination.

Another trend that has emerged is that the Congress party that used to dominate the political scene in the country receded into the background as it could win only 44 Lok Sabha seats in 2014 election. and had not been able to regain its lost ground. On political front also the decade of the 1990s was marked by an arrival of coalition politics in place of one party dominance system. There was apprehension that India may enter into an era of instability due to the fractured mandate. Initial experiences somewhat endorsed this but later on three successive governments with a large number of coalition partners completed their terms that once again proved the skeptics wrong. Meanwhile, Voters have shown enough maturity as they have not allowed political parties to remain complacent. Even though, identities still play an important determining role as caste-based voting is still going on but along with that development and governance have become new watchwords. Parties have learnt the lesson that identity-based politics may help them win power in one or two election but to sustain their victory they will have to deliver and fulfil the promises made to the people. It has resulted into pro-incumbency instead of anti-incumbency that is again a new trend, especially in state elections. Governance has occupied a pre-eminent position in Indian politics, and it played a very crucial role in Narendra Modi-led BJP government victory in 2014 Lok Sabha election. However, challenges to Indian democracy are far from over. Poverty, inequality, illiteracy, social, ethnic and religious tensions, corruption and criminalization of politics still pervades which questions the credibility of democracy and democratic institutions.

Therefore, the conclusion may be drawn from Indian example that in India, democracy never had a smooth journey, and this trend can be observed at the global level as well. As in all democracies, groups and some individuals held a very wide range of power *vis-á-vis* government (Oldenburg 2007). Despite all these stumbling blocks, it has not only been able in successfully establishing democracy, but deepening and consolidating it as well. Given the size, complexities as well as diversities that India had, even die-hard India fan can also not think of its smooth journey. Barring one exception, i.e. 1975, democracy was never threatened in India. It does not mean, however, that all is well with Indian democracy as governance remains an issue. Similarly, its track record on some key frontiers like land reform, health and education looks pretty dismal. Therefore, what makes Indian democracy unique is the fact that it is a classic example of a democratic regime that formally believes in the values of liberty and equality, but society and polity remain segmented and fragmented which makes the journey of democracy very complicated and difficult (Vora and Palshikar 2004).

Despite all the lacunae which are explained above, if we compare India's track record on governance front in comparison to other developing countries, it looks better as it has dealt with the challenge of ethnicity extremely well under the rubric of federalism. Similarly, it has had a sound economic and foreign policy along with growing middle class. Many regionalists, secessionists, separatist movements have been contained. However, some grey areas still persists. Therefore, on the one hand, we are experiencing growth, but along with growth, inequality is also widening that makes the entire exercise questionable.

Bringing everybody to a commonly accepted platform is a daunting task, but consistent and well thought out strategy may help in diagnosing and addressing the issue. In other words, while devising programmes for the welfare of ordinary people, they need to be consulted, the absence of which leads to its failure to yield the desired result. It has been a major area of concern so far as Indian democracy is concerned. As highlighted earlier, our Land Acquisition Policy, Forest rights act, Naxal problem, Ethnic conflict in Assam, North-East, Kashmir issue etc. are some of the examples where government failed to involve the stakeholders in thoroughly debating/discussing and devising policies as to how to address them. In other words, Indian democracy has passed through many turbulent phases, and the process of democratic consolidation is still going on.

**Review of the Contributions**

The essays in this volume provide a broad insight into various facets/ aspects of India's democratic experiment. They are not based upon a single explanatory framework as scholars from different streams of humanities, and social sciences have tried to examine Indian democracy in myriad ways. They have picked up a variety of issues and themes and have attempted to argue convincingly as to why and how democracy has taken shape in India against conventional wisdom. It has also dealt with new challenges being encountered by Indian democracy in recent times. Against this background, the book will discuss the contributions by scholars to this volume on various facets of Indian democracy.

The present volume is divided into four sections. The first section entitled engaging with the ideas begins with the question of interdisciplinarity of democracy and its Indian interpretation. In this chapter, *Ravindra K.S. Choudhary* has dealt with the subject of interdisciplinarity that has gained salience in recent times as it has struck a cord in many areas of intellectual's pursuits. It involves interface among different disciplines. The chapter has dealt with the conceptual framework of mutualism between interdisciplinarity and democracy. It believes that this relationship is mutually enriching. The chapter has also highlighted that interdisciplinary studies are largely dominated by Western ways of thinking which have certain inherent problems. It has suggested that it needs to incorporate the Indian perspective to it.

The next chapter deals with the question of secularism. Secularism is a complex and vexed issue of Indian democracy that remains unresolved. *Madhurendra Kumar* has dealt with this subject in the present context and questioned the viewpoints of the certain section which believes that secularism is alien to Indian context as religion has been an integral part of people's daily lives. He has questioned the prevailing viewpoints that religiosity and secularism are antithetical to each other. He argues that it is fallacious to equate religion with communalism. The chapter has argued that nature of secularism as a principle needs scrutiny in the context of politics of communalism. It ends with the suggestion that in order to be secular politically the Indian state need not withdraw from dealing with religion and religious communities and religion should not be allowed to accrue political mileage.

The second section has dealt with the question of rights and conflicts. Movements and struggles to question government policies has been a subject of critical enquiry in the study of Indian democracy. Marginalization has assumed new forms but democracy has provided avenues to demand the socio-economic rights denied to marginalized groups. The second section has tried to understand the marginalization of different forms and the modes of protest in some cases. It has dealt with variety of issues that have cropped up in recent times and how Indian democracy is dealing with these challenges? It begins with the chapter written by *Henrik Berglund* and *Sofia Helander*. The chapter is based on an empirical study involving Coca-Cola Company in Plachimada, Kerala and alleged environmental damages and water depletion that was caused by its production of soft drinks. It has explored the role of civil society in Indian democracy and presents its empirical finding. The chapter has elaborated on those factors that were responsible in galvanizing people, especially Tribal people whose homogeneity as a group proved advantageous in their mobilization. Prolonged discrimination by the Indian state along with flawed practices of Private Corporation has had a cumulative effect. The movement succeeded because of its ability to make ample use of local, regional, national and global civil societies. It also succeeded because of its internal strength, the competent leadership, its ability to strike alliance, and also its ability to present the presence of Coca-Cola as a case of capitalist exploitation. The chapter has shown how civil society can play a very effective role in democracy. The next chapter in this section has touched upon the question of individual and group rights that has been a debatable subject right from its inception. In fact, this issue came up for discussion during the meeting of Constituent Assembly itself and since then it has been occupying the minds of the political class in India and yet remains unresolved. *Shashikant Pandey* in his chapter tried to deal with this subject by using a historical analytical framework. The chapter has made an effort to locate the issues involving individual/group rights by applying theoretical as well as the analytical method. It has also made an effort to understand how the Indian state has dealt with the issue of individual *versus* group rights. The chapter explains that in the Indian context, the juxtaposition involving individual/group rights is misunderstood to be in opposition. It concludes with the assumption that although they are not complimentary to each other, but they are not the polar opposite either. Another very interesting exploration about the links between economic inequality and political conflicts comes prominently in *Sarabjit Kaur's* chapter. She has argued that political and economic grievances are repeatedly linked to conflict processes in the qualitative literature on conflicts, however, the plethora of quantitative studies found no robust relationship between economic inequality and conflict. Citing Indian examples, she has explained that political, economic and social factors have operated in such a way that it has facilitated the functioning of the political system without any threat from the economically deprived. Thus, the universal assumption that an inequitable distribution of resources and wealth will provoke violent rebellion has not proved correct in the context of Indian democracy.

The Third section begins with the chapter by *Swarnamayee Tripathy*. She has discussed the changing dimensions of rural politics within Indian democracy. The chapter has focussed on the changing dimensions of rural politics and the role played by women in it. The chapter is based on a field study conducted in one of the backward states of India that is Odisha. The main research question of this study is "have women been successful in changing the power configuration in rural society of our country?" Will these developments ultimately result in a proactive civil society and give 'voice' to the 'silenced ones'. It has adopted an empirical approach to arrive at the findings. The chapter is divided into three parts. The first part deals with the changing socio-political dimensions of rural India. The second part has given a theoretical understanding of the concept 'politics'. The third part of the chapter has addressed the main research question by which the gender dimension of politics in rural India has been analyzed.

The next chapter in this section is written by *Sudhir Kumar*. The main objective of the chapter is to explain the phenomenon of suicides and its linkages with political processes or more specifically with political emotions in India. The chapter argues that disappearance of a particular kind of political emotions may result into emergence of a 'stress society.' The existing studies on suicides in India (more specifically studies on farmers' suicides) provide an economic or sociological explanation of the problem. Though the existing scholarship does try to bring in political factors by relating it with the larger question of policy efficiency, however, a 'political perspective' of this entire problem is still lacking. It has made an attempt to argue that political processes tend to create certain kinds of political emotions that bring varieties of attachments, associations and embeddedness for the political system in the individuals. The chapter is divided into three sections. The first section provides an overview of the problem of suicides in India. The second section looks at the existing analysis of democratic institutions and how do they generate political emotions. The third section provides a framework for understanding psychological implications like suicides and its interrelationship with a political system and institutions. In the next chapter in this section, *Roshni Sengupta* has dealt with the subject of Democracy and the new media. She has referred to various communication theories and history of mass media. New Media, she explains encompasses the range of so-called digital media which are informal, primarily social and are not easily reducible to specific categorization. Of late, it has emerged as a preferred tool of political communication. New Media offers space for a conversation about dominant discourse outside the hegemony of established institutions such as government or traditional media. Political parties are making good use of it and there increasing dependence on new media for political messaging and campaigning reveals a trend towards greater democratic deepening that is brought about by an enhanced reliance on technology-enabled methods. However, *Siddhartha Mukerji* in his chapter argued that technology has further depened the gap between elite and the masses which is called digital divide. In his chapter, he has dealt with this subject at great length. He argues that technology has emerged as a new mode of public activism. However, in India, it remained a prerogative of technocrats, scientists, and the business class. Attempts to decentralize technology began during Rajiv Gandhi's regime when he talked about bringing technology closer to the masses and its current manifestation is e-governance. The emergence of IT and new social media has democratized technology by facilitating democratic movements, public consciousness, and public activism. Examples of Arab Spring and the Anna Hazare anti-corruption crusade have been cited as good examples. In the end, he argues that even though, technology has penetrated in rural areas, due to illiteracy and ignorance among rural populace, they have failed to learn and adopt new technology.

The fourth and final section deals with current economic pathways and its socio-political implications with major focus on the post-liberalized period. Economic equality and the ability of the state to redistribute resources in a just and fair manner is a vital element of modern democracy. The inability of the Indian state to address economic marginalization has therefore interrogated the success of Indian democracy. *Sanjay Gupta* in his chapter has evaluated the role and impact of globalization on India's growth and development in the post-1990 period. He has argued that India, today, is in a position to largely counter the negative effects of globalization and to navigate and calibrate the speed and direction of globalization suiting its own development requirements. However, in spite of developing this capability and notching up some impressive gains from the neo-liberal driven economic policies in the post-1990 period, it is still debatable whether India has discovered the right kind of economic model that caters to a balanced growth and development or whether it has achieved an imperfect economic growth devoid of humane face and leading to a greater inequality? He has also probed whether the growth pattern that India has adopted is regionally more lop-sided, urbanized and concentrated in the privileged sections, than an equitable, humanized and sensitized growth? The author believes that most of the South Asian countries who got liberated in the twentieth century, including India, have been struggling to find a right kind of developmental model that caters to the needs of social justice as well as rapid economic development. While acknowledging that rapid economic growth is must for a nation, the chapter ends up with suggesting solutions that can initiate a developmental model that carries equity, humanity and inclusiveness within itself. *Surendra Meher*, has dealt with the Indian Agriculture, the mainstay of the Indian economy with special reference to small farmers. His focus is largely on post-reform period. Indian Agriculture after a satisfactory growth during 1980s has experienced a slowdown in the post-reform period which has been indicated by its growth and the proportion of population depending on it. This has accelerated inter-sectoral inequality and poses a threat to the livelihood security to the farmers especially the small and marginal segments. Against this background, by utilizing secondary data, the chapter analyses the agrarian structure, the trends and pattern of agricultural growth and concerns over livelihood security of the vulnerable sections of India's population. The chapter finds that in the post-reform period, there was poor performance of agriculture, accompanied by the poor agrarian structure and lack of adequate rural infrastructure supporting agricultural growth. A decline in public investment was found to be the important reason for such sluggish performance in agriculture. Therefore, it suggests that agricultural sector must be given attention with the due focus on small and marginal farmers so as to ensure food and livelihood security for them. The final article of this volume is written by *Amit Kumar Singh*. The chapter has dealt with the issue of nexus between political elite and the corporate sector. It believes that state in India is acting like an MNC, and it only visualizes, considers and understands different issues in the binary conclusion of economic profit or loss. It has led to a sense of despair and alienation among marginalized groups. The author has also explained that weak democratically elected governments cannot regulate the market forces that always try to maximize its profit by making an unholy alliance between corrupt bureaucracy and weak elected governments.

## Notes

1. (2014): *Pratiman* (New Delhi: Vani Publication), Vol. II, Issue I, pp. 14-15.
2. http://www.newstatesman.com/politics/2014/05/narendra-modi-man-masses, site visited on 8.9.2015.
3. "Crimes Against Women". National Crime Records Bureau, 2013. http://ncrb.gov.in/CD-CII2012/cii-2012/Chapter%205.pdf (accessed July 28, 2015).
4. http://sahoo.wordpress.com/category/democracy, Viewed on 17.7.2015.
5. http://www.humanrightsinitiative.org/index.php?option=com_content&id=199%3Asupreme-court-directives-on-police-reform&Itemid=98, Viewed on 10.9.2015.
6. S.R. Bommai *Vs*. Union of India (1994).
7. (2007): India's Democratic Challenge *Foreign Affairs*, Vol. 86, No. 2, pp. 93-106.

## References

Bardhan, Pranab "*Democracy and Distributive Politics in India*" (2010) http://eml.berkeley.edu/~webfac/bardhan/papers/BardhanDemoDist.pdf, Viewed on 10.7.2015).

Bhargava, Rajeev (2010), "What is Political Theory and why do we need it?" (New Delhi: Oxford University Press).

Chandoke, Neera (2009): "Deepening the Democratic Culture in India" in Rajesh M. Basrur (ed.) *Challenges to Democracy in India* (New Delhi: Oxford University Press).

Dahl, Robert A. (2001): "*On Democracy*" (New Delhi: New-West Press).

Jayal and Mehta (2010): "*The Oxford Companion to Politics in India*", (New Delhi: Oxford University Press).

Jayal, Neeraja Gopal (2001): "*Democracy in India*" (New Delhi: Oxford University Press).

Kohli, Atul (1988): *India's Democracy, An Analysis of Changing State-Society Relations* (USA: Princeton University Press).

Kohli, Atul (2007): *State, and Redistributive Development in India* http://www.princeton.edu/~kohli/docs/UNRISD.pdf, downloaded on 13.7.2015.).

McMillan, Alistair (2008): "Deviant Democratization in India", Volume 15, Number 4, pp. 733-749(17) Routledge.

Mukherjee, Sanjeeb (2009): "Indian Democracy: Puzzle of Unanswered Questions" *Economic and Political Weekly*, Vol. XLIV, No. 43.

Oldenburg, Philip (2007): *Indian's Democracy: Illusion or Reality*, https://www.asian-studies.org/eaa/Oldenburg-12-3.pdf, Viewed on 11.7.2015).

Pai, Sudha, and Avinash Kumar (2014): *The Indian Parliament: A Critical Appraisal* (New Delhi: Orient BlackSwan).

Palshikar and Vora (2004): *Indian Democracy, Meaning and Practices* (New Delhi: Sage Publication).

Parekh, Bhikhu, (2011): The Crisis of Indian Democracy https://www.cambridgetrust.org/assts/documents/lecture_32.pdf, site visited on dated 23.7.2015.

Rudolph, Lloyd and Susanne Rudolph (1987): *In Pursuit of Laxmi* (Chicago: University of Chicago Press).

Rudolph, Susanne and Lloyd Rudolph (2002): New Dimensions of Indian Democracy, *Journal of Democracy*, pp. 52-66.

Shankar and Rodrigues (2011): *The Indian Parliament: A Democracy at Work* (New Delhi: Oxford University Press).

Sharma, Shailendra (1994): "*Indian Democracy and The Crisis of Governability*", dl.tufts.edu/file_assets/tufts:UP149.001 00035.00012, Viewed on 21.7.2015.

Spary, Carole (2010): "Disrupting Rituals of Debate in Indian Parliament". *The Journal of Legislative Studies* 16 (3): 338-51.

Suri, K.C. (2008): "*The State of Democratic Governance in India*" : *An Asian Barometer Conference on State of Democratic Governance in South Asia*, http://www.asianbarometer.org/newenglish/publications/ConferencePapers/2008 conference/sec.6.1.pdf, Viewed on 15.7.2015-Right Pattern.

Varshney, Ashutosh (2013): *Battles Half Won: India's Improbable Democracy* (London: Penguin Books India).

Vora, Rajendra and Suhas Palshikar (2004): "*Indian Democracy: Meaning and Practices*" (Sage: India).

Yadav, Yogendra (2000): "Understanding the Second Democratic Upsurge: Trends of Bahujan Participation in Electoral Politics in the 1990" in Francine Frankel *et al., Transforming India, Social and Political Dynamics of Democracy* (Place: Oxford University Press).

Yogendra Yadav, (2011): *Democracy and Diversity in India,* https://www.youtube.com/watch?v=al3lEi9DsPM, site visited on 15.7.2015.

Zoya Hasan (2009): "Indian Democracy and Social Inequalities" in Rajesh M. Basrur (ed.) *Challenges to Democracy in India* (New Delhi: Oxford University Press).

# SECTION I
## Engaging with the Ideas

# 2
# Interdisciplinary Democracy
## An Indian Engagement

*Ravindra K.S. Choudhary*

### Introduction

Interdisciplinarity is nowadays very popular with people in academia, mainly because it seems to have struck a democratic cord in many areas of intellectual pursuits. Democracy is in fact not confined to political arena; it can very well flourish as a full-fledged way of life and as such it can foster general participation and promote equality among the participants from diverse backgrounds on different levels, e.g. body politic as well as intellectual pursuits. We thus hear frequent calls from several quarters for more interdisciplinary study and research. Such calls are often prompted by the criticism of undemocratic insularity and compartmentalization of knowledge growing within the rigid disciplinary structure.

It is in fact not difficult to realize that different disciplines represent oversimplified views of issues involved in life at large, and also that none of them is self-sufficient; they all are always in need of each other for putting forward a world-view. The need for interdisciplinary studies is basically due to these mutual complementarities of different disciplines. Obviously, interdisciplinarity is an ever expanding field open to all, and it is as vast, varied and vibrant as life itself. This brings interdisciplinarity into a symbiotic relationship with democracy. Democracy is a multi-dimensional and multi-level phenomena or process, and interdisciplinarity helps us understand it better with all its richness and diversity. Democracy fosters perspectival pluralism, and so it provides interdisciplinarity with an appropriate socio-politico-cultural setting to flourish. Interdisciplinarity in its true spirit has a remarkable democratic character. Democracy too, in its turn, is not a simple phenomenon or linear process; it is too complex a process or phenomena to be dealt by one discipline alone. Any exercise in understanding democracy, particularly as it is practiced in a vast, variegated and vibrant country like India, naturally calls many different disciplines into play.

The present chapter seeks to put forward a conceptual framework of this mutualism between interdisciplinarity and democracy. If seen in the right perspective, this relationship is so mutually enriching for the two that a new dimension of democracy, namely Interdisciplinary Democracy, comes to the fore. But, besides disciplinary compartmentalization, there is a significant problem on the way to interdisciplinary democracy. The widespread format of interdisciplinary study and research has overwhelmingly been dominated by Western ways of thinking. This format has in fact been formulated in the postmodern West and all the rest of the world, wittingly or unwittingly, took it up through colonial legacy. In this format, interdisciplinarity is inextricably bound up with science and technology so much so that the methodology of interdisciplinary study and research is modelled on the methods and techniques of current techno-science. Despite its much-publicized advantages, the dominant framework of interdisciplinarity has certain inherent problems. Such problems can be mitigated significantly by contextualizing democracy and interdisciplinarity through the incorporation of Indian perspective of the two phenomena in question. We will look here into this end as well. Of course, there is a plethora of related problems, which I do not propose to go into at the moment.

## Interdisciplinarity and Democracy

Interdisciplinarity refers to a particular set of activities that is marked by interface and interaction between/among different disciplines. It is often understood in a contrastive relation to disciplinarity. Disciplinarity is suggestive of boundary, isolation, self-centredness, singularity, monologue, specialization, regimentation, control, policing, monotony and the like; whereas interdisciplinarity suggests openness, diversity, self-transcendence, community, dialogue, freedom, collaboration, potentialities, novelties and many more. Interdisciplinarity widens our intellectual horizon by ranging across disciplines; it keeps us open to innovations and breakthroughs taking place in other disciplines; it also facilitates democratic dialogue among different disciplines. Hence, interdisciplinarity is seen nowadays as an academic virtue.

The idea of democracy springs to mind first of all—voting is the royal road to public participation; violation of voting right in any form is a serious blow to freedom. But democracy is not just the total of votes taken among isolated individuals; it is much more than that. In a democracy, we have to be open-minded and sensible enough to accept and respect diversity with all civility; we must not turn a deaf ear to any voice that is dissimilar to ours. Being democratic thus amounts to accepting the variety of viewpoints as something to be encouraged, and not something to be destroyed or obliterated. What is required in it is a culture of respecting diversity and plurality where a citizen tends towards creative engagement of the self with others.

Public participation is essential for the formation of a democratic society, but it has to be fostered through 'dialogic model' in which collective choices are made on the basis of 'public reasoning'. Citizens participate beyond all unreasonable barriers and boundaries without any discrimination. So, it has been observed that "the tradition of public reasoning is closely related to the roots of Democracy across the globe" (Sen 2005: 12). Democracy is thus a dialogue in which public participation is governed by principles of equality and freedom. It depends to a great extent upon the political communication among the various stakeholders.

It is well-known that political communication has a significant impact on civic engagement. The news media and party campaigns have traditionally been two major modes of political communication. Recent years have experienced not only a wide variety and criss-crossing practices in political communication, but its sources, content, and range have also gone far beyond traditional boundaries. For instance, it is usually expected that

> ...the news media should provide citizens with political information at a variety of different levels, ranging from the most technical and thorough details to the simplest accounts.

> The reason is that citizens come to politics with different backgrounds (Norris 2000: 31).

Thus, citizens may belong to diverse socio-cultural backgrounds having widely varying education, training, and leanings. This diversity makes it necessary for the main actors of representative democracy to adopt interdisciplinary approach while developing political communication.

Many political scientists and a few institutions of higher learning have timely recognized far-reaching implications of these changes and resulting requirements. Consequently, they are instrumental in initiating 'Democracy Studies' whose primary aim is to approach the multidimensional phenomena of democracy from as broad an outlook as possible. Democracy is thus viewed as more a way of life than a particular form of government. And, as a way of life, democracy calls for a much wider educational experience and broader treatment than our received wisdom has granted it so far. Attempts are thus being made to develop interdisciplinary understanding of democracy by drawing together the experts from many different disciplines. Seldom has democratic theorizing allowed so wide a spectrum of perspectives, e.g. ranging from politico-legal to psycho-philosophical, from socio-economic to anthro-cultural studies, and so on.

In interdisciplinarity, we need continuous efforts and experiments to negotiate with disciplinary boundaries. These negotiations can be seen as the extension of the democratic process on the intellectual plane. Different disciplines, in a real sense, represent various walks of life and so we have a variety of territorial studies of life and the world. To bridge these considerably isolated constituencies, one needs not only to bring necessary changes in the intellectual landscape but also to have an actual engagement in practice. It has quite correctly been argued that

> ...transcending disciplinary boundaries is not possible if their practitioners are not partners in the wider struggle for a more democratic society (Giri 2006: 147).

Once we allow interdisciplinarity to play a significant role in shaping our intellectual landscape, we welcome perspectival pluralism with open arms. Hence, interdisciplinary approach towards problems, whether theoretical or practical, is seen as a great facilitator of democracy. Elizabeth Anderson in her case study of community forest management groups in India and Nepal includes the local women's point of view, and she demonstrates how this inclusiveness of many marginalized viewpoints have led to successful creation of a richer knowledge base. This regard for and reliance upon widely diverse domains of information and insights amounts to a significant mode of being democratic at the epistemological level (Anderson 2006: 8-22).

A number of reasons can account for this happy change. From the postmodern perspective, this increasing intimacy of democracy and interdisciplinarity seems to be a new achievement. Its origins are marked by the fundamental changes of 1970s, which led to unprecedented intensification of worldwide interconnectedness in all aspects of life at all levels—local and global, intellectual and socio-political (Choudhary 2012a: 105). These changes are the ramifications of newly emerged technoscience, which substantially challenge our old ways of theorizing about public communication and civic engagement. As I have elsewhere tried to show,

> The convergence of computers and satellites has revolutionized our life and the world leading to a transformation of our Weltanschauung altogether. The world-view thus emerged calls for politics and governance that are simpler, faster, more effective, yet more democratic and transparent than conventional ones (Choudhary 2012b:202).

New technologies challenge boundaries of many kinds—between nations, social classes, cultural forms, academic disciplines and so on. The spectacular advances in information and communication technology, in particular, have created the widespread view that our traditional ways of public participation are behind the time, and we now need new ideas and ideals to make sense of our socio-political life at large. For instance,

> Internet has provided a remarkable increase in the infrastructure of horizontal and lateral communication capacity within and across borders… these developments do imply that many new forms of connection and media range in and across borders, linking nations and people in many news ways. Accordingly, the capacity of national political

> leaders to sustain a national culture has become more difficult. For example, China sought to restrict access to and use of the Internet, but it has found this virtually impossible to do (Held 1996: 350-51).

In effect, the very notion of relevant constituency or community, which was so central in the classical democratic thought, now seems to be rather inadequate or even redundant. The notion of citizenry confined within a geographically demarcated specific constituency that was once thought to be essential to democracy holds no good any longer.

> ...the very idea of consent through elections, and the particular notion that the relevant constituencies of voluntary agreement are the communities of bounded territory or a state become open to question as soon as the matter of national, regional and global interconnectedness is considered and the nature of so-called 'relevant community' is contested (*ibid.*: 338).

The questioning of the notion of fixed and well-demarcated constituency has not been confined to the political arena; it features quite prominently also in the intellectual landscape. The very notion of relevant constituency or community, whether geographical, or social, or intellectual, which was so vital in the classical thought, now seems to be largely outmoded for the current modes of participation in general. The bounded rationality on which disciplinary structure of divergent knowledge pursuits was based has lost much of its significance in the current knowledge scenario.

The point is that the rise of interdisciplinarity and the way in which classical democracy is being challenged are not isolated phenomena; they are parallel developments as the struggle for freedom from barriers, borders, and boundaries. Society today is characterized by unprecedentedly increasing the complexity of overlapping organizations, interest groups, and socio-cultural forms. The dynamics of these diverse elements and divergent factors strengthens democracy to a great extent because it no longer remains so easy for any one of them to dominate the scene for long. Obviously, this dynamism can be best understood only in the interdisciplinary context. As a result, democracy too is now viewed as a multi-level and multi-dimensional phenomenon that calls for an interdisciplinary approach for its adequate understanding.

## Dynamics of Bounded Rationality

Why is disciplinarity not intellectually as conducive to democratization as interdisciplinarity? Rigid disciplinarity is wrong-headed because of its confinement and border maintenance giving rise to exclusivist tendencies ultimately leading to a cult of monolithic knowledge elites. In such a situation, one cannot help but think that intellectual horizons are artificially narrowed by a too strict policing of this boundary line (Norris 2000: 1). It misses the life-experience of the human living in a highly complex society and the world marked by increasing interactions in myriad ways. The dimension of power that is inextricably linked with the modern conception of discipline-bound knowledge is also responsible in this regard.

This linkage of power and knowledge is particularly interesting for the present. It is noticeably evident that the pursuing knowledge under the rigid disciplinary framework, reinforcing its actual practice and dissemination through the departmental structure, inevitably lead to power, position, and privilege. It has rightly been observed:

> There is a connection between viewing knowledge as leading to power and putting the pursuit of knowledge in bounded disciplines. If knowledge is considered as giving us power rather than a better preparedness to participate creatively in the dynamics of relationships in life, then there is an inherent tendency to project the boundaries of this guarantor of power and to rigidify these. Disciplinary boundaries become a servant to the will to power of the men of knowledge (Giri 2006: 147).

Hence, we are required to look into the linkage of knowledge and power which has developed in the modern knowledge situation as a result of the practice of disciplinarity.

The modern mind gradually categorized knowledge as falling within distinct disciplines. Hence, as Stephen Toulmin points out, "issues that do not fall within the scope of a recognized discipline are scarcely seen to qualify as 'academic' at all (Toulmin 2005: 189). Underlying this pigeonholing process, there has been a 'disciplinary criterion'. This criterion has become a tool of legitimizing suitable bodies of knowledge and marginalizing the unsuitable ones. Any piece of knowledge must have the ability or adaptability to the set criterion. If the indigenous knowledge of non-Western people does not suit to any disciplinary department, it is most likely to be discarded as 'non-knowledge'. Thus,

> Western compartmentalization of Knowledge delegitimizes knowledge that does not fit into established disciplinary compartments (Chew 2000: 126).

The disciplinary criteria are affected through several means. The specialized curriculum for each discipline and grooved ways of studying it set the patterns for a newcomer to the subject to follow. The cognitive classification, such as bibliographical categories, has been helpful in reinforcing the disciplinary criterion. Professional practices such as Association, Conference, etc. have also been conducive to compartmentalization. But the organizational divisions made among different departments of the modern universities have been the most decisive factor. "The modern university represents its knowledge and expertise to the public primarily in disciplinary terms" (Appadurai 1996: 18). Obviously, what is missing in this framework is an open, egalitarian and holistic conception of knowledge that is essential to reflect a democratic spirit.

Even interdisciplinary ventures take place in this dominant framework against the background of disciplinarity and compartmentalization of knowledge. The interdisciplinary format widely in use nowadays is, by and large, issued from this 'comdepartmentalization'[1] of knowledge, and so it is equally problematic:

> For inherent in the interdisciplinary format is a mechanistic and aggressive, at best integration, process rather than the transformative process that is what is taking place. What happens is perhaps better described as transdisciplinary or extra-disciplinary knowledge rather than interdisciplinary orientation (Kothari 1988: 34).

It is thus important for us to look into the genealogy of this dominant framework of knowledge within which we all are usually set to carry out our varied intellectual pursuits including the interdisciplinary study and research. The first thing to be noted about this framework is that it was formulated in the West under the deep influence of the logic of modernity. It relies heavily on the capacity of rationality that is regarded as the prized possession of humans. The capacity of humans to arrive at rational solutions to worldly problems has been reinforced by science and technology that have been seen as originally a Western achievement (Rosenberg 2000: 14). Further, mainly due to the historico-cultural reasons, the scientific paradigms of the West hold a hegemonic position in the various knowledge pursuits of all the rest of the world.

As a result, we have a particular sort of worldwide homogenization of knowledge. It can generally be observed that "whenever the agents of the modern societies confront traditional culture that may have more comprehensive embedded notions of natural knowledge, they are likely to screen such knowledge for useful information and appropriate the information into the modern framework" (Daele 2005: 408). But all this is an exercise in the *ex situ* treatment of the alternative ways of understanding life and the world. The information thus wrenched away from the truth of the situation degrades even the nature of knowledge into mere an instrumental. It promotes a "narrowly utilitarian view of science based on a conception of knowledge as an instrument of power in man's search for control and domination" (Kothari 1988: 3).

It is a matter of great democratic concern that the dominant framework of knowledge is extremely utilitarian, authoritative and anthropocentric in character. It takes little notice of other traditions of knowledge such as Indian, Chinese, Arabian, African and Caribbean to name a few. This is democratically dangerous and philosophically unacceptable. Thus, the dominant framework of knowledge needs to be contextualized keeping in view the changing contours of the intellectual landscape. So, some social scientists now urge to incorporate non-western ways of thinking; for, one can easily experience in them a conception of knowledge that is far more integral and nearer to life.

> Individualistic cultures, like the United States, do not emphasize context as a variable while analyzing different situations. Subsequently, the emphasis is on the outcomes and quantifiable accomplishments where compartmentalization of

> actions is the norm. Collectivistic cultures, like Japan, China, and India, emphasize relationships and take a more holistic approach to life and learning (Kapur 2002: 25).

Interdisciplinarity must be faithful to inclusive approach, in general, and it should ultimately lead us towards a holistic and integral conception of life and the world.

The point to be noted about the dominant framework is that disciplinary boundaries are not just for the sake of creating administrative divisions; they have much more to do on the part of practitioners and participants. Rosenberg rightly wrote, "It is the discipline that ultimately shapes the scholar's vocational identity. The Confraternity of his acknowledged peers defines the scholar's aspirations, set appropriate problems and provides the intellectual tools with which to address them; finally it is the discipline that rewards intellectual achievements" (Rosenberg 1979: 444). It is against this backdrop of disciplinary compartmentalization and the attending notion of knowledge as a power that interdisciplinary studies seem to make much more sense.

In the process of knowledge production and dissemination, these disciplines thus function as the *loci* of power, position and privilege in the modern university system. The undercurrent of will to power at times becomes so intense that certain sorts of groupings among the practitioners of disciplinarity begin to creep into the exercise. Disciplinarity develops a kind of 'ethnocentrism' around itself, which in its turn often causes "a redundant piling up of highly similar specialties, leaving interdisciplinary gaps" (Campbell 1969: 328). Consequently, separate disciplines are often formed despite having almost indistinguishable problematics, analogous methods, and identical goals.

**Need for New Sort of Expertise**

There are many other related features of disciplinarity that often turn to be undemocratic in its spin-offs. For, the rigid disciplinary structure inevitably leads to over-specialization and compartmentalization of knowledge. And,

> ...the excessive insistence on specialization may result in lopsidedness among its adherents and produce skewed

> citizenry whose tunneled vision may lead to misunderstanding and even clash of opinions about phenomena (Singh 2010: 44).

In fact, understanding consists in attending the 'other' sensibly and openly enough on equal footings; it is rooted in the dialogue with the other. The disciplinary criteria give rise to a cult of expertise, and consequently to the increase of a class of 'knowledge elites'. Harold Laski once said:

> ...special knowledge and highly trained mind produce their own limitations...Expertise...sacrifices the insight of common sense to the intensity of experience ... It has a certain caste-spirit about it, so that experts tend to neglect all evidence which does not ...belong to their own rank.[2]

This 'caste-spirit' that can commonly be experienced in expert behaviours gives us one of the reasons why disciplinarity has not been found so democracy-friendly.

Political thinkers have long been trying to reconcile the need for expertise and the egalitarian demands of democracy. In one of his dialogues, Plato considers the issue of expert testimony; in another, he speaks of the importance of expertise in democratic context by way of the famous metaphor of ship and true navigator.[3] Life and thought have changed a lot since the time of Plato, yet the basic issue in this regard seems to be unresolved.

There is no denying that we cannot do without professional experts in this age of techno-culture. Increasingly growing complexities in the world of affairs necessitate expert consultation in all walks of life. Their unavoidable necessity has bestowed them with a privileged position in society at large. For instance, many believe in comparing doctors with God, but if considered democratically, that is too high a privilege. Democracy demands of such experts to prove themselves, first of all, as common citizens having no exalted status. But this is an ideal to which they often seem to be least committed to. Democracy is not just political; it is socio-cultural too. And,

> ... socio-cultural democracy ... also includes active participation in the production and presentation of

> information and culture. Democracy thus means a systematic opposition to knowledge elites as well as economic elites (Mosco 1990: 216).

By becoming interdisciplinary, we significantly depart from the discipline-bound elitist model of knowledge production and dissemination. Interdisciplinarity, in fact, calls different sort of experts into play. In a situation where boundaries are blurring and even vanishing at times, where the paradigms of expertise are shifting rapidly, we are moving towards an era of experts who are no longer monolithic, authoritative and unshakable. Because,

> ...if disciplinary boundaries are fluid, then there are fluid ways of becoming expert in a field, and proof of expertise, of any stripe, will come from continuous and changing standard of negotiations (Selinger 2006: 14).

Such negotiations need to be essentially democratic in the sense that they must be inclusive and participatory to the greatest possible extent. Thus both, democracy, and interdisciplinarity, urge to reconcile "the demands of professionalism with those of citizenship" (Katz 1995:876).

Insofar as life-experience is concerned, the specialist and the generalist ways need not be at loggerheads. Specialization and generalization can be rendered as complementary processes; we can very well posit them as relative movements towards the opposite ends of our varied cognitive experience (Choudhary 2013: 21). If democracy is not just a political belief but a way of life, then it would require a transformation on the part of its practitioners at the intellectual level as well. Particularly, one must go beyond the discipline-bound perspective of knowledge as power meant for establishing dominance over nature and others. Interdisciplinarity, through its inclusive and integrative approach, opens up this much sought-after Democratic horizon.

But why has the dimension of power been so crucial in the production and dissemination of knowledge? The main reason behind it is that there prevails a conception of knowledge as information (Daele 2005: 406). Since, knowledge is reduced to information, it inevitably leads to the play of and will to power. "Reductionism remains the ruling mentality of technoscience and commodification its structural form," says Best (Best 2001: 102). It thus turns knowledge into a sheer commodity like any other marketable item. Hence,

> Once viewed as commodity to be bought and sold, knowledge itself became merely a means to an end, and culture became wholly a commodity disseminated as information without permeating the individual who acquired it (Outram 1995: 10).

It is also clear from the recent researches in the field of symbolic logic that the reduction of knowledge into information leads to a propositional view of knowledge, and thus propositions are logically thought to be the bearer of truth-value in the sense that they are either 'True' or 'False'. The propositional view has been found to be very helpful in quantitative and computational conceptualizations, but all this is achieved by sacrificing the matters of value altogether.

In parallel with the dominant framework of knowledge, there is also "the dominant model of democracy today," which "relies on the unhampered pursuit of self-interest and, politically, on competitive elections where voters choose delegates maximally committed to promoting their interests" (Dallmayr 2007: 12-13). Fred Dallmayr convincingly shows how this model is inextricably bound up with the idea of liberal democracy and he goes on to question the very plausibility of the idea:

> ...the Western world calls itself, somewhat boastfully, the "Free World," while America celebrates itself as the "land of the free." As a corollary of this development, democracy as a political regime has come to be equated with an area of free individual choice—that is, liberal or libertarian democracy. But how plausible is this outcome? Has freedom in the modern world completely replaced such traditional categories as virtue and the "good life"—with the result that Aristotle's distinction between just and unjust regimes would be levelled into that between free and unfree forms of life? (*ibid.* : 2).

Liberals advocate minimum governance to expand the arena of free individual choice. What is more, many leading theorists of this model argue that ethics has nothing to do now in the matters political.

In Robert Dahl's view, public affairs and larger concerns are matters to be governed by external or procedural checks rather than traditional internal checks such as conscience and ethical dispositions (Dahl 1956). "Democracy begins with demo-power," says Sartori (Sartori 1987).

The 'democratic minimalism' just outlined brings the typical minimalist liberal at the Centre stage which can be viewed as "an individual with no roots and little connectedness to the community". He or she is thus a highly competitive individual fixated on narrow purposes whose practice is marked by expedience rather than conventional ethics (Boisvert 1998: 51-52). This insularity is not only reminiscent of but also connected with the isolation of different knowledge-domains about which inter-disciplinarians have been so scathingly critical. John Dewey anticipated the dangers of this reckless individualism when he said that "The clear consciousness of a communal life, in all its implications, constitutes the very idea of democracy." Taking clues from Dewey, an attempt can be made to revise the state of affairs in democratic theorizing:

> Whereas old-style individualism connotes "both isolation and self-interestedness," "individuality" in the revised Deweyan sense identifies "the distinctive manner in which someone participates in communal life"; it recognizes "the irreducibility of community and the multiple perspectives associated with it." Such individuality and multiple perspectives to which it gives rise are not opposed to, but constitutive of democratic life (Boisvert 1998; Dallmayr 2007).

This perspectival pluralism and concern for community, rather than rigidity and singularity, brings democracy near to interdisciplinarity. It is at this juncture that Indian wisdom may add many illuminating perspectives indeed.

**Indian Perspective**

From the very beginning of her history, India is a country of many languages, many races, and many religions—a truly multicultural nation. Given this socio-cultural milieu, one of the first things that a child learns here is to respect other's point of view. In effect, Indians never believed that there is only one way of approaching the truth and those who think differently are inspired by the devil. Such an intellectual landscape rich in cultural diversity and adequately accommodating to perspectival pluralism has been very much conducive to integrated learning. If diversity and Openness, tolerance and synthesis, freedom and transcendence are essential to interdisciplinary studies, then India has all the potentials to provide an ideal setting for interdisciplinarity to flourish (Choudhary 2014: 20-21).

Knowledge has been practiced and disseminated in India basically in the interdisciplinary spirit of the very ancient times. Specialization and compartmentalization through rigid disciplinary structures are foreign to India's intellectual tradition. Some social scientists have also taken note of it:

> The categorization of knowledge into well-defined, formalized disciplines having institutionalized mechanisms for creation, communication and diffusion in the present form is basically a western model (Singhi 1987: 3).

Contrastingly, in the Indian context, one is required to take many facts or factors into account in reaching one's conclusion. In the *Sushruta Samhita*, for instance, we are explicitly warned against jumping to conclusion by studying just one *Shastra* or discipline:

> *Ekam shastramadhiyano na vidyat shastranishchayam,*
> *Tasmad bahushrutah shastram vijaniayacchikitsakah.*[4]

Different *shastras* or disciplines, in a significant sense, represent various cultural forms, and being interdisciplinary amounts to supporting the plea for a dialogue of civilizations. For, entering into a dialogue with the other is an important part of transcending boundaries. It is no good, according to Bhartrihari, to remain confined to one's own tradition. On the path of one's intellectual and spiritual development, such an insular approach is a big stumbling block. Hence, his suggestion is:

> The intellect acquires critical acumen by familiarity with different traditions. How much does one really understand by merely following one's own reasoning only?[5]

We have already seen that it is the public reasoning that keeps a democratic society ever moving ahead. A dialogic interaction of diverse elements and factors is of vital importance in the formation of public reasoning. In the Indian context, Jainism, Buddhism and Charvaka have contributed enormously to the dialogic process and the formation of public reasoning. As Amartya Sen puts,

> Heterodoxy deeply influences Indian politics and is particularly relevant to the development of democracy in India and the emergence of its secular priorities (Sen, 2005: 12). Sen goes on to argue, "in philosophical discourses throughout Indian history, atheists and skeptics make frequent appearances, and even though, in many cases, their points of view are ultimately rejected they do get their say" (*ibid.*: 25).

However, we should also realize that public reasoning does not amount to propaganda; it has an inbuilt normative rationality. It is instructive in this regard to recall "Gandhi's conception of public reason characterized by three basic things, *viz.*, *vichara* (rational discernment and thought), *sanchara* (communication) and *prachara* (propagation)" (Chattopadhyaya, 2003: 12). The Indian approach to democracy seeks to combat the problem of public reasoning at the source, rather than superficially. This goal cannot be achieved unless we nurture virtues and values.

Against the value-neutral or amoral character of the dominant model of democracy, Fred Dallmayr turns his attention to "non-Western intellectual contexts". Particularly, he finds Gandhi and his idea of self-rule (*Swaraj*) immensely relevant. "Profiled against dominant Western approaches," Dallmayr points out, "Gandhi's idea of *Swaraj* discloses a conception of democracy—an ethical conception—sharply at variance with interest-based models of liberal or libertarian democracy" (Dallmayr 2007: 11). In *Swaraj*, one is not simply in the pursuit of individual or collective self-interest but on the path of transformation. Gandhi says,

> It is *Swaraj* when we learn to rule ourselves. ... Swaraj has to be experienced, by each one for himself. One drowning man will never save another (Gandhi 2003: 56).

*Swaraj* is of great relevance for democracy and interdisciplinarity as well. This is mainly because of the common reason that *swaraj* involves self-transcendence and a diligent training in the ways of freedom (Dallmayr 2007: 11).

We have already seen at length how the Western tradition puts human beings at the centre of the universe and induces them to utilize knowledge merely as an instrument for establishing domination over nature and others. This whole outlook towards life and the world needs to be transformed if we want to transcend boundaries in a fruitful and democratic manner. Indians, by tradition, believe that knowledge is not concerned with sheer professionalism and power pursuit. Instead, it is meant to bring a change in life and our Weltanschauung. Hence, "the primary concern in India," has always been, "not information, but transformation" (Zimmer 1990: 4).

Knowledge thus transforms here into higher wisdom. Such an approach goes far beyond the conception of knowledge as information and makes knowledge a way of life meant for service to society at large. Thus,

> What we need now is a new ethics of servanthood, and it is easier for those man of knowledge who conceptualize their pursuits as those of a servant to break their disciplinary boundaries than those who think of themselves as masters (Giri 2006: 147).

For this much-needed transformation, the lessons of *Advaita Vedanta* can be of great help. "*Advaita Vedanta* represents a paradigm of the Indian way of life. *Vedanta* philosophy leaves to every man a broad spectrum of real usefulness" (Choudhary 2007: 11). According to *Advaita Vedanta*, humans and nature, subject and object, self and others—such binaries do not constitute alien domains. Also, some Western social scientists now urge, "to recognize that they both form part of a single universe" (Wallerstein 1995: 84). Hence, the upholders of this view regard the dialogue of civilizations as an essential part of our ventures to transcend disciplinary modes of thought. The questions they raise, in this respect, are not only pertinent for the present but highly suggestive too:

> Is there a deeper universalism of modern societies and modern thought, one that accepts contradictions within its universality? Can we promote a pluralistic universalism on

> the analogy of the Indian pantheon wherein a single God has many avatars? (*ibid.*: 66).

Philosophy, for Indians, has never been an arid zone of intellectualism. Indian philosophy is above all a philosophy of life and is deeply concerned about the problem as to how a person should plan his or her life in an ideal way. Any exercise in sheer professionalism cannot provide us a far-going solution to this problem. "For answering it, man must develop his reflective abilities. He must have time for reflection. But impartial reflection is not possible so long as man is carried away by the needs, duties and responsibilities of daily life in family and society" (Raju 1985: 3). The life of a professional is bounded by formal disciplinary training and characterized by appropriate expertise and competence. The main motivation for professional pursuits is simple enough. It is will to power, prestige, and prosperity that keep professionalism alive and kicking.

What is important to realize is that such a bounded life can be significant only as a stage of life; it cannot, and should not, encompass a person's whole course of life. One also has to take into account wider social responsibilities that make human life meaningful. As Radhakrishnan has observed,

> Our age is the age of specialists. Each one knows more and more about less and less. We concentrate on some narrow field and forget the larger context in which we can see the meaning of our specialism. Modern specialization has led to the fragmentation of knowledge. We should be not only the specialists but also have the sense of the meaning of life and social responsibility (Radhakrishnan 1997: 154).

Hence, in the ancient Indian tradition, a person's life was divided into four stages (*ashramas*). They are the student, the householder, the forest-dweller, and the wandering ascetic. The third of these four stages of human life (i.e., *vanaprastha*) is particularly interesting for the present because it adds a new perspective to interdisciplinarity.

To lead a successful household life one has to earn money for livelihood and achieve power and prestige for social recognition. The household stage of life and professional career, therefore, mostly go hand in hand even today. All this, however, is not the end of the story.

Thus, "The perspective of *vanaprastha* states that after one has accumulated one's wealth and power one should abandon all these and search for truth. This seems to be an immense enriching suggestion for our task of abandonment at hand. Academic disciplines provide wealth, prestige and power and acclaim to the practicing professionals. But having gained all these through our respective disciplines, at particular stage, we have to abandon our assuring grounds in order that we can discover the unexpected truths of reality in the borderland and wilderness, as it were" (Giri 2006:150-51).

Indian wisdom can play a crucial role in breaking down boundaries and barriers and open up quite new horizons. For, the emphasis here is very much on "developing spiritual alternatives to the logic of power" (*ibid.*: 148). That is why; the stage of *vanaprastha* gets importance as a transformative phase in an individual's life. It provides a person time, environment and mindset necessary for impartial reflection that help one go beyond all insularity evolved from self-centredness.

Even some Westerners recognize the ultimate significance of this perspective. They find a 'real contradiction' in the Western way of thinking about the Subject in the sense that "it is indeed impossible to reconcile an appeal to the freedom of the Subject with an ethics of duty." For, "The Subject is centred on the individual, and the individual's will to autonomy and freedom is an essential part of its formation." Hence, the question arises: How is the Subject related to another subject? This question is a crucial one because the Self-Other relations and ordinary social relations are not always of the same piece.

> The understanding of the Other establishes a relationship that is of a different order to professional and economic relations, and it is also the relationship existing between people who belong to the same cultural community. It gives rise to a counter-society, to the beginning of a political society that is no longer a community of citizens, but a voluntary association of social actors who resist all the impersonal logics of power (Touraine 2000: 80).

At first blush, this may seem to be too idealistic and thus not in consonance with real politik or the actual functioning of democracy. But we must realize that democracy is not mere a state of a polity to be achieved once and for all; democracy is also an ideal that is always in the making. Ideally, a democratic society must be able to provide every citizen with equal opportunity and prospects of progress.

The very idea of a pretty good, informed and conscious 'Citizen' around which the whole of our democratic discourse revolves is logically not a reality but a dream, no matter how dear and desirable this goal is for us all. Such a citizen is supposed to be an idealized entity that is faceless and nameless. He or she cannot be located in any country or at a particular place and yet presumed to be fit for and even essential to Democracy. There is thus a significant sense in which

> ... democracy must be defined as the politics of Subject, as the regime that grants the greatest possible number the greatest possible opportunity to succeed in individuating themselves, or living as Subjects (*ibid.*: 158).

Thus, Indian experience of democracy is suggestive of many illuminating aspects. It invites a democratic theorist to update his conventional wisdom that democracy can flourish well only in widespread prosperity and literacy. It also challenges the notion that monolithic socio-cultural milieu is best suited for democratization. Indian experience has shown to the world that democratic experiment can successfully be carried out on a large scale even having so much diversity. Above all, Indian experience suggests that the emphasis on freedom and equality is not the benchmark of real democracy; neither are these concepts capable of leading us to an adequate understanding of democracy. The 'Subject' is required to undergo a profound transformation to be a worthy citizen, and accordingly, one is always in a need for reconstruction of one's relationship with the 'Other.'

It goes without saying that 'the unity in diversity' that India has down through the ages is of great interdisciplinary significance. The dynamics of democracy in India parallels that sort of interaction that generally occurs in interdisciplinary ventures. And, it can be better understood and expressed only by employing interdisciplinary approach. The challenges to Indian democracy are also unique in many ways. The main difficulty in the current context can be identified as to "how to relate and join the deeper drives of Indian citizens and communities to the broader challenge of socio-political transformation and emancipation; how to engage in preservation of freedom and autonomy in the face of both corporate and transnational varieties, and the confrontations found within the nation state such as economic divides based on class and caste, and the more threatening communal drives (Kothari 2007: 2).

**Critical Remarks**

Interdisciplinary Democracy is a nascent and an ever-evolving realm. The issues involved in it are many, and most of them are naturally far from being settled. Criticisms of interdisciplinary democracy are therefore likely to be found in plenty. Some of them deserve our special attention here.

(1) In the first place, many may be critical of the Indian view of interdisciplinarity and its intimate relations with democracy. Critics may say there is more 'a pious hope' in it than any effective intellectual strategy. In response to this critical point, it may be said that Indians never cared about interdisciplinarity as an autonomous inquiry—we do not in fact need to arrive at yet another discipline through the paradigmatic practice of interdisciplinarity. From the Indian point of view, "interdisciplinarity is not an end in itself"; instead, it is "a means to a process of knowledge that is integral, sensitive to the challenge of a fast-changing human condition, problem-oriented and capable of creative interaction with reality and liberating" (Kothari 1998: 43). What we as humans require now is a transformation through liberation from discipline-bound ways of thinking.

(2) Interdisciplinary Democracy seems to place much of the burden of social change in the technology-generated sophisticated modes of interactions than in humans and their time-honoured institutions. The real challenge lies in the problem of creative engagement with contemporary complexities. Democracy demands of us to reach decisions amicably without sacrificing diversity in a socio-political arena as well as in our intellectual pursuits. But, in the wake of tremendous changes that the postmodern situation brought in, all this no longer remains an easy-going task.

Contemporary context of democracy is characterized by the highly complex nature of many policy affairs, rise of technical managerialism, increasing the power of the corporate world over nation-states and growing apathetic forms of citizenship. All these factors are closely knit together in the current socio-political situation that can no longer be conceptualized in terms of democracy alone. Such is the view supported by some social scientists who opine that ours is an age of 'post-democracy', rather than that of democracy as such. For them, political practices in this age of high technology and managerial solutions are inevitably underpinned by post-democratic values.

(3) There is yet another side to the matter. Democracy is also regarded as a value in itself requiring no other system for its justification. Of course, there are significant issues involved in democracy but they need to be addressed democratically. It is thus sometimes contended that "the only cure for the evils of democracy is more democracy". This is the widely held view about the value of Democracy. Democratization is no doubt good but how much of it is suitable and sustainable? With the widespread participation of people, organizations and interest groups across all traditional boundaries and regulatory mechanisms, governments are often confronted with unrealistic expectations at large leading to 'political overload'.

Such a situation has been viewed by Huntington as an "excess of democracy". There is thus a need, in his opinion, to strike a balance by disciplining our overwhelming democratic aspirations. According to him, "A value system that is good in itself is not necessarily optimized when it is maximized. We have come to recognize that there are potentially desirable limits to the extension of political democracy. Democracy will have no longer life if it has a more balanced existence" (Crozier *et al.,* 1975: 115). Huntington's view is, in fact, well-founded; it is based on Aristotelian Virtue Ethics, according to which virtue is "the mean by reference to two vices: the one of excess and the other of deficiency" (Rachels 1978:159-79).

Similar is the situation on the educational front where we hear frequent calls for becoming more and more interdisciplinary often propelled by inadequate critical considerations. Hence, it has been emphasized that "A fight must also be waged to alter the balance between standardization and variety in the curriculum. Diversity carried to its extreme could produce a non-society in which the common frames of reference would make communication between people even more difficult than it is today. The dangers of social fragmentation cannot be met by maintaining a highly homogeneous education system while the rest of the society race towards heterogeneity" (Toffler 1970: 411).

(4) In interdisciplinarity, we are required to recognize the diversity of knowledge domains, yet the existence of the dominance of certain disciplines at the expense of others should not escape our attention.

For instance, technoscience is the dominant note of the day that is further fuelled and fostered by market forces. In a sense, there is a real danger for societal life posed by the pressure of market imperatives. Interdisciplinarity is a double-edged sword, and market-friendly forces know well how to manipulate it for profit enhancing. Education is often considered to be the last hope of humankind and interdisciplinarity is regarded as the future of higher education. But what is going on in the name of the interdisciplinary study and research is "the development of an increasingly interdisciplinary general humanities amid a cluster of vocational schools". This merging of disciplinary departments into engineered interdisciplinary programmes has been seen in actuality as "a form of downsizing and cost cutting" (Readings 1999: 174,191).

Obviously, the prevailing interdisciplinary format marked by a preponderance of high technology is not always conducive to democracy. Martha Nussbaum has plausibly shown why democracy needs humanities. She makes a distinction between education for profit-making through the excessive thrust on economic growth and education for developing an enlightened and inclusive citizenship. Most of the countries nowadays are focused on promoting the education of the first kind ignoring the latter almost altogether. The value of becoming a good citizen occurs nowhere in the priorities of the dominant model of democracy across the globe. What is emphasized in the name of education is the promotion of domain-specific knowledge and specialized skills that could be applied in wealth creation.

But democracy does not call for this short of citizenry skewed towards pecuniary advantage alone. Democracy demands a strong base of education with a thrust on humanities. Accordingly, interdisciplinarity too has to be more inclusive in scope and more critical in its concerns. An interdisciplinary research must not be a pick-and-mix market-friendly programme. Thus, the model of education that democracy demands marks a sharp departure from "passive assimilation of facts, and cultural traditions, but about challenging the mind to become active, competent, and thoroughly critical in a complex world" (Nussbaum 2010: 18). A healthy democracy requires citizens who have nerve and knowledge, who can think critically and act unwaveringly to counter any unjust and authoritarian regime, who are sensible enough to the human predicament at large and ever eagre to arrive at a creative engagement with others.

## Notes

1. This less used word is meant for emphasizing that compartmentalization and departmentalization go hand in hand in academia. *Vide*, Aronowitz, S., *et al.*, Eds. Technoscience and Cyberculture. NY & London: Routledge, 1996, p. 26, n. 16.
2. *Vide*, Laski, Harold, "The Limitations of the Expert," Harper's Magazine, December 1930; as cited in N. Stehr and R. Grundmman (eds.), Knowledge: Critical Concepts. Vol. II, London & NY: Routledge, 2005, p. 101.
3. The issue of expert testimony was addressed by Plato in his dialogue The Charmides, and it has recently attracted the attention of Alvin I. Goldman, "Experts: Which one should you trust?" in Selinger, E. and R.P. Crease (eds.). The Philosophy of Expertise, NY: Columbia University Press, 2006, p. 14. The metaphor of ship and navigator occurs in Plato's The Republic, and David Held has discussed the metaphor at length in his Models of Democracy. 2nd Edn., California: Stanford University Press, 1996, pp. 29-30.
4. *Sushruta Samhita*, I.4.7.
5. Bhartrihari, *Vakyapadiya*, 2. 484.

## References

Anderson, Elizabeth (2006): "The Epistemology of Democracy," *Episteme: A Journal of Social Epistemology*, 3.1.

Appadurai, A. (1996): "Diversity and Disciplinarity as Cultural Artifacts," in C. Nelson and D.P. Gaonkar, *Disciplinarity and Dissent in Cultural Studies* (NY & London: Routledge).

Best, S., and D. Kellner (2001): *The Postmodern Adventure: Science, Technology and Cultural Studies at the Third Millennium* (NY & London: The Guilford Press).

Boisvert, Raymond D. (1998): *John Dewey: Rethinking Our Times.* Albany (New York: State University of New York Press).

Campbell, Donald T. (1969): "Ethnocentrism of disciplines and fish-scale model of omniscience," M. Sherif and C.W. Sherif (ed.) *Interdisciplinary Relationships in Social Sciences*, (Chicago: Aldine Publishing Company).

Chattopadhyaya, D.P. (2003): "Difference Principle, Demoted Democracy and Globalization without Hegemonism," *Journal of Indian Council of Philosophical Research*, Vol. XX, No. 2.

Chew, Mathew (2000): "Politics and Patterns of Developing Indigenous Knowledge under Western Disciplinary Compartmentalization," M. Kusch, (ed.), *The Sociology of Philosophical Knowledge* (Dordrecht: Kluwer Academic Publishers).

Choudhary, Ravindra K.S. (2007): *Wittgensteinian Philosophy and Advaita Vedanta: A Survey of the Parallels* (New Delhi: D.K. Printworld).

______. (2012a): "Going Global after Wittgenstein," *Indian Philosophical Quarterly*, Vol. 39. Nos. 3-4.

______. (2012b): "Digital Democracy: Gandhi with Satellites," *Dialogue*, Vol. 14, No. 1.

______. (2013): "Specialization and Generalization–Considered as the Two Extremes of our Educational Experience," *Las Perspectivas*, Vol. 2, No. 2.

______. (2014): "An Indian View of Interdisciplinarity," *Prabuddha Bharata*, Vol. 119, No. 9.

Crozier, M.J., S.P. Huntington, and J. Watanuki (1975): *The Crisis of Democracy*. (NY: New York University Press).

Daele, Wolfgang von den (2005): "Traditional Knowledge in Modern Society" in N. Stehr and R. Grundmman (eds.) *Knowledge: Critical Concepts*, Vol. II, (London & NY: Routledge).

Dahl, Robert A. (1956): *A Preface to Democratic Theory*: (Chicago: Chicago University Press).

Dallmayr, Fred (2007): "Liberal Democracy and its Critics: Some Voices from East and West," *Journal of Indian Council of Philosophical Research*, Vol. XXIV, No. 4.

Gandhi, M.K. (15th Rpt., 2003): *Hind Swaraj*: (Ahmedabad: Navajivan Publishing House).

Giri, A.K. (2006): *New Horizons of Social Reality: Conversations, Transformations and Beyond* (Jaipur: Rawat Publications).

Held, David (2nd Edn., 1996): *Models of Democracy* (California: Stanford University Press).

Kapur, Vijay (2002): "Education Sans Frontier—Yankee Cola or Knowledge Vaccine", *Studies in Humanities and Social Sciences*, Vol. IX, No. 1.

Katz, Stanley N. (1995): "Do Disciplines Matter? History and the Social Sciences," *Social Science Quarterly*, Vol. 76 (4).

Kothari, Rajani (1988): *Rethinking Development: In Search of Human Alternatives* (Delhi: Ajanta).

______. (2007); *Rethinking Democracy* (London: Zed Books).

Mosco, Vincent (1990): "Computers and Democracy", in J. Berleur, A. Clement, R. Sizer, and D. Whitehouse, (eds.), *Information Society: Emerging Landscapes* (Canada: Springer-Verlag, Captus University Publications).

Norris, Christopher (2000): *Deconstruction and the 'Unified Project of Modernity'* (London: The Athlone Press).

Norris, Pippa (2000): *A Virtuous Circle: Political Communications in Postindustrial Societies* (Cambridge: Cambridge University Press).

Nussbaum, Martha (2010): *Not For Profit: Why Democracy Needs the Humanities*. (NJ: Princeton University Press).

Outram, Drinda (1995): *The Enlightenment: New Approaches to European History* (UK: Cambridge University Press).

Rachels, James (1978): "The Ethics of Virtue" *Elements of Moral Philosophy*, (New York: McGraw-Hill).

Radhakrishnan, S. (1997): *Religion and Culture* (Delhi: Orient Paperbacks).

Raju, P.T. (1985): *Structural Depth of Indian Thought* (New Delhi: South Asian Publishers).

Readings, B. (1999): *The University in Ruins* (Cambridge, MA: Harvard University Press).

Rosenberg, A. (2000): Philosophy *of Science* (London: Routledge).

Rosenberg, C. (1979): *Towards an ecology of knowledge: On discipline, Contexts, and History:The Organization of Knowledge in Modern America: 1860-1922.* (Baltimore: John Hopkins University).

Sartori, Giovani (1987): *The Theory of Democracy Revisited* (NY: Chatham House Publishing).

Selinger, E. and J. Mix (2006): "On Interpretational Expertise: Pragmatic and Ontological considerations," in Selinger, E. and R.P. Crease (eds.) *The Philosophy of Expertise* (NY: Columbia University Press).

Sen, Amartya (2005): *The Argumentative Indian* (New Delhi: Penguin Books).

Singh, A.K. (2010): *Towards Interdisciplinarity* (New Delhi: Creative Books).

Singhi, N.K. (1987): "Some Issues in the Conceptual Articulation of the Indian Intellectual Tradition," in Daya Krishna (ed.) *India's Intellectual Tradition* (New Delhi: Indian Council of Philosophical Research in Association with Motilal Banarasidass).

Toffler, Alvin (1970): *Future Shock* (New York: Bantam Books).

Toulmin, Stephen (2005): "The Invention of Disciplines," in N. Stehr and R. Grundmman. *Knowledge: Critical Concepts*, Vol. II (London & NY: Routledge).

Touraine, Alain (2000): *Can We Live Together? Equality and Difference* (California: Stanford University Press).

Wallerstein, I. *et. al.*, (1995): *Open The Social Sciences* (Lisbon: Report of the Gulbenkian Commission).

# 3
# Secularism Revisited
## Issues and Options

*Madhurendra Kumar*

## Introduction

Secularism is an evolving concept with varied interpretations and different implications for different people. Juxtaposed to western notion of secularism, which suggests religious neutrality of the state, Indian secularism stands for religious tolerance, liberty of faith and equality. It does not portray the Indian state as anti-religious rather it stands for symmetric treatment with all religions. In spite of secularism being the guiding principle of the Indian state, it is still being questioned today. After recent elections to the Lok Sabha, the victory of rightist forces, under the stewardship of Shri Narendra Modi, has been hailed as victory of Hindu nationalism and defeat of pseudo-secularism in some discourses published in the leading dailies of the country. It is argued that secularism is alien to Indian soil as religion is an integral part of peoples' everyday life. But what is ignored in this kind of arguments that religiosity and secularism are not antithetic to each other. It is a fallacious notion to equate religious faith with communalism. The real discourse on the nature of Indian secularism is often viewed through the lenses of vote bank politics whereas this pertinent issue calls for a dispassionate and objective appraisal of the theory and practice of secularism in India.

Therefore, the primary focus of this chapter is to examine the ideology of secularism practiced in India and to evaluate its role in the functioning of the democratic polity. It has been argued in this chapter that nature of secularism as principle and practice needs scrutiny in the context of politics of communalism. Finally, it is suggested that in order to be secular in political sense, the Indian state need not withdraw from dealing with religion and religious communities rather there should be symmetric treatment and religion should not be allowed to accrue political mileage.

Secularism has been a central issue of political discourse in the post-Independent India. Although, the founding fathers of our Constitution made it the cardinal basis of the post-Independence policy yet it is the most debated issue today. It faces multipronged attack leading to the question what it means to the citizens of a pluralistic democratic country like India.

As an ideology of the Constitution, secularism was intended to check absolutism, religious bigotry, and fanaticism. "It aimed at imposing limits on the political expression of cultural and religious conflicts between Hindus and Muslims (Bhargava 1998:1). But contrary to it, rise of religious fundamentalism and communalization of politics indisputably pose a serious challenge to secularism as it has failed to attain the objectives for which it was unanimously opted as one of the pillars of the state in the post-Independent India. In brief, secularism has not only failed in assuring the people to practice religious beliefs of their choice but the politics of vote bank has exacerbated the very problem that it was devised to overcome" (*ibid.*).

## Theoretical Aspect—Occidental and Oriental

In its origin secularism is a Western concept. The word secular is derived from Latin word 'Sacculum' which "implies the age, the world". In due course of time, it was interpreted as the opposite of 'Sacred'. During the Medieval period when there arose a conflict between state and church, temporal authority ultimately got victorious, and authority of the king was established. Consequently, it was established that religion and politics are two different domains and authority of the state should be irreligious (Madan, 1998:359-60).

As a concept, secularism is the product of liberal-democratic tradition. The underlying assumption of this theory is simply that religion and the state function in two different areas of human activities. It is none of the duties of the state to promote, direct or otherwise meddle with religion.

In a historical perspective, the word secularism was first used in 1648 at the end of the thirty years war in Europe. Again on 2nd, November 1789 Talleyrand accounted to the French National Assembly that all ecclesiastical goods were at the disposal of the nation. Later in 1851, George Jack Holyoake coined the term secularism and led a rationalist movement of protest in England. Thus, the idea of secularization was incorporated into the idea of progress.

What do we mean by secular and secularism? Various scholars have attempted to define these terms in different ways[1] however; they construed almost the same thing. The *Encyclopaedia of Religion and Ethics* describes it as a movement intestinally, ethical, negatively religious with political and philosophical antecedents. George Ostler, in the *Oxford Dictionary of Current English*, defines Secular as about this world or the present life not ecclesiastical. Secular can, therefore, be explained as worldly related to thing connected with the present life only. In the negative sense, it implies disassociation from religion or religious teachings. In the *Encyclopaedia Britannica*, Secularism is defined as a branch of utilitarian ethics that described the physical social and moral improvement of mankind which neither affirms nor denies the theistic premises of religion. According to *Encyclopaedia of Social Sciences*, "secularism in the philosophical sphere may be interpreted a result against theological and virtually against metaphysical absolutes and universals. In the political sphere came to mean that temporal ruler was entitled to exercise power in his own right."[2]

In a nutshell, secularism seeks human progress and improvement through material means. Secular knowledge is founded upon the experiences of life and cannot be tested by reason. It is entirely unconcerned with the unknown world. In fact, secularism is an offshoot of rationalism and seeks the physical moral and intellectual development of man through material means.

In the western setting secularism in its intellectual and political aspects has undergone different phases. The first stage marked a tendency to carry over to secular realm some older idealistic elements that had been identified with religion. In the second phase, several types of compromises between secularism and religion was made. For instance, John Lock tried to fuse Renaissance Humanism, State Natural Law system and Eurasian conception of Christianity as a primarily system of ethics into one integrated system while in third stage disparities between different nation-states led to the development of exclusive particularism and revival of nationalism. Further the revolt against particularism led to the revival of juristic universalism based on theories regarding the universality of human nature and humanitarianism and emphasized the maximization of social justice and welfare. So, secularism guarantees individual and corporate freedom of religion and deals with the individual as a citizen irrespective of his or her religion.

A peep into history of political and social philosophy depicts that the term secularism acquired a new significance and wide currency in British thought and literature as a result of the writings of G.C. Holyonike, an associate of Charles Bradlaugh (noted for his atheism) brought out his principles of secularism in 1859. These principles won the whole-hearted approval of the celebrated political philosopher J.S. Mill. In the opinion of utilitarian thinkers secularism was virtually an offshoot of utilitarian philosophy enunciated in the eighteenth century which laid emphasis on the utilitarian value of law and politics that must be determined by human welfare (Beg 1969; Gajendragadadkar 1966).

Thus, secularism, as developed in the West, does not permit the state to interfere in the religious domain. It is supposed to maintain complete neutrality in religious matters. Contrary to Western tradition, the Indian secularism is different in the sense that it stands for tolerance and accords equal respect to all religions. The spirit of toleration is the basic underpinning of the ideology of secularism.

A look into the Indian history and civilization provides a comprehensive account of secular tradition. Although religion and politics were closely linked yet, there was a freedom of thought with remarkable tolerance towards heterodox opinions and latitude. There are numerous instances of secular provisions in the ancient Indian tradition. Of course, there is an emphasis on '*Dharma*' in Hinduism but it is a mistaken notion that '*Dharma*' is synonymous with Hindu religion. '*Dharma*' is, in fact, duty not 'theism' or belief in divine. It is noteworthy that there is hardly any reference to right in ancient texts such as *Shanti Parva* or *Mahabharata* or *Anushashan Parva* or in '*Arthshastra*' of Kautilya. It may be regarded as one of the earliest secular code of law in the world. It provides a complete secular approach to political and legal problems. Its contents and approach to the problems of governance is totally secular. Besides it, there is evidence of secular jurisprudence in ancient India. Brihaspati refers to two modes of proof: supernatural and secular[3] 'द्विप्रकारा क्रिया प्रोक्ता, मानुषी दैविकी तथा' According to Katyayana when one party offers to prove his case by secular evidence, while the other offers supernatural (divine) proof, the court should accept the secular evidence and reject the supernatural (Dhawan, 1966:124).

यद्येको मानुषीं ब्रूयादन्यो ब्रूयात्तु दैविकीम्।
मानुषीं तत्रे गृहणीयान्न तु दैवीं क्रियां नृपः ॥

These references buttress the existence of secular tradition in ancient India. It is again a noteworthy fact of Indian history that Jainism, Buddhism and even Islam co-existed. Even the imperial powers did not interfere in religious matters. Further, recognition of the rule of law during the British period laid the foundation of the secular polity.

During freedom struggle also leaders like Dada Bhai Naoroji, Ranade, Surendra Nath Banerjee, Shri Aurobindo, Gokhale, Ferozshah Mehta, etc. though advocated the concept of moral foundation of political authority, but their sole emphasis was on religious, cultural unity. Even Mahatma Gandhi did not believe in the dichotomy of religion and secularism. He was deeply religious yet was a votary of the secular state. He found in the synthesis of religion and politics, but through his experiment aimed at secularizing religion and spiritualization of politics. His religion was not a propagation of theism rather his religion was truth and righteousness. He said in 1946 "If I were a dictator, religion and state would be separate. I swear by my religion and die for it. But it is my personal affair. The state has nothing to do with it. The state would look after your secular welfare, health, communications, foreign relations, currency and so on but not your or my religion. That is everybody's personal concern". The assertion of Gandhiji candidly shows that he had no faith in state religion. He further maintained "The state should undoubtedly be secular. Everyone living without it should be entitled to profess his religion without hindrance so long as they as citizen obeyed the common law of the land" (*Harijan*: 1947).[4]

Secularism as an ideology of state in India is not a historical accident rather it was a conscious choice of the nation despite occasional spasms of sectarian violence, communal politics, and partition. This decision of the founding fathers of the Constitution was inspired by our glorious cultural tradition of tolerance and the principle of live and let live which is so deeply ingrained in the historical experiences and cultural dynamics of the Indian society (Pannikar 1997:50-53). It is worthwhile to recall here that culturally and demographically India was not exactly a melting point, the indigenous culture and religion did not absorb or assimilate all that came from outside. Both co-existed, mutually influencing as well as mutually contending. Diversity rather than homogeneity in that what history gave to the people of India? In fact, this sense of history exercised a profound influence on the minds of the makers of the modern secular India (*ibid.*: 5). Secondly, Congress under whose aegis India attained Independence from colonial rule was also committed to pursuing a secular approach. Behind this kind of approach was the realization of the reality of the pluralistic society in India. Jawaharlal Nehru, the Chief architect of modern India, expressed his abiding faith in secularism. He asserted, "I believe in India being a secular state with complete freedom for all religions and cooperation between them. He declared in a letter to the Nawab of Bhopal on 8th July, 1948 "I believe that India can only become great if it preserves that composite culture that it has developed through the ages." (Gopal) His objective was to create a secular state through democracy. He made a dispassionate analysis of history and reached the conclusion that India lost its age-old glory owing to mutual distrust, disbelief, and communal approach. So, it would be difficult to safeguard democracy without fostering unity in the country. To this end, secularism was a very powerful mechanism for maintaining unity and integrity of the country. His concern for the unity of the country was very much reflected in the objective resolution that was the foundation of the Constitution of India. Explaining it further he said, "the resolution that I am placing before you define our aims. It has ever been and shall always been our ardent desire to see the people of India united together so that we may frame Constitution which will be acceptable to the masses of the Indian people." (Hasan, 1997:135-36). Outlining his views on secularism he clearly said that "India is a secular state does not mean it is anti-religious instead it implies respect for all irrespective of their religion and faith. Secularism was the only way for progress.[5]

Thus, Nehru put his personal stamp on secularism. It was seen as countering the internal threat to national unity unleashed by communalism as well as differentiating progressive India from reactionary Islamic Pakistan. "It will be with pride, a constituent assembly member declared in May 1949, that our nation will be remembered by the nations of the world that we have kept no room for communalism in our Constitution and that we are in real sense of the word a secular state" (Hasan 1997:141). In fact, in the prevailing situations when religious and regional division were posing a threat and a challenge to Indian unity and integrity in a traditional society with its rigid caste system, religious revivalism, and obscurantist way of thinking, secularism was the only alternative for the further governance in India.

Participating in the debate on the Hindu Code Bill in Provisional Parliament Dr. Ambedkar, explained the concept of secularism as follows: "If secular state does not mean that we shall not take into consideration the religious sentiments of the people. All that a secular state means is that this Parliament shall not be competent to impose any particular religion on the people. That is the only limitation the Constitution recognizes (*Parliamentary Debates* 1956).[6]

So, it is due to historical and political reasons the framers of the Constitution declared India to be a secular state. Secularism was thus justified not only to sustain intercommunity solidarity, but to protect the democratic structure of the Indian state. It is interesting to note that originally the text of the Constitution did not contain the word Secularism anywhere. It was inserted into Constitution only in 1976 vide the forty-second Constitutional Amendment. However, the philosophy of secularism was enunciated in the Preamble to the Constitution and the chapter on Fundamental Rights. Constitution establishes no state religion, creates no category or preferred citizens, throws citizenship open to all (*Constitution of India*: Art, 5) which guarantees equality of status and opportunity and promise to promote dignity of the individual. It throws open to all creeds and castes all publications including the highest office of the President (*Constitution of India*: Article 15-1) prohibits discrimination by any agency on the basis of religion, guarantees equality of representation, forbids discrimination on the basis of religion in educational institution. (*Constitution of India*: Article 16-2) Constitution forbids even non-governmental agencies such as shops public restaurant hotels and places of public entertainment to discriminate against citizens on the ground of religion, race, caste, sex and place of birth (*Constitution of India*: Art. 15-2). It also provides that a citizen shall not be denied admission to any educational institution maintained by state funds on the grounds of religion, race, and caste languages (*Constitution of India*: Art. 15-8).

Further the right to franchise is guaranteed to every adult citizen irrespective of religion and caste etc. The Constitution provides one electoral roll for every territorial constituency. Article 325 says that no person shall be ineligible for inclusion in any special role for such constituency on grounds of religion, race, caste, sex or any of them. (*Constitution of India*: Art. 8) Communal electorate have been held unconstitutional and further our Constitution provides that state may make any law for providing for social welfare and reform or the throwing open Hindu religious institutions of a public character to all classes and section of Hindu. The Constitution also guarantees the right of religious and charitable organizations to manage their affairs in matters of religion (*Constitution of India*: Art. 26). Besides, these provisions "The dominant themes of secularism, i.e. freedom of religious belief and conscience, equality of all religions and equidistance of the state from all religions were backed up by special provisions for minority rights. It was realized by the political leadership that mere proclamation of secularism may not have been able to create a supportive social and political environment for minority cultures. Hence, a congenial atmosphere was created by the institutionalization of protection for minority rights (Chandoke 1999: 56).

The Constitutional provisions show that abundant care was taken by the makers of the Constitution to avoid any hindrance to the state's endeavour to secularize and modernize the Indian Society. But in practice Indian secularism owing to the marked departure of state from the ideology of secularism has been challenged in the post-Independence India. It is alleged by Bharatiya Janata Party and like forces that "with the aid of a series of legislation, the State has attempted to neutralize the communal identity of Hindus". Hindus are forced to be non-religious while Muslims are permitted and often encouraged to frame their identity purely in terms of their religion. So, Indian secularism, in fact, is far from neutral (Bhargava 1998 : 487), or it is pseudo-secularism. In another attack on secularism, it is argued that "the Indian Constitution and political and legal tradition actually favour minority community of Muslims giving them a privileged status not enjoyed by the majority community of Hindus (Sen 1996 : 458). Allegations are leveled even on the grounds of practices of personal laws of Hindus and Muslims particularly in the cases of marriage and divorce. Therefore, demand for a common civil code is often made to remove this kind of biases.

In fact, the practice of secularism by political dispensations has developed several fault lines due to which it has often become a convenient weapon in the hands of fundamentalists and communalists. The rise of communalism and fundamentalism; be it Hindu fundamentalism, Sikh fundamentalism or Muslim fundamentalism; all have tended to weaken secularism and inter-community faith. It threatened the unity and integrity of the nation and put a question mark regarding Constitutional commitment for a secular polity. It is also indicative of a breakdown of secularization process in India. It has brought about the escalation of ethno-religious conflicts and national disintegration. So, one is forced to ponder whether the principles of secularism embedded in our Constitution are properly understood and adhered by the citizens, or there is a deviation from the principled stand? The rise of communal parties in India marks this deviation. The statements and public speeches delivered by separatist and communal forces and sectarian appeal made by political leaders during elections and tremendous impact they exercise on the masses, recurring communal riots in various parts of our country, such as Godhara, Muzaffarnagar, Meerut, Mumbai or Aligarh clearly exhibit the strength of communal forces and relative weaknesses of secularism and buttress the charge that there have been deviations in the practice of secularism.

During the past seventy years of Independence, communalism has provided to be both ritualistic and institutionalized as it has been directly or indirectly supported by the governing elector for the cause of identity and consolidating vote banks. The very fact that state agency, in the name of minorities under the Constitutional load has sustained communalism in our polity and therefore, the Indian leaders have morally failed to control the scourge of communalism. Frequent occurrences of communicable violence are a severe blow to secularism. Paul R. Brass blames the organs of the Indian state for riots and calls it structured violence. He writes, "....it was.... Now, clear enough to me that what have been called Hindu-Muslim riots in India of the past several decades are misnamed that they could not have been carried out with such force in so many places in many cases for extended periods of time and repeatedly without the complicity of the police and failure of the political parties in controls of government and the administrative and police officers. Therefore, he regards secular values essential for maintenance of a just and peaceful social order in India.[7] (*The Hindu* 2006).

Unfortunately, the quest for sustaining secular values as a cornerstone of polity faced attacks from the so-called champions of *Hindutva* after the BJP- led government assumed power. Supernatural elements are being revived and revitalized which gives birth to plethora of misgivings in to minds of the people if India is tending towards desecularization? It is due to attempts made by a section of society to equate Hindu cultural symbols as the national culture. Shri Narendra Modi's *Ganga Arati* at Varanasi and its telecast by media, Sushma Swaraj's proposal to declare the *Bhagwad Gita* as national book, public utterances of the RSS Chief Shri Mohan Bhagwat in favour of Hinduism, the diatribes of Sakshi Maharaj and Yogi Adityanath show that an avenging rage is attempting to found ancient theology. Apart from that, growing attack on churches in different parts of the country is enough to plant this misgiving in the minds of those believing in pluralistic society and composite culture that current political dispensation is trying to impose its cultural agenda on the nation that was long drafted by its think tank RSS. It is certainly the most serious challenge to Modi Government. It is further exacerbated by cultist fringe groups for whom Hinduism is nothing, but a political sledgehammer to bash others. These forces seek to stereotype any dissent as anti-Hindu in the same way as the so-called secularists tend to brand any alternative viewpoint as communal. In this war of two feuding schools of secularism, it is difficult to ascertain what is wrong and what is right? *Hindutva* agenda projects secularism as elite irreligious Marxist fade while any concession to minorities sits the secularists.

In fact, the drift in the Indian secular discourses is also due to the role of media. Modi's *Aarti* became an issue in secular discourse simply because his performing of *Aarti* was not treated as personal and private religious act. Thus, media contributes in distorting the picture of Indian secularism. It is unfortunate that even national issues such as common civil code and Article 370 become communal symbols due to politics of secularism. Virtually, all political parties are accountable for the perversion of secularism. Rajiv Gandhi was regarded as a secular Prime Minister, who unhesitatingly overturned Shah Bano judgement, banned Satanic Verses of Salman Rushdie and at the same time allowed to unlock the gates of Babri Masjid and permitted *Shilanyas*. It was certainly an attempt to appease both the

Muslims and the Hindu. It was a projection of silly secularism creating grounds for the massive backlash of rampaging identity politics. It also paved the way for Hindu consolidation, and so-called secularists sought to appease the identity-driven instincts of the Muslim community. Even Mamta Banerjee's decision to dole out honourarium to Imams and overt leaning of Samajwadi Party government in Uttar Pradesh towards Muslims inevitably leads to a backlash of majoritarianism. Now, the Narendra Modi government is using the same means to appease the Hindu majority. It is the greatest challenge to Indian secularism that is founded on the principle of equal protection to all faiths. So, it seems that perversion of secular discourse is likely to continue if the meaning of religion and its relationship with politics is not correctly understood and proliferated in the real sense in the Indian context. We must bear this fact in mind that modernization of secular society is not merely a political process. It is futile to cherish the hope of cultural and ideological transformation simply through political and economic change. The disintegration of the former Soviet Union and present plight of vanishing socialist states of Eastern Europe should be an eye opener for our ruling elites where caste and communal issues are still unresolved.

It is incumbent upon the political class to dispassionately address caste and communal questions. There is a dire need to create a congenial situation where political misuse of religion is not permitted because it is the political misuse of religion that has given rise to several fissiparous tendencies disrupting a harmonious social living. Whether becoming religious is communal? Whether a man automatically becomes communal having practiced his religion? These are a few pertinent issues that need to be addressed widely? Unfortunately, a deliberate confusion has been created between religion and secular; between Hindu and Indian, between Muslim and Indian, etc. whereas cultural dimension of secularism is often entirely neglected. As a result, we have neither attempted to develop a composite Indian culture based on true amalgam of all religions and subcultures nor have we developed a new political culture of tolerance and co-existence based on secular values with emphasis on secular symbols.

The greatest strength of our political system, in fact, lies in democracy and secularism. In a religiously pluralistic society, democracy cannot flourish without secularism. The State, however, for political reasons has not been able to maintain equal distance from all religions. Sometimes, it plays Muslim card and sometimes Hindu card whatever suits in a particular context for sheer electoral benefits. The role of the State in the Shah Bano case, Ayodhya dispute, demolition of Babri Masjid are oft quoted instances of the partisan role of the state. Consequently, a big inter-religion and inter-cultural hiatus was created, and it has shaken the very foundation of secularism.

To sum up, it may be said that awareness and consciousness about the values of secularism are still in its infancy, and we prefer to look upon ourselves more as a Muslim or Sikh or Hindu than Indian citizen. The politics of religion has decidedly weakened the fabric of secular politics in India. So, secularism has to be strengthened politically by combating communalism, and it must be strengthened socially by advocating progressive social change in every religious community. At political level what is required is broadening of democracy and its attendant concepts such as freedom, equality and justice as it ensures both inter-group and (Chandoke 2010: 344-45) intra- group relations along the norms of equality that is virtually the cornerstone of secularism.

## Notes

1. See Charles Taylor, *Modes of Secular*ism in Rajiv Bhargava, *op. cit.*, pp. 31-32.
2. *Encyclopaedia of Social Sciences,* Vol. XIII, MacMillan, New York, 1954, p. 631.
3. *Brihaspatismriti,* IV. 1. 16.
4. *Harijan,* 24 August, 1947, p. 292.
5. *Constituent Assembly Debates,* Vol. III, p. 37.
6. *Parliamentary Debates,* 1951, Vol. III, Para II, p. 211-66.
7. *The Hindu,* 23rd August, 2006.

## References

Beg, Heg (1969): Islamic Jurisprudence and Secularism in G.S. Sharma (ed): *Secularism Implication for Law and Life in India*, (Bombay: N.M. Tripathi Private Limited); Bhargava, Rajiv (1998): *Secularism and its Critics*, (New Delhi: Oxford University Press).

——"What is Secularism?" *Economic and Political Weekly*, July 9, 1994, p.487.

Brass, Paul R. "Organized Riots and Structured Violence in India", *The Hindu*: 23 August, 2006.

Chandhoke, Neera (1999): *Beyond Secularism: The Rights of Religious Minorities*, (New Delhi: Oxford University Press), p. 56.

Dhawan, S.S. (1966); Secularism in Indian Jurisprudence in G. Sharma (ed.): *Secularism Implications for Law and Life in India* (Bombay: N.M. Tripathi Private Limited), p. 124.

Gajendradadkar, P.B. (1966): *The Constitution of India: Philosophy and Basic Postulates*, (Bombay: N.M. Tripathi Private Limited), p. 140.

Hasan, M. (1997): *Legacy of a Divided Nation; India's Muslims since Independence*, (New Delhi: West View Press ) pp. 135-36. Madan, T. N. (1998): 'Secularism in its place' in Rajiv Bhargava (ed.) *Secularism and its Critics* (New Delhi: Oxford University Press), pp. 359-60.

Madan, T.N. (1998): 'Secularism in its Place' in Rajiv Bhargava (ed.) *Secularism and its Critics*, (New Delhi: Oxford University Press), pp. 359-60.

Pannikar, K.M. (1997): *Communcial Threat, Secular Challenge* (Madras: Earthworm Books), pp. 50-53.

Sen, Amartya (1996): Secularism and Its Discontents, in Basu, K., Subramahmyam, S. (ed.): *Unraveling the Nation: Sectarian Conflict and India's Secular Identity* (New Delhi:Penguin Books), p. 8.

# SECTION II
# Question of Rights and Conflicts

# 4

# Protest and Participation

## The Popular Struggle against Coca-Cola in Plachimada (Kerala)

*Henrik Berglund* and *Sofia Helander*

### Introduction

In accordance with global norms, India decided in the early 1990s to open up parts of its economy for foreign investments. While this process is by no means completed, the increased presence of multinational corporations has had significant consequences for Indian society, primarily within the political and economic spheres. One sector that has witnessed rapid globalization is the Indian soft drink market, as local brands have gradually been overtaken by two global conglomerates, Pepsi Co and the Coca-Cola Company, which now hold at least 95 per cent of the Indian market between them. The Coca-Cola Company has in several cases been accused of violating laws for environmental protection, and for excessive usage of water, harming public access to water for drinking and irrigation. The campaigns against the companies have usually started as local initiatives, but many of them have gained support from national and international NGOs.

While protests against allegedly flawed practices of private and public corporations are by no means new to Indian society, the protests against foreign companies often has a different edge, drawing on discourses of domination, dependency and nationalism, with expected support from both left and right. In the campaigns against Coca-Cola it is also fact that the company in itself symbolizes the Western style of capitalism and consumerism, perhaps more so than any other corporation. The Coca-Cola company also has a history of conflicts with the Indian authorities as it was basically thrown out of the country in 1977 after refusing to follow the existing currency legislation and being accused of routinely shifting its huge profits outside of the country. The corporation re-entered as late as 1993 and its current expansion in India has included the opening of several new bottling plants, and at present operates fifty two plants all over India.

This article analyzes a campaign launched against the company in Plachimada, northern Kerala, where the bottling plant has been shut down after intense pressure from various NGOs, and focuses on the effects of the protests. The following issues are addressed in the article: *How was civil society used as a platform for this struggle and what was the outcome? Did this campaign have any long-term effects on political participation?* The research problem relates to vital debates on the effects of globalization, and on the role of civil society in the development and strengthening of democracy. While the effects of the globalization process in developing countries are contested, the claim that civil society plays a major role in the construction of consolidated democracies is increasingly recognized. The article contributes to the understanding of how actors within civil society work together against perceived injustices and how they include both the political sphere and the state in this struggle.

## Political Protests and Participation

Social movements are, according to Sidney Tarrow, best defined as "...collective challenges by people with common purposes and solidarity..." (Davis *et al.*, 2005:75). India has ever since its colonial period witnessed various forms of protest movements, focussing on both the struggle against colonial ties, as well as on various forms of social issues. Throughout history, we have seen both elite dominated as well as mass movements, earlier often tied to the Indian National Congress or other groups within the anti-colonial movement, later usually working more independently. Since, the 1980s we have also experienced the phenomena of "new social movements", indicating a shift from larger movements with clear material gains in focus, such as e.g. trade unions, to smaller and more ideologically motivated groups, often with strong local connections. Examples of such groups are many of the "green" NGOs which have emerged in India, and the anti-Coca-Cola campaign in Plachimada is a case in point. It should however be noted that no clear distinction can be made between ideological NGOs and those primarily focussing on material issues. What is at stake for many of those engaging in environmental protests is not necessarily an alternative view of life, or a critique of a materialist or capitalist society, but rather an urge to protect his/her livelihood. Environmental damages may threaten whole communities and radically alter their ability to provide for themselves and their families, hence the strong resistance.

Even though the research concerning political participation and social movements has thoroughly examined how participation is initially triggered when social movements are formed, there is a gap in the knowledge concerning how the movement and participation in itself affects long-term participation among the involved individuals (Giugni *et al.*, 1999: xi). There are three potential scenarios of what could be the long-term effects of social movement on individual participation: no effect on participation, continued participation through the movement and continued participation in other forms. Research in the area of political participation has led to insights in what constitutes political participation as well as how it can be measured. Most definitions contain some central elements, such as emphasizing action rather than motivations, ordinary citizen rather than bureaucrats or political elite and focus on influencing *political* outcome and government activity on any level rather than on influencing non-political actors (Brady 1999: 737). In one of the more recent studies by Verba *et al.*, participation is divided into six main modes of participation: voting, campaign work, other collective activities, contacting, protesting and political organization.[1] Participation is measured separately in each mode, as well as in an aggregated index.

### Equal Participation, Political Equality and Democracy

According to Robert Dahl, five criteria have to be met in order to attain the ideal type democracy: effective participation, equality in voting, enlightened understanding, control of the agenda and inclusiveness (Dahl 2000:38). All of these criteria, in particular effective participation and inclusiveness, are connected to the concept of equal participation. Effective participation is defined by citizens having adequate and equal opportunities to form their preference and place issues on the public agenda and it is clear that political participation, and especially *equal* political participation, is strongly connected to the concept of democracy. It is, therefore, not surprising that, in the research field of political participation, much focus has been placed on studying equality in participation and how it can be enhanced. In the late 1970s, Sidney Verba, Norman Nie and Jae-on Kim formed the basis of a new discourse on political participation through their seven nation comparison: *Participation and Political Equality*, in which they argue that even though democratic systems often are equalitarian in principle, differences in social and economic resources result in unequal levels of political activity and influence, which creates a democratic deficit.

Verba *et al.,* suggested that even though political rights provide opportunities for participation they are not in themselves enough to trigger participation. In order for an individual to participate she has to choose to use this opportunity and have the resources necessary in making a particular activity possible. Consequently, activity depends on resources and motivations, and the authors identified two different processes which result in mobilization: individual-based, depending on individual motivations and resources, and group-based, depending on group-based motivations and resources (Verba, 1978:5). Individual motivations differ from group-based motivations by not involving preferences for policies beneficial to a group in which one is a member. Instead, individual motivations could be a sense of obligation, confidence in one's own political competence, general political interest and knowledge or personal problems that could be affected by government officials. The group-based process of mobilization is triggered by membership in a particular group. The group could be based on a variety of factors, such as economic position, race, ethnicity, region or religion, and its main common resource is organization—the more organized the social category is, the more capable it is of participating politically (*ibid.*:12).

## Coca-Cola in India—The Case of Plachimada

Political participation is often organised around various forms of protest movements and the anti-Coca-Cola movement in Kerala is a case in point. The Coca-Cola bottling plant in question is situated in Plachimada, a small village under the Perumatty *panchayat* (local council) of Chittur block, Palakkad district, in northern Kerala, bordering the State of Tamil Nadu. The area is very dry with an average rainfall of one half of the Kerala state average and consists mainly of agricultural land with coconut and rice as the dominating crops. Most of the households in the area depend on agriculture for their survival, as farmers or agricultural labourers (Nair *et al.*, 2008:33). The district has a sizable tribal minority and the area surrounding the plant is populated almost exclusively by tribals from the *Eravalan* community. Compared to the state average the area lags behind in development with illiteracy as high as 32 per cent and with incomes far lower than the state average (*ibid.*: 29-38). The Congress Party and the Janata Dal (S) has dominated local politics for the last decade, with the Congress as the winner of the three last State Assembly elections in the Chittur constituency, but with the Janata Dal (S) controlling the *panchayat*.

Already in 1998 Coca-Cola started to plan for a new plant in Kerala, and after securing a land lease from the local *panchayat*, as well as the necessary state licenses, the company started production in the year of 2000. According to most estimates 300-500 workers were employed when the plant was working at full capacity, but official figures from Coca-Cola Company (henceforth CCC) are unavailable. The Plachimada Solidarity Committee, one of the NGOs engaged in the campaign against the company, claims that only a handful of these are directly employed by Coca-Cola, and that the vast majority are instead contract labourers, with both poor wages and insecure employment.[2]

After less than two years the communities living near the plant started to complain about both the quality and the quantity of water in the village wells. A villager interviewed for this article also claimed that it had a direct and negative effect on the health of the villagers, especially the children.[3] In the autumn of 2001 the first collective protests were organized outside the factory, demanding its closure, and full compensation to the villagers. This was the starting point for a movement which was—and still is—grass root based, but with links to the national and global level. The Coca-Cola Company tried to disrupt the protests by issuing statements in which they refuted the accusations of water depletion and pollution, referring to tests conducted by independent laboratories, but paid for by Coca-Cola. The Coca-Cola Company also arranged for some social programmes to boost its image among the local population, e.g. free health camps, rain-water harvesting systems and free meals for school children (Nair *et al.*, 2008 : 98). In April 2002 the campaign against Coca-Cola was formally launched with the formation of the Anti-Coca-Cola Peoples Struggle Committee (Coca-Cola Virudha Janakeeya Samara Samithy) in connection with a blockade of the factory, which was disper sed by the police. The target of the protests was of course the Coca-Cola Company, but also the state authorities, the political parties and the public. The core of the Plachimada movement is the Anti-Coca-Cola Peoples Struggle Committee (henceforth called the Committee), sometimes called the Plachimada Struggle Committee or similarly, or CVSS, an acronym of its Indian name. This group includes the grass root supporters of the cause, almost solely tribals. Outside, but in close cooperation, we find the Plachimada Struggle Solidarity Committee with the task of generating outside support the campaign, also on the national and global level. In October 2008, 92 different organizations had registered as members of the Solidarity Committee.[4]

From 2002 and onwards both the Anti-Coca-Cola Peoples Struggle Committee and other NGOs and various journalists tried to establish a link between the plant and the problems experienced by the villagers. The claim that the water level was sinking was validated, but Coca-Cola claimed that the variations were natural and due to poor monsoon rains, and the Central Ground Water Board (CGWB), representing the Government of India, supported the company. Concerning the alleged pollution of the water the claims made by the Committee have been substantiated by a number of tests, both in Indian and in foreign laboratories. Two different forms of contamination were suspected: first, the leaching of contaminated waste water into the ground water reserves, thereby polluting the wells in the surrounding villages; secondly, high toxic levels in the solid waste produced. The waste was dumped in open fields around the factory, but was also used as a fertilizer by many farmers. Both Coca-Cola and the CGWB rejected the initial complaints of polluted wells. The sludge was analyzed in a British laboratory and in July 2003 the BBC reported high levels of both lead and cadmium. Less than two weeks later the state authorities demanded that the Coca-Cola Company should keep the sludge in safe containers as further tests by the Kerala State Pollution Control Board (KSPCB) had shown that the sludge contained even higher levels of toxicity than in the BBC tests (Bijoy 2006:4332-39).

Due to pressure from the villagers the Perumatty *panchayat* started to change its mind concerning the presence of Coca-Cola. In the interviews made for this article leaders and activists stated that the relation to the local *panchayat* was now very good, but that there had been suspicions of corruption when the plant was established.[5] One example is the claim that the Coca-Cola Company contributed financially to the election campaigns of some local politicians.[6] The sentiments of the leaders of the *panchayat* however changed gradually and already before the BBC-report and the intervention by the KSPCB the *panchayat* had in May 2003 decided to cancel the license under which Coca-Cola was producing. This was immediately disputed by the company, and the case took a dramatic turn when a Single Bench of the Kerala High Court ruled in favour of the villagers and urged Coca-Cola not to overexploit the local water reserves. The company appealed, but was forced to stop its production in March 9, 2004. Later the same month Coca-Cola received a further set-back when the *panchayat* of Perumatty refused to renew the licence for the bottling plant. 1, June, 2005 a Division Bench of the Kerala High Court overturned the previous court ruling and ruied that the Coca-Cola Company had the right to exploit the local water resources as long as it did not do so at the inconvenience of others. The Court further ruled against the *panchayat's* decision to refuse to renew the licence, since it had been done without scientific proof of the alleged misuse of water resources. The licence was also later renewed, but the *panchayat* set several conditions which were later rejected by the company which again started production on August 8. The State Government however reacted quickly and on August 19 the KSBPC ordered the plant to stop production immediately. Coca-Cola has challenged the decisions by both the *panchayat* and the KSBPC, so far without success, and the plant remains closed. The matter now rests with the Supreme Court of India and its ruling is expected to have wide consequences also for other current conflicts related to water issues.

## Explaining the Success of the Anti-Coca-Cola Peoples Struggle Committee

The struggle of the people in Plachimada is by many accounts exceptional, but when visiting the activists outside the factory gates one may wonder whether their struggle has been a victory at all. The water is still polluted and they remain uncompensated for the illness, and even deaths, inflicted by the poisoning. Their daily life is still disturbed by the shortage of water and their incomes as day labourers have been reduced, as the task of collecting drinking water is very time-consuming.[7] Some of the activists are also still facing legal charges due to their involvement in the protests. Largely based on grass root activism amongst tribal villagers with little or no formal education, the movement's victory over a large multinational corporation seemed unlikely at any stage of the conflict.

The Anti-Coca-Cola Peoples Struggle Committee attracts its members from a very limited geographical area around the Coca-Cola plant in Plachimada. The members are almost solely agricultural workers from *Eravalan* tribe, and the leaders have strong connections to the villagers. The current chairperson of the committee, Vilayodi Venugopal, is not himself a tribal, but he has been engaging himself in the life of the community long before the Plachimada struggle and is highly respected amongst the villagers (Nair *et al.*, 2008 : 90-91). The homogeneity of the group has been used as an advantage in the mobilization, forming a good basis for local protest and the constant presence of activists outside the factory gates, which continues still today. The identity of the Committee has been kept intact also by the arrangements with supportive groups, primarily the Plachimada Struggle Solidarity Committee, which has allowed outsiders to lend their support and work for further alliances on local, national and global level, but which has not "diluted" the local committee by allowing outsiders to join as members. While the strong tribal identity of the Committee was a strength when mobilizing support within the *Eravalan*-community, it may have been a disadvantage when seeking broader support in the area, given the often strict boundaries between religious communities, castes and sub-castes in India. It was also a fact that the movement initially did not attract people outside the tribal community. The farmers with holdings surrounding the factory were affected by the water shortage and have supported the movement, but rarely participated in agitations. Their lack of commitment may be explained by the fact that the prime concern of the farmers was not the pollution, but the lowering water levels, an issue on which they also influenced the *panchayat* to act against the company (*ibid.*: 95). This passive attitude may be explained as a rational action: an agent pursuing his self-interest, but also by a lack of solidarity with the tribal community.

The social context of the struggle must also be seen in larger perspective, as an issue with relevance to the whole tribal community. The State of Kerala has a tribal population of only 1.14 per cent, most of them landless and far poorer than the average. Indian law provides for the possibilities to protect the tribal population by notifying tribal areas as "scheduled areas," thereby putting restrains on the selling and buying of land and property originally belonging to members of the Scheduled Tribes. Unlike other States in India, the State of Kerala has failed to implement these measurements, resulting in widespread resentment amongst the tribal population, but also political mobilization (Bijoy 2006: 4332-39). The Plachimada struggle benefited from these experiences, and to some extent the movement was an offshoot from an already existing tribal NGO (Nair *et al.*, 2008 : 88). The previous experiences of political organization within the tribal movement proved valuable also when cooperating with other groups, and the Plachimada movement did from the beginning work within civil society on various levels. While having a hard time convincing even local farmers to join the campaign, the Plachimada movement early on cooperated with local NGOs who supported their cause and helped with the first technical analyses of the well water. The movement also formed links to outside groups such as NGOs active within human rights, environmental issues, and with anti-globalization groups on both national and global level. The prominent human rights organization People's Union for Civil Liberties (PUCL) gave attention to the Plachimada struggle as early as in November 2002 and has continuously covered the issue, as has important anti-globalization web-sites such as CorpWatch and India Resource Centre. Local, national and international NGOs were able to present the Plachimada struggle as a case of bad globalization, in which a multi-national corporation, with the support from state officials and politicians, was exploiting the local population. In the competitive political climate of Kerala, with a strong and organized political left, the political parties soon realized that it would be poor judgement to continue to support the claims of Coca-Cola. The cause of the movement has no doubt been helped by the apparent vulnerability of the villagers. Not only are they poor, they also belong to a community which has been exposed to severe and pro-longed discrimination. While the resources of Coca-Cola certainly helped when establishing the factory, and in the early stages of the campaign when it tried to contain the movement by filing charges against the activists, leading to a lengthy and costly legal battle, the might of the company may well have backfired later. The image of the poor tribal villagers pitted against the super-rich, foreign private conglomerate no doubt raised sympathy for the campaign, helped to strike alliances and perhaps also to change the stand of both Government agencies and political parties.

## Effects on Participation

The initial section of the analysis is focused on creating a general picture of the participation in the village and on establishing whether a change in the overall level of political participation can be observed. Subsequently, the two main steps of the analysis are conducted. The first step aims at testing different aspects of the hypothesis of the spin-off effect of political participation. In the second step, the mechanisms explaining the effect are identified. Finally, the results are summarized in a model and conclusions are drawn.

### *Case Selection and Generalizations*

For the study 80 informants were chosen through a stratified selection. The overall goal was to create a representative picture of the village as a whole and receiving a diversity of cases. The selection was made taking into account the sex, caste, religion, living area and household of the informants. In practice, the selection was made after interviews with local *Panchayat* representatives. Through these interviews, information was collected concerning the composition of the village. As discussed in the background section, the main differences in income corresponded with differences in caste. The main dividing line could be found between the tribal population and the non-tribal population, and the sample was divided equally between these two groups. Moreover, the aim was to interview an equally large proportion of men and women and to find informants of different ages. In conclusion, the result will be generalized to the village of Plachimada.

The study is focused on two main periods of time: before the end of factory production and after the end of factory production. The political participation in the protest against CCC is the main independent variable in the study; the political participation after the end of factory production is the dependent variable. In order to be able to control for several variables there is a need to isolate for the political participation before the protests against the CCC.

Consequently, the level of political participation in three different periods of time is measured:

- $t_0$: Before the establishment of the CCC bottling plant (before the year of 2000).
- $t_1$: After the protests against the CCC started, before the end of production (approximately the year of 2001-2005).
- $t_2$: After the cessation of factory production, specified as the last 12 months (approximately autumn 2011 and spring 2012).

Every question concerning level of participation will be formulated for every period. In order to distinguish the different periods, years will be given, as well as important events, such as elections.

### *Operationalization of Political Participation*

In measuring political participation, distinctions are made regarding different dimensions of participation, periods of time and the connection to the struggle against the CCC. This study applies Verba (1978) *et al.*'s specification of political participation, where it is divided into six main modes of activity: voting, campaign work, contacting, protesting, political organization and other collective activities. Subsequently, an index is created, using Verba *et al.*'s model as well as taking into account the specific context studied. An aggregated index with a scale from 0 to 6 is used. Participation in every mode of political participation is weighted equally and yields one point. In categorizing the answers, every activity could be classified only into one mode of activity. For example, protest action within the struggle committee only yields a point as protest activity and not as community activity. Below, each mode of political participation is listed.

- *Voting*: Voting in state, national or local election.
- *Campaign work*: Working as a volunteer for a candidate running for national, state, or local office.
- *Contacting*: Contacting government officials.
- *Political organization*: Being a member of a political organization.
- *Protest activity*: Taking part in protest, march, or demonstration.

- *Other Collective activities*: Working formally or informally with others in the community to deal with some community issue or problem (One point is given for each mode of political participation).

### *Operationalization of Participation in the Struggle against the CCC*

The struggle against CCC during the time period of $t_1$ is mainly measured with a dummy variable: participated or did not participate. However, in examining whether there is a threshold value that triggers a spin-off effect, a scale of participation is created. The informants had, in general, a very vague time perception and found it difficult to specify their level of participation in concrete terms. Consequently, measures of frequency are generally avoided. Participation in the protest against the company was measured in a simple scale, letting the informants answer whether they participated "never", "sometimes" or "often".

The analysis will begin with a description of the participation in the village during the relevant periods of time, with the aim of determining whether the intense and focused struggle resulted in change in the overall level participation among the village population. The first step aims at testing different aspects of the hypothesis of the spin-off effect of political participation. If such an effect can be observed, a second step is conducted. In this step, the mechanisms explaining the relation are identified. Two aspects of the spin-off effect of participation will be tested. Firstly, it will be examined whether there is a significant correlation between the participation in the movement during $t_1$ and the level of political participation in $t_2$. Secondly, the aim is to find out whether participation in the movement could result in an increase in participation in *general* and not just directly connected to the initial action.

### *Testing the Hypothesis of the Spin-off Effect*

In the first step of the study, the hypothesis that political action in itself could lead to more political action is tested. The test is conducted through linear multivariate regression analysis (OLS) with the dummy variable of participation in the struggle during $t_1$ as independent variable and the index of political participation during $t_2$ as the dependent variable.

In the regression analysis, several dummy variables are used. Dummy variables consist of dichotome values and are in the study coded so that they can take on the value of zero or one. An ordinary linear regression analysis will assume a line where all values are possible and with infinite scale. Consequently, there are several problems with applying OLS on dummy variables. While the dummy variables only can take on two different values, the regression analysis will generate several values between zero and one, which are lacking real significance. In addition, the regression analysis will generate a line that goes beyond zero and one, thereby risking resulting in intercepts off the scale. In order to isolate the effect of the participation during the time period of $t_1$, a number of potential antecedent variables are controlled for. The variable selection is based on results from earlier research. The main criteria when choosing antecedent variables are their potential risk of affecting the independent and dependent variable, the participation in $t_1$ and $t_2$. These variables are mostly demographic, such as socio-economic background, religion and caste. In addition, it is important to isolate for the participation before the establishment of the bottling plant; the participation in $t_0$. By controlling for this variable, a number of other potentially misleading effects are also excluded (such as income, level of education, political knowledge, level of confidence etc.). If the correlation still proves to be significant, it is implied that the relation is not spurious. The hypothesis of the spin-off effect of participation will be confirmed given that the coefficient is positive and significant at a 95 per cent level.

### *Spin-off Effect on Participation in General?*

A central aspect in studying a potential spin-off effect is finding out whether participation in one specific issue can result in participation in other areas as well. Consequently, it will be examined whether the participation in $t_2$ is directly connected to the struggle against the CCC, or if the political action in $t_1$ has resulted in a long-term, broader political participation. The test is conducted through two separate linear regressions, where in the first, the participation in the CVSS is analyzed as dependent variable, and in the second, participation outside of the CVSS is the dependent variable. The correlation will be considered statistically secured if the coefficient is positive and the correlation is significant at a 95 per cent level.

### *Description of the Participation in the Village*

In Figure 4.1, the level of participation during the three time periods examined is presented. Since, tribal identity is one of the main dividing lines in the village, the differences in level of participation between the tribal and non-tribal population is highlighted.

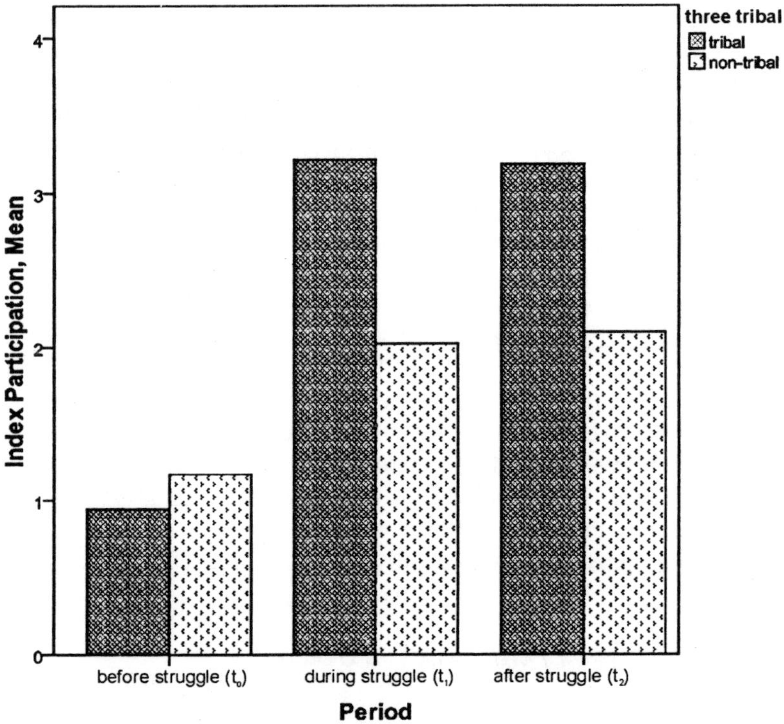


**Fig. 4.1:** Average Level of Participation

The data presented in figure 4.1 indicates that there was a considerable increase in political participation in connection to the struggle against CCC. Interestingly, a high level of participation remains during the period after the initial goal of the struggle was reached. However, it should be noted that, in reality, the time spent on political activity among the informants decreased considerably going from the period of $t_1$ to $t_2$. This is not evident in Table 4.1 since frequency of participation is not measured in the index. The decrease in activity is mainly connected to decrease in activity in the CVSS.

Overall, the tribal population seems to have been the most affected by the struggle. In the initial phase, the villagers belonging to the ST caste participated less than members of other caste. During the struggle and in the period after the struggle, the activity among the ST population increased to the extent that it surpassed the level of activity among other groups. Even though the participation among the non-tribal population did not increase as notably, it remains at a higher level in $t_2$ in comparison to in $t_0$. In order to examine how the patterns of participation have changed in connection to the struggle, the participation in each mode is presented in Table 4.2. Since, activity in each dimension of participation is measured with dummy variables, the data is presented in the form of percentage of informants participating in each mode during each time period.

**Table 4.1:** Percentage of Informants Participating in Each Mode of Political Activity

| *Activity* | *Percentage participating (%)* |
|---|---|
| *Voting* | |
| $t_0$ | 87.5 |
| $t_1$ | 88.7 |
| $t_2$ | 87.5 |
| *Campaign activity* | |
| $t_0$ | 6.3 |
| $t_1$ | 10 |
| $t_2$ | 10 |
| *Contacting* | |
| $t_0$ | 2.5 |
| $t_1$ | 3.8 |
| $t_2$ | 7.5 |
| *Political organization* | |
| $t_0$ | 6.3 |
| $t_1$ | 66.3 |
| $t_2$ | 58.8 |
| *Protest* | |
| $t_0$ | 2.5 |
| $t_2$ | 67.5 |
| $t_3$ | 48.7 |
| *Community activity* | |
| $t_0$ | 1.3 |
| $t_1$ | 26.3 |
| $t_2$ | 45 |

As evident from table 4.1, there are no larger changes in patterns of voting, campaigning or contacting. As could be expected, the percentage of informants participating in protest activity and political organizations have considerably increased, with more than 60 per cent participating during the time of the struggle and with high levels of participation remaining today.

In the initial phase of the struggle most members of the struggle committee participated nearly everyday. The activity constituted mostly of meetings and sit-ins in a hut outside of the factory. Today (2012), the participation constitutes of some sit-ins outside of the, now closed, factory as well as some larger events and meetings. Some of the most active members of the struggle committee travel around to protest at different soft drink factories in the nearby area. In addition, with the aid of economic contribution from NGO's, some longer trips are made, such as to New Delhi. The struggle committee members then meet national and state politicians to raise the issue of the CCC and water derogation.

Interestingly, the level of other collective activities has also notably increased, being even higher today (45%) than during the period of the struggle (26%). While participation in the CVSS meetings and protests has been coded as participation in political organization and as protest activity, no activity in connection to the CVSS has been coded as other collective activities. The main type of activity categorized as other collective activities is instead participation in what the villagers call the "collective tribal meetings" or the "tribal union". Even though most villagers found it very difficult to categorize each activity into different periods of time, most informants stated that the tribal union was formed after the start of the struggle against the CCC. Even though, it is not very common, some of the villagers not belonging to the ST also participate in these meetings. The success of the CVSS was an inspirational source leading to increased activity in the tribal union.[8] Today, the union focus on issues commonly facing the tribal population, particularly concerning land rights and environmental protection, but also regarding education of tribal children.[9] In conclusion, the activity in the tribal union could be an indication of a spin-off effect of the participation in the struggle, possibly through empowerment and increased awareness of group belonging and common problems.

Concerning the factors that might affect and be affected by participation, potentially intervening variables, an overall change among the informants can be observed. In Table 4.2, the change in motivation and resources between the time period of $t_0$ and $t_2$ is described.

**Table 4.2:** Percentage of Informants Noticing an Increase in Resources and Motivations

| *Resources and motivations* | *Informants* % |
|---|---|
| *Individual* | |
| Increased general political interest | 51 |
| Increased political knowledge | 53 |
| *Networks* | |
| Mobilizing networks increased | 43 |
| *Group based* | |
| Increased sense of group belonging | 46 |
| Increased awareness of common problems | 46 |

Overall, it is clear that there has been a significant increase in all the variables described in the table. Consequently, it is implied that the political participation in the social movement and the general increase in political awareness in the village might have resulted in a considerable empowerment of the poor village population. Considering the low level of political participation before the beginning of the struggle, this might not be surprising. However, even though the villagers were asked to notify solely increases connected to the struggle, it might be difficult to separate changes that occur with time and age from changes related to the struggle. Therefore, this factor might have slightly obstructed the results. These effects are later controlled for in the regression analysis.

In conclusion, a fundamental change of the political climate in the village of Plachimada can be observed. Following the social movement against the CCC, many villagers noted an increase in general political interest and knowledge as well as in mobilizing networks and awareness of common problems. In addition, there is a clear increase in the overall political activity among the informants. In the following steps of the analysis, the potential causal relations explaining this change is examined, and more specifically, the hypothesis of the spin-off effect of participation is tested.

### *Testing the Hypothesis of the Spin-off Effect*

In the first regression analysis, the basic relation between the participation in the struggle during the period of $t_1$ and the political participation in $t_2$ is tested. In addition, by controlling for potential antecedent variables, the link is isolated. In order to separate the effects of different potential antecedent variables, which might influence one another, four different models are created. In the columns for each model, the values of the unstandardized coefficients are noted.

**Table 4.3:** OLS Regression on Index of Political Participation in the Time Period of $t_2$

| *Indenendent variable* | *Model 1* | *Model 2* | *Model 3* | *Model 4* |
|---|---|---|---|---|
| Dummy participation in the struggle, $t_1$ | 1.834*** | 2.129*** | 1.656*** | 2.147*** |
| Index political participation, $t_0$ | | 0.798*** | | 0.916*** |
| Age | | | –0.001 | –0.001 |
| Sex | | | 0.128 | 0.106 |
| Tribal identity | | | –0.149 | 0.038 |
| Education | | | –0.059 | 0.004 |
| Party identification | | | 0.408 | –0.347 |
| Membership in non-political organization | | | –0.144 | 0.010 |
| | N 80 Adj-$R^2$ 0.420 | N 80 Adj-$R^2$ 0.596 | N 80 Adj-$R^2$ 0.415 | N 80 Adj-$R^2$ 0.577 |

*Note*: * = result significant at a level of 90%,
** = result significant at a level of 95%,
*** = result significant at a level of 99%.

*Source*: Dependent variable: Level of political participation $t_2$ (measured through index of political participation).

In Model 1, the effect of the participation in the struggle against the CCC during the time period of $t_1$ on the political participation during the time period of $t_2$ is examined. The result indicates that the level of participation in the struggle against the CCC positively affect the level of political participation during $t_2$. The correlation proves to be significant at a level of 99 per cent. The value of adjusted $R^2$ indicates that the model has a rather strong explanatory power. The variation in the independent variable would explain approximately 42 per cent of the variation in the dependent variable.

The significant association between the participation in the struggle against CCC and the level of political participation during $t_2$ is also confirmed in Model 2, where the level of political participation during the time period of $t_0$ is controlled for. In addition, the analysis of Model 2 confirms that the political participation in the period of $t_2$

is significantly affected by the level of participation in the period of $t_0$. Interestingly, as indicated by the steeper slope in Model 2 than Model 1, the effect of the participation in $t_1$ on the independent variable is stronger when controlling for participation in the period of $t_0$. Consequently, it is implied that the participation in the struggle against the CCC in itself could have an effect on the participation in the time period of $t_2$. In addition, it could be mentioned that the value of the adjusted $R^2$ suggests that Model 2 would explain approximately 60 per cent of the variation in the participation during $t_2$, proving the variation of participation during the two earlier periods to be important factors in explaining the participation in $t_2$. Considering that the suspected antecedent variables are chosen because of their possible influence on political participation, they are likely to be correlated to the political participation in $t_0$. Therefore, the correlation between each of these variables and the dependent variable is tested separately. Model 3 includes the variables of age, sex, tribal identity, education, party identification and membership in non-political organization. In the multi-variate analysis, none of these variables prove to be significantly correlated to the participation in $t_2$. In addition, the value of the adjusted $R^2$ of the model is not considerably larger than the value of the adjusted $R^2$ of Model 1. Consequently, the analysis indicates that these variables do not have a strong explanatory impact on the participation during the time period of $t_2$.

In Model 4, all of the chosen variables are added. The result is in line with the analysis of the earlier models, proving the correlation between the participation in the struggle and the participation during the last 12 months to be even stronger when potential antecedent variables are isolated for. The coefficient is approximately 2.147 suggesting that going from not participating in the struggle to participation in the struggle generates an approximate increase in the overall political participation with two units of the index. An increase in two units could for example be to become a member in a political organization and starting to participate in a community activity. Consequently, the results imply that the participation in the struggle in a focused issue for a limited period of time could generate a real change in the future political participation. In conclusion, the results of the second step of the analysis indicate support of the hypothesis that political action for a particular cause and a limited period of time could have a long-term spin-off effect on political participation.

### *Spin-off Effect on Participation in General?*

The results of the previous regression analysis indicated support for the hypothesis. However, it is still not examined whether the effect found was only reflecting participation in the same issue. Can political participation during a limited period of time and focused on a certain issue also have a more general effect on participation? In order to answer this question, the long-term effect on political activity directly connected to the initial action is tested separately from the long-term effect on activity indirectly or not at all connected to the initial action. In the first regression analysis the correlation between the participation in the CVSS during $t_1$ and the participation directly connected to the same issue is tested.

**Table 4.4:** OLS Regression on Index activity in connection to the struggle against the CCC, $t_2$

| *Independent variable* | *Model 1* | *Model 2* | *Model 3* | *Model 4* |
|---|---|---|---|---|
| Dummy participation in the struggle, $t_1$ | 1.592*** | 1.615*** | 1.590*** | 1.683*** |
| Index of political participation, $t_0$ | | –0.031 | | 0.029 |
| Age | | | –0.003 | –0.004 |
| Sex | | | 0.164 | 0.121 |
| Tribal | | | –0.022 | 0.078 |
| Education | | | –0.044** | –0.033 |
| Party identification | | | –0.107 | –0.201 |
| Membership in non-political organization | | | 0.209 | 0.176 |
| | N 80 Adj-$R^2$ 0.646 | N 80 Adj-$R^2$ 0.669 | N 80 Adj-$R^2$ 0.662 | N 80 Adj-$R^2$ 0.678 |

*= result significant at a level of 90%,
** = result significant at a level of 95%,
*** = result significant at a level of 99%.

Dependent variable: index activity in connection to the struggle against the CCC, $t_2$.

Model 1 proves the two variables to be significantly correlated at a level of 99 per cent. Moreover, the participation in struggle against CCC proves to have a strong explanatory power regarding the dependent variable, explaining approximately 65 per cent of the variation. In Model 2 the level of political participation in $t_0$ is added as independent variable. The correlation between the participation in the anti-CCC struggle and the dependent variable remains strong. However, regarding the correlation between the participation in $t_0$ and the dependent variable, the correlation is not statistically secure at 95 per cent level. The result of this analysis, clearly, differs from the study of the effect on general participation in $t_2$. In Model 3, participation in $t_0$ is excluded, while the rest of the potential antecedent variables are added. Interestingly, level of education proves to have a significant negative effect on the CVSS related participation in $t_2$, suggesting that less well-educated individuals are more keen to continue the struggle regarding the same issue as the initial action. However, this effect is no longer present when the variable of participation in $t_0$ is added in Model 4. Overall, it could be observed that the correlation between the struggle in $t_1$ and the related participation in $t_2$ remains significantly correlated when controlling for potential antecedent variables. In addition, the level of struggle in $t_1$ proves to be an important variable in explaining the related participation in $t_2$. In the second regression analysis the correlation between the participation in the struggle during $t_1$ and the participation not directly connected to the same issue during $t_2$ is tested.

**Table 4.5:** OLS Regression on Index of Political Participation in $t_2$ not directly Related to the Struggle against the CCC

| *Independent variable* | *Model 1* | *Model 2* | *Model 3* | *Model 4* |
|---|---|---|---|---|
| Dummy participation in the struggle, $t_1$ | 0.242 | 0.514*** | 0.066 | 0.464** |
| Index political participation, $t_0$ | | 0.829*** | | 0.887*** |
| Age | | | 0.002 | 0.003 |
| Sex | | | –0.036 | –0.015 |
| Tribal | | | –0.127 | –0.040 |
| Education | | | –0.015 | 0.037* |
| Party identification | | | 0.515*** | –0.147 |
| Membership in non-political organization | | | –0.353 | –0.166 |
| | N 80 Adj-$R^2$ 0.009 | N 80 Adj-$R^2$ 0.508 | N 80 Adj-$R^2$ 0.059 | N 80 Adj-$R^2$ 0.490 |

* = result significant at a level of 90%,
** = result significant at a level of 95%,
*** = result significant at a level of 99%.

Dependent variable: index, activity not directly related to the struggle against the HCCB, $t_2$.

In Model 1 the relation is analyzed but not isolated. The result is distinguished from the earlier regressions, finding no significant correlation between the participation in the struggle and participation indirectly or not at all connected to the struggle.

However, in Model 2, when the level of political participation in $t_0$ is controlled for, a significant correlation between the participation in the struggle and the dependent variable appears, proving the link to have been hidden by the antecedent factor of earlier levels of participation. The correlation is now significant at a 99 per cent-level. The political participation in the period of $t_0$ is also significantly correlated. Not surprisingly, the observed value of the coefficient (approximately 0.51) is considerably smaller than the corresponding value in table 4.5 (approximately 1.62). This suggests that the effect of the participation in the struggle is stronger on participation directly related to the same issue as the initial action than to indirectly or non-related action.

In Model 3, participation in $t_0$ is excluded while the rest of the potential antecedent variables are added. Consequently, the correlation between the participation in the struggle and the dependent variable is once again obstructed. Worth mentioning is that a significant correlation could be observed between party identification and the dependent variable, implying that this might be a factor explaining some of the participation. Most likely, party identification could also explain some of the participation in $t_0$, since this connection could no longer be observed in Model 4 when level of participation in $t_0$ was added. When, in Model 4, all the chosen potential antecedent variables are added, the dependent variable remains significantly correlated to the participation in the struggle during $t_1$. However, the relation is somewhat weaker and significant at 95 per cent-level. Interestingly, the effect of education has a significant positive effect on participation in $t_2$, suggesting the general long-term effect of participation to be stronger among villagers with higher levels of education. The spin-off effect seems to have a slightly different effect on individuals depending on their level of education. While more educated individuals seem to be prone to engage in activities related to new issues, less educated people to a higher extent continue to participate in activities related to the initial action.

In conclusion, the results indicate that participation in the struggle against the CCC triggered more participation in activities directly as well as not directly related to the initial activities. Consequently, it is implied that participation regarding a specific issue for a limited period of time could have an effect on political participation in a more general sense.

## Conclusions

Looking at this campaign from the outside it looks like a clear-cut case: accusations of environmentally hazardous production are found to be corroborated and results in the closure of the plant. To some extent this is also the view of the activists interviewed for this chapter; no one can stand against the will of the people. For observers of local Indian politics the success of the movement must, however, be seen as a surprise. Similar complaints as those in Plachimada have been made against Coca-Cola plants in other parts of India. In Mehndiganj, Uttar Pradesh, the company has since 1999 been heavily criticised for alleged pollution, water depletion, tax evasion and crimes against the labour laws. Despite an intense campaign with strong local support the plant remains open. Accusations of pollution and water depletion have been levelled also against the production unit in Kala Dera, Rajasthan. All over India we have reports of violations far worse than in the case of Plachimada: the establishing of industries, dams, mines and various infrastructure projects result in the eviction of people and pollution of the environment without any action taken from the government, sometimes without even being reported by the press. The fact that the villagers represent a marginalized community have raised sympathy for their cause, but would in normal circumstances also have worked against them, as these groups generally face huge difficulties in influencing the decision-making process. The relative success in Plachimada must be seen as an exception produced by several factors working together, such as the internal strength of the movement; the competent leadership and its ability to strike alliances; the double vulnerability of the poor tribal villagers which was turned into political capital; and the ability to present the presence of Coca-Cola as a case of foreign and capitalist exploitation. When challenging Coca-Cola the Plachimada movement has made ample use of the local, regional, national and global civil societies, using its ability to strike alliances and secure outside support for its cause. These alliances were developed in a space outside the immediate influence of the state, the market economy, and the political parties, suggesting the importance of such a sphere. The Plachimada case also shows the importance of striking civil society alliances which have the capability of influencing also the political parties and the state. While giving full credit to the hard work and well found strategies of the movement, success would have been difficult without linking the struggle to the political sphere and thereby gaining a direct effect on the decision-makers.

This study further indicates that there is a way into the political world for also for the most disadvantaged social groups. Though a political struggle may be more difficult due to the lack of socio-economic resources such as education, wealth or political confidence, the threshold into that world is not as high as it is often perceived to be. In our analysis, a spin-off effect of participation among the informants was identified. In addition, the participation in the struggle resulted in a spill-over effect into participation in other areas not directly connected to the struggle against the CCC. In accordance with the guidelines for drawing conclusions discussed in the method section, the results are generalized to the population of the village of Plachimada. In addition, the results indicate that a spin-off effect of participation might be found among disadvantaged groups in general. However, further research is needed in order to draw any definite conclusions. The participation in the struggle was noted to have a direct effect on further participation as well as an indirect effect through the strengthening of group-based motivations. The result is in accordance with Verba *et al*'.s theory that group-based motivations are of particular importance in the political mobilization of disadvantaged groups. The results of this study can be seen as a complement to Verba *et al*'.s findings, proving that these effects do not only trigger participation, but is generated by the participation in itself, thereby resulting in the spin-off effect. Even though the group-based effects might be particularly strong in the collectivistic society of the tribal population, they do provide some indication of what kind of mechanism might explain the spin-off effect among disadvantaged groups in general.

In conclusion, participation for a limited period of time and for a specific cause might be enough to empower individuals from socio-economically disadvantaged groups and to generate broader political awareness. Social movements are found to have a potentially important role to play. Even though some research has pointed at the instability of these movements, their particular ability to mobilize disadvantaged groups into specific causes might be a way to trigger long-term political participation outside of the movement itself. By empowering individuals lacking in individual resources, political activism can lead to increased equality in participation, thereby strengthening democracy.

## Notes

1. The index originally included the category "communal activity" which has a very different connotation in an Indian context. The title of the category was therefore altered to "other collective actions".
2. Interview with K.V. Biju, Convenor, Plachimada Struggle Solidarity Committee, Plachimada, October 2008.
3. In the interviews for this article one of the villagers claimed that there had even been deaths due to the pollution: at least four children were claimed to have died after drinking well water near the plant. This claim has not been corroborated by other sources, but was confirmed by other villagers during interviews in October 2008.
4. Interview with K.V. Biju, Convenor, Plachimada Struggle Solidarity Committee, Plachimada, October 2008.
5. According to Nair *et al.*, some *panchayat* officials later admitted that the promises of tax revenues had initially stopped them from acting against the company (Nair *et al.*, 1978 : 99).
6. Interviews with Parvadi, activist and member of the Anti-Coca-Cola Peoples Struggle Committee, K.V. Biju, Convenor, Plachimada Struggle Solidarity Committee, Plachimada, and Vilayodi Venugopal, Chairman, Anti-Coca-Cola Peoples Struggle Committee, Plachimada, October 2008.
7. Interview with Parvadi, activist and member of the Anti-Coca-Cola Peoples Struggle Committee, Plachimada, October 2008.
8. Interview with activist Kaniama, Plachimada, March 2012.
9. Interview with activists Shanti and Mutulekshmi, Plachimada, March 2012.

## References

Bijoy, C.R. (2006): "Keralas Plachimada Struggle—A narrative on water and Governance Rights", *Economic and Political Weekly*, 14 October, 2006, pp. 4332-4339.

Dahl, Robert (2000): *On Democracy*, (New Haven: Yale University Press), p. 38.

Gerald F. Davis, Doug McAdam, William Richard, Scott Meyer and Nathan Zald (2005): *Social Movement and Organization Theory*, (Cambridge: Cambridge University Press), p. 75.

Henry Brady (1999): "Political Participation", in John P. Robinson, Phillip R. Shaver, and Lawrence S. Wrightsman (ed.), *Measures of Political Attitudes* (*my* Diego CA: Academic Press), p. 737.

Marco Giugni, Doug Macadam and Charles Tilly (1999): *How Social Movements Matter*, (University of Minnesota Press: Minneapolis), p. xi.

Nair, K.N., Antonyta Paul, and Vineetha Menon (2008): *Water Insecurity, Institutions and Livelihood Dynamics: A Study in Plachimada, Kerala, India,* (Delhi: Daanish Books), p. 33

Verba, Sidney Norman H. Nie and Jae-on Kim (1978): *Participation and Political Equality—A Seven Nation Comparison* (Cambridge: Cambridge University Press), p. 5.

# 5

# Individual *versus* Group Rights

## The Paradox of Indian Democracy

*Shashikant Pandey*

### Introduction

Reconciling individual and group rights were one among many challenges that India experienced even before it attained Independence. Diversity and separatedness had been its hallmark and one of the most significant and enduring disputes across twentieth Century (Jayal 2011:185). Indian society was not a homogenous society as discrimination as well as disadvantages were being encountered by those social groups identified differently. Equal opportunity provision was not sufficient enough to deal with group-based differences as multiple layers of inequalities were lying concealed beneath the mask of formal equality (*ibid.*: 186). Therefore, the notion of group-differentiated citizenship was introduced in the Constitution of India to meet the challenges associated with difference-based inequalities. It was certainly a courageous decision on the part of Indian leadership that they never shied away from acknowledging and according differential treatment to different disadvantaged groups. It has helped in overcoming multiple challenges associated with cultural as well as material inequality, but at times, it has also led to animosity and violent conflict among majority and minority groups.

The present chapter makes an effort to locate the issues involving individual/group rights by applying theoretical as well as the analytical method. It would also make an effort to understand as to how Indian state has dealt with the issue of individual *versus* group rights. Since, India is home to diverse ethno-religious groups where different groups experience various levels of development and encounter multiple challenges in the socio-economic arena. The chapter explains that in the Indian context, the juxtaposition involving individual/group rights is misunderstood to be in opposition. However, the result in the end reflects that for a diverse and plural country like India, recognition of group rights along with individual rights are a must. It concludes with the assumption that although they are not complimentary to each other, they are not the polar opposite either.

## Individual and Group Rights: Theoretical Discourse

Recently, there is an upsurge in interest worldwide so far as questions of identity, culture and differences are concerned. However, prior to dealing with individual and group rights in India and its complexities, it is essential to understand the modes of interpreting and analyzing group rights. An Individual gets rights by virtue of being human whereas group rights deal with the rights of the peoples and groups. Individual rights that do not believe in differential citizenship prove advantageous for majority community as it helps them to see their values, customs, and traditions find representation in public institutions. Contrary to individual rights, group rights deals with the issues where the person is defined not by his individuality, but by his/her ethnic, cultural or religious identity. It believes in granting greater recognition and accommodation of distinct identity of minority groups in public institutions. In other words, individuality is not the focal point within the narratives of group rights as they regard identity-based difference as the most suitable basis for making the claim to group rights. It also finds institutional expression in the form of guaranteed representation in institutional governance, minority rights, affirmative action and another symbolic mode of representation (*ibid.*). It poses a paradoxical situation as, on the one hand, group rights is a valid move to address the group-based differences and to safeguard minority from the homogenizing tendency implicit in the universal notion of citizenship. On the other hand, it also has the potential to institutionalize the entrenchment of identities that may lead to weakening of social cohesion and in its extreme form may result in demand for secession (*ibid.*).

Moreover, in a liberal scheme rights belong solely to individuals, as their "trumps" against the power of the group. Thus, any theory that suggests that the group may itself be a holder of rights appears inherently anti-liberal and, therefore, incompatible with the usual "Western" formulation of human rights (Oestreich 1999:108-132). However, in recent years, many western scholars such as Charles Taylor, Yale Tamir, Joseph Carens (2000), Kymlica and Wayne Norman (1995), Iris Marion Young (1989, 1995) etc. have acknowledged group—differentiated rights. Kymlica has addressed it as "Liberal Culturalism" where all liberal-democratic states along with upholding and protecting civil and political rights must also adopt group-specific rights to recognize the distinct identities of various groups (Kymlica 2002: 338-342). Similarly, Iris M. Young asked for making an effective representation of those groups that are distinct and feel disadvantaged or oppressed (Young, 1995:199).

Liberals, as well believe in recognizing diversity/differences, but at the level of individual only. Over the years, however, they have also softened their stance and now rarely oppose minority rights comprehensively. At the same time, they continue to resist such rights where these right come into conflict with liberal commitments to individual freedom (Bajpai, 2010:5). Explaining it further, Bhikhu Parikh argues that in contemporary western multicultural society, cultural diversity manifested in art, literature, music, customs, and traditions, but not their values or visions of real life. It does not appreciate non-liberal ways of life which might embody worthwhile moral values and visions. So, what we find that even though, they understand cultural diversity, but not moral difference and pressurize cultural minorities to adopt dominant liberal values or liberal way of life (Parekh, 2011:66). It creates problems of acceptance by the group rights advocates. Advocates of liberal ideology try to universalize and justify their way of life which creates suspicion among minority groups. Many immigrant groups in the western liberal democracy are experiencing this difficulty as they feel that they are being pressurized to adopt and emulate the civic culture and way of life of the dominant community. For example, the liberal American state recognized religious diversity; but does not recognize linguistic diversity by forcing the immigrants to learn English.

It poses a challenge for the supporters and detractors of individual and group rights and the challenge is how to reconcile the two set of rights. This problem gets further compounded as group rights do not fit in the classical-liberal framework as it believes and promotes individual rights and have the tendency to interpret things from an individualist perspective. Apart from that, liberal states tend to adopt ethnocultural neutrality where the state is supposed to remain neutral concerning ethnocultural differences as they are considered private sphere and forbidden terrain for state interference (Jovanovic, 2005:625-651). Though, scholars like Will Kymlica in his *magnum opus* "Multicultural Citizenship" has questioned this viewpoint and refers to the inevitable non-neutrality of the state when it comes to culture and identity. He argues that state can handle religious diversity through its refusal to give preferential treatment to any religion. However, the same yardstick cannot be applied to deal with cultural diversity. The state cannot always remain neutral and will have to take positions in matters such as language, public symbols, school curriculum and so on. All of which work to the advantage of some particular cultures and identities and not others. Its definite manifestation can be observed in Indian democracy where very often conflicts occur when a state has to deal with cultural issues.

An exciting puzzle worldwide in which right should be given preference and why? Group rights advocates argue that since there is no uniform culture, there cannot be uniform rights (Tharoor, 1999/2000). Therefore, different identity groups cannot be judged by putting them on the same pedestal. The groups, which are facing an identity crisis, be given special safeguards in the form of collective exemptions and entitlements. This view also finds supports from liberals like John Rawls and Ronald Dworkin, who believe that pursuit of equality may require special consideration. They believe that in the absence of a level-playing field equality of opportunity cannot exist and, therefore, to rectify it, extraordinary measure in the form of group rights is required (Mahajan 2011:7). On the contrary, the critic of this approach believes that individual should have freedom to choose his/her identity. They point out that, group entitlements imprison people and societies, and there may be an occasion when a person may require protection against the actions of groups. The advocates of individual rights question that when one category of persons is singled out for granting certain privileges, are not the rights of others get violated. Charles Taylor has offered an explanation in this regard. He takes the example of the Canadian province of Quebec. The Francophone group has regulations forbidding the French-speaking population and immigrants to send their children to English-language schools to safeguard themselves from the threat of the Anglo-Saxon majority culture. Taylor shows how the promotion of collective goals conflicts with the theory of individual rights. He then suggests that restrictions under certain conditions on individual rights may be placed to maintain the integrity of endangered forms (Bhargava 2010:107). One may not agree with Taylor. However, one thing is clear that a way out has to be found out as per the particular cultural context.

Critics of group rights believe that state institutions have to be "colour-blind" and extending benefits on the basis of membership in ascriptive groups by the state is seen as morally arbitrary and inherently discriminatory. However, many authors defended such kinds of group-specific rights (Young 1990, Parekh 1990, Phillips 1992, Taylor 1992). They argue that difference blind institutions try to be neutral amongst different ethno-cultural groups. They are also implicitly tilted towards the needs, interests and identities of the majority groups by using the majority's language, calendar and symbols that create stigmatization and further alienation of minority groups. In India, there are numerous examples where the secular state follows majoritarian cultural practices. Therefore, they argue that minority rights do not constitute unfair privilege to minority groups rather it compensates for unfair disadvantages (Kymlica and Norman 2000:34-35).

In this regard, it would be pertinent to highlight the recent changes in background theoretical conditions of liberalism where a significant intellectual shift is being witnessed from the mainstream tradition of Enlightenment political philosophy. The concept of freedom, equality and justice with pronounced individualist orientation is being questioned in last few decades by communitarian writing that recognizes the relevance of cultural/group rights (Bhargava 2010:104). The communitarian critique of liberalism has supported the community against individualism. They believe that all groups should not necessarily follow each and every law. For example, in the name of uniformity, we cannot expect that Sikhs should abandon their turban. Fair treatment entails a slightly different dress code be acceptable if their religion so required. This viewpoint also finds an endorsement from multiculturalists who support community power over individual freedom (Mookherjee 2008:223). Kymlica takes these rights to be an important aspect of 'differentiated citizenship' which entails that, in order to treat people fairly; governments should recognize that their groups have different needs and goals (*ibid.*).

The abovementioned description regarding individual and group rights clearly reflect that there is no unanimity concerning these two sets of rights. Disagreement exists even among liberal scholars as to which right is to be preferred and under what circumstances. If India applies this yardstick, it reflects the conflicting position of the state as it has the provision to deal with the issue of group-differentiated rights. However, problems do appear very often in the form of conflict between majority and minority community. It also appeared in the form of demand for a separate homeland, demand by various underprivileged groups such as women, minorities, backward castes, homosexuals, etc.

### Individual and Group Rights: Tracing its Historical-Constitutional Roots

The legacy that it inherited from the British colonial power made its task more difficult as their emphasis was on managing the empire. Being outsiders and having an altogether different cultural background, they failed to deal with problems of a nation full of diversities in terms of language, religion, and ethnicity. They had not experienced differences of this magnitude, nor was it on their priority list. For them, group-based cleavages deny any possibility of commonality that can be best served by taking into consideration the viewpoints of each group in decision-making. Therefore, they introduced separate electorate to address this problem which created rift between majority and minority community and ultimately led to the partition of the country. Being a colonial power, they were least concerned with the long-term consequences of their actions on Indians as their primary motive was to maintain their hold on its territory. Therefore, the methods that they employed to address the myriad problems being encountered by Indians in various spheres were guided more by their personal interest rather than addressing them. They were least concerned with social complexities of India and the issues associated with it. Although, it is not difficult to establish as to what were the real motives behind their lacklustre approach towards India's pressing social problems. However, one thing was sure that their strategies towards minorities and other disadvantaged groups had no long-term planning and its future repercussion. For example, they introduced communal electorate to include almost all minority groups. It led to a feeling of distinctness among all the minority groups that propelled them to ask for separate representation that ultimately culminated into the partition of the country. However, partition did not address the problem rather it worsened the situation. The large-scale violence that followed left an indelible scar between majority and minority community.

The cause of conflict between individual and group rights can be traced to the colonial policy. They opted for a method of selection of Indian representative through the principle of representation of communities, not individuals (Acharya 2010:51), as they treated Indian society as an ethno-cultural mosaic.[1] The classificatory schemes adopted by the colonial powers in the gazetteers and the various Census Reports between 1881 and 1931 led to caste and community consciousness. It got further consolidated with the codification of Hindu and Muslim law.[2] Moreover, they failed to understand the diverse and plural character of Indian society and tried to segment different groups by reserving seats in legislatures and granting quotas in government employment for religious minorities.[3] It resulted in burgeoning demands by various groups. When they realized their fault, they called for roundtable conference in London to address this issue, but failed to convince Muslim League as well as Indian National Congress and various other groups.

Their entire effort was focused not to bring about unity between different groups, but to divide the nationalist front. INC strongly disapproved this decision by the government in its Lahore Session (1909) and later on British government realized its mistakes in Montagu Report (1919) and Simon Commission Report (Wolpert 1967: 200). However, it was too late as it ultimately culminated in the partition of the country. However, after Independence, the separate electorate was abolished as it went against the secular character of the country and legislative as well as employment quotas came to be restricted mainly to Scheduled Caste and Scheduled Tribes.

It can be inferred that colonizers on the one hand, unified the Indian sub-continent, but on the other side instilled a sense of majority-minority divide among Indians. The communities that were living together for centuries with their distinct identities were reorganized in such a way that led to the feeling of doubt and suspicion among them. Therefore, it was an important challenge before the Constituent Assembly to bridge the rift created between various communities especially Hindus and Muslims.

Efforts to accommodate diverse groups began with the formation of the Constituent Assembly itself. While constituting the Assembly, it was composed in a manner that not only reflected the diversity of

India in terms of ideas, but also to give an opportunity to various groups. Members were so chosen so that diversity that was the hallmark of India gets represented. The Constituent Assembly tried to incorporate those principles into the Constitution, which could bring about a sense of integration and oneness among minority groups. Interests of minority groups like Sikhs and Muslims were taken care of even during the formation of the Constituent Assembly itself. Similarly, most of the resolutions were passed by the Assembly through consensus. Constituent Assembly tried to resolve many complex and vexed issues through negotiation, discussion, etc. During deliberation, concerns of various groups came up for discussion and due attentions were paid and discussion took place in a very transparent manner. Constituent Assembly took special care to ensure the protection of various groups especially of Muslims and Scheduled Castes and Scheduled Tribes.

When India attained Independence, it was a daunting task as to how to accommodate these groups within the liberal framework which India has adopted. Since, there was no precedence from the past as liberal doctrine, though believed in diversity never promoted diversity based on groups. To address these myriad challenges, India took the calculated risk of introducing liberal-democratic model, but never copied it in its entirety, therefore, quasi-liberal spirit pervades the Constitution of India.

When Constituent Assembly began its deliberation, reconciling the two sets of rights appeared to be a daunting task before the members of Constituent Assembly. There were differences of opinion within Assembly. One group that claimed to represent nationalist opinion was deeply influenced by western liberal ideals that believed in the absence of discrimination on grounds of religion, race or gender. They believed that everybody is equal before law. For them, granting group rights would be suicidal as people will show precedence to their group loyalty than national loyalty, and this may threaten national unity. Therefore, initially, within Constituent Assembly, group identities were viewed with suspicion and considered as antithetical to the kind of national identity being espoused by the nationalist. Nationalist looked upon group identities with suspicion, as distinct from, and potentially in competition with, shared citizenship identities. They opposed it tooth and nail as they were in favour of creating a sense of shared nationality among Indians which would transcend group identities based on caste, creed, and religion. For them, safeguards involved recognition of group identities in the political realm which may promote identification with particular groups at the cost of the nation. Therefore, group rights in the form of political safeguards were also opposed from a nationalist perspective.[4] Moreover, there was a strong resentment against political guarantees provided by Britishers as its underlying intention was to promote division within society. Protections of minority rights through political safeguards were also seen to violate the principle of justice in the liberal framework. While defining justice in liberal terms, they stated that all individuals should have similar rights. Differences in the political rights of people deriving from their cultural group membership were seen to contravene the state's commitment to treat all its citizens as equal.[5] They opposed on the ground that "in a secular state, minorities based on religion is the very negation of secularism" (CAD 1948:899).

The nationalist interpretation within the Constituent Assembly was that Indians constituted themselves into a nation by all becoming members of the same state. Therefore, they were grossly against the granting of cultural and educational rights of minorities or reserving seats for minority religious groups in legislatures. The strong advocates of this viewpoint were leaders like Rajkumari Amrit Kaur and G.B. Pant, who wanted to ensure that all other identities like sex, religion, language and culture be made subservient to the national identity. They demanded that uniform civil code be accepted as a fundamental right, against imparting religious instruction in any state or state-aided schools. They demanded further that state should not recognise any minority on religious, linguistic, or sexual ground and no political safeguards for any minority be made the rule. They based their interpretation largely on liberal-individualist premise that the new Indian state was to be made up of individuals, not of communities (Jha 2010:340). They were of the opinion that "community-specific rights will encourage a spiralling estrangement between social groups" (Bhargava 2010:32).

However, this nationalist position was opposed by the proponents of group rights as minorities especially Muslim community made the demand to be governed by their personal laws.[6] They also made demands for providing all kinds of cultural, educational and political safeguards to religious minorities. However, in due course of time, Constituent Assembly not only focused on recognizing rights of various groups, but it also made effort to give due recognition to individual rights. It was so arranged that in the Constitution the cultural and educational rights of religious minorities assume the form of the rights of individual members of minority communities as well as that of minority group rights (Bajpai, 2008:358). However, group rights based on differential identities were recognized to ensure equality of rights and equality of treatment. Disagreements remained about what kind of differences would be accepted and what kind of concrete measures were needed to sustain these differences. But ultimately Constituent Assembly arrived at the consensus and tried to accommodate group differences to the overall satisfaction of all the affected groups (Rodrigues, 2008:180).

Granting of group rights to minorities and other deprived groups was a visionary move on the part of Indian leadership. It not only instilled a sense of confidence among minorities but also in a single stroke tried to allay the fears among minorities like Muslims, regarding their future in Independent India. Hence, the demand for cultural autonomy on the part of minority groups and its acceptance paved the way for national unity.

## Negotiating Individual *versus* Group Rights in Indian Democracy

Like other traditional societies, in India too, the political discourse was dominated by community rights. In other words, group rights in India preceded individual rights that made it a unique successful experiment in history where modern notion of individual rights were introduced in a country strongly influenced by community values. Indian approach was distinctive in the sense that it linked equality for the person with equality for diverse communities.[7] In other words, it felt that individual cannot enjoy equal rights and opportunities so long as the community to which he or she belongs remains marginalized. Therefore, provisions were made in the Constitution so that no community could feel marginalized. Arrangement were deliberately made to accommodate the claims of historically disadvantaged groups on the grounds of protection or compensation for disadvantage, rather than because they had distinct interests that required special representation in the political system.[8]

India stands as a United Nation simply because of the way it handled its diversity. It negotiated diversity in such a manner that it no longer looks like its weakness. Although, it is yet to turn out as its strength as inter-community conflicts still prevail. Going against the prevailing wisdom that diversity may lead to balkanization of the country, India believed that the strong nation-state can be built by acknowledging the difference. Group rights were recognized and granted to diverse communities that find reflection in the form of various group rights measures in the Constituent Assembly.

Constitution of India is an amalgamation of individual as well as group rights although it does not give primacy to either person or group rights. Rajeev Bhargava points out that in the Constitution of India both sets of rights were recognized and it does not provide any clear guidelines when one is to override the other. Instead, an attempt was made to strike a balance between the two with the scales marginally tilting in favour of individual rights (Bhargava 2010 : 10) as various measures were adopted to protect and safeguard them.

India, like many other liberal democracies such as the United States and South Africa, has recognized affirmative action policies with the aim of ameliorating the conditions of deprived groups. They were allocated a disproportionate share of jobs or other opportunities to bring them at par with the rest of the society. In this way, India is one among few liberal democracies in the world which commits itself to liberal democratic norms, and yet it has recognized group rights. Constituent Assembly did try to settle this issue by going against the prevailing views that group-sensitive provisions may not be entrenched in a liberal Constitution. The Indian constitutional experiment attempted to accommodate various claims of identity by different groups (Acharya 2010:50). However, in the post-Independent India, this debate is still not settled and very often conflict appears between these two sets of rights. The gay community in India has been fighting a legal battle where they have been asking to be treated as a distinct group that is still not recognized. There are many other groups who feel isolated, marginalized like AIDS patients, the differently-abled person who needs special care and protection.

While Constitution was being framed, many such problems did not exist like granting reservation to Other Backward Castes, Reserving 1/3 seats for women in Parliament, recognizing group rights of the Lesbians and Gays and so on. However, an effort has to be made to reconcile individual, and group rights as different groups have different group based requirements. Therefore, it can be assessed only by the state as whether they require distinct category status or not. Series of initiatives have been undertaken to settle this complex issue though it has failed to resolve the issue entirely. For example, the Constitution of India, defined minority, yet it remained silent about majority rights and therefore on many occasions majority do not get those privileges and rights which minority gets and it creates animosity between communities. For instance, in India, Christians, Muslims can approach court both as a citizen of this country and also as a member of minority community whereas a Hindu can approach court as a citizen only. Similarly, the way the term minority is defined is questioned by the followers of majority religions as Hindus do not constitute a homogenous group. They have different castes and sub-castes category. If understood from this point of view, then everybody is in minority at some places or other and therefore advocates of majority community argue that while defining minority, this point must be taken into consideration.[9] However, this viewpoint has not many takers as differences and division exist between majority religions, their sense of belongingness comes to the forefront at the time of crisis.

Indian society, apart from multicultural, multilingual and multi-religious, is also one of the world's most unequal societies as well. Therefore, to negotiate individual rights with group rights a very cautious approach was required to deal with this issue. In an unequal society, Fundamental Right to equality is compatible with special benefits for the disadvantaged groups. Even though, India is committed to ensuring equality, the policy of providing benefits to historically disadvantaged groups permits departure from formal equality for the purpose of eliminating social discrimination. In a nutshell, it can be stated that Constitution tried to strike a balance between individual and group rights. Although, it is a different matter that while granting group rights, Constitution followed different strategies for different groups or in other words, institutionalized two sorts of distinct rights. It made an essential distinction between the cultural rights of minorities and group rights for communities who feel discriminated on the basis of caste. While minorities were located in the framework of religion, disadvantaged castes were removed from this realm and situated in the context of social justice (Hasan 2009:5). Therefore, one thing is clear that while formulating group rights, the Constitution of India made a departure from the traditional liberal conception of individual rights. It was guided by its needs and requirements and tried to negotiate between an individual and group rights. For instance, Right to Religion under Articles 25-30 manifest an unusual amalgam of individual and group rights. Whereas Article

25 gives religious rights to individuals, Article 26 addresses collective rights practiced by establishment of institutions.

Critic of group rights argue that state has to ensure the dignity of each and every individual and granting of group preferences denies such opportunities to a person not belonging to a particular group. Similarly, recognizing religious/cultural rights of minorities with regard to their personal laws is questioned on the ground that it violates the rights of women as a group and also as an individual to claim alimony from her estranged husband. It has also been observed that since, Islam permits triple marriage, many people belonging to other religion got converted to marry for their convenience. Therefore, negotiating individual and group rights is an imperative and should not be treated as antithetical to each other.

There is an always a danger implicit in the interpretation of group rights. For example, it has been observed that Group rights of an ethno-cultural group has the tendency to harm individual rights leading to gender injustice especially among Muslim women who feel marginalized. Whereas Group rights as affirmative action programme has proved advantageous for marginalized groups, Indian liberal democracy has not been able to make a distinction or to find a way out to address this problem. Similarly, the Constitution of India, emphasizes upon inter-group equality and justifies special consideration for marginalized groups and minorities. However, it has left the issue of intra-group equality unattended which is very often used by the cultural groups to protect structures of domination and patriarchy.[10]

## Contestation and Negotiation in Minority Rights Especially Muslims

Recognizing group rights for minorities in colonial India might have been easy as they were not accountable to anyone. However, in Independent India, granting exclusive rights to cultural minorities was a very complex and serious issue for various reasons. First, India was a Hindu majoritarian state and country got partitioned on communal lines, and thousands of people lost their lives in communal clashes. The scar was so deep that granting political or any other safeguards, especially to Muslims, could have resulted in further clashes between the two communities. Second, for those Muslims, who decided to remain in India, their identity as a Muslim was very crucial, and they were not in a mood to compromise on this issue. On the whole, it was a very complex issue, and the major challenge was how to deal with it. If India opts for universal rights; minorities lose out on their specific rights to culture and access to opportunities. Whereas, by going for minority rights, there is a real danger that we may land up in ghettoisation and loss of a sense of political community (Chandoke 2011).

In liberal democracies around the world, an upsurge of interest in the rights of minority groups can be observed. India is no exception to it. While Constitution of Independent India was being framed, the term "minority" was employed which did not denote the numerical status of the group as much as the group suffered from some disadvantage concerning others that entitled it to special treatment from the state (Bajpai, 2008: 356). In other words, efforts were made to integrate all the marginalized groups. Instead of focusing on numerical strength, they emphasized the disadvantageous position of the various marginalized groups. Initially, Constituent Assembly recommended reservation in the State legislature and quota in Government services for religious minorities. However, in the final draft, these provisions were dropped, and it was restricted to Scheduled Castes and Scheduled Tribes. The logic advanced in this regard was India, being a secular democracy cannot grant safeguards on religious ground. However, minorities were given freedom to impart and administer religious instruction. In other words, citing subjection to oppression as a pre-eminent reason Scheduled Caste and Scheduled Tribes were given reservation. However, it remains unanswered as to why the political safeguards to Muslims were, on the one hand, considered threat to national unity and against our secular fabric and on the other side same was granted to them in the form of cultural and educational rights. The question that it raises is as to why the concept of secular democracy has space for one, but not the other (*ibid.*: 342). It happened mainly because distinction was made between caste and minorities for the purpose of preferential treatment, making it clear that reservations were matter of compensation and beneficiary groups were constructed and perceived in terms of social justice and equity. On the other hand, the concerns of minorities were anchored in the political framework of secularism-communalism and majority-minority syndrome, resulting in their exclusion (Hasan, 2009:342).

Group rights in case of Muslims are also questioned on the ground that it favours Muslim men by allowing them to practice triple *talaq*, which enables them to divorce a wife with immediate effect. This situation raises serious concerns for the rights of Muslim women as a group (Mookherjee, 2008:227-228). The problem is that minority communities ask for exclusive rights, particularly about marriage, divorce, or reproduction. It is done to limit women's freedom that puts minority women in a dilemma as to whether to remain in their culture or to fight for achieving self-respect for their individual rights (*ibid.*: 228). Although, at present, they have been granted choice under special Marriage Act to be governed either by their personal laws or by the state laws, it has not turned out to be very effective due to the variety of reasons one of which being that Muslim women are not self-reliant to take an independent decision.

In India, the conflict between individual and group rights can also be seen in the context of Uniform Civil Code *versus* Personal Laws. Minority community opposed Uniform Civil Code as it would reflect majoritarian beliefs and would hence erode the identity of minority groups such as Muslims, Christians, Parseis and Jews (Mansfield, 207-246). In the Constituent Assembly, Dr. Ambedkar proposed that civil rights should be given precedence over religious practices. He argued that the provision of uniform civil code should find a place in the chapter on fundamental rights (Balkrishnan 2009). However, ultimately it was placed within Directive Principles of State Policy.

Differential treatment in the context of Muslim communities in India is also questioned by majoritarian communities on the ground as to why certain groups are allowed to have multiple spouses, or granted special autonomy in education. It is also asked as to why such freedoms are not awarded to all citizens? If the rationale for not doing so is that polygamy is socially harmful, or that regulation of educational institutions is needed, then why such detrimental rules are allowed in case of Muslim communities? (Mantra and Gupta, 2013). Why Hindu Code Bill was introduced to bring social reform in Hindu community by curtailing caste and gender-based discrimination that is prevalent in customary laws, and similar amendments were not made for changing Muslim personal laws. Customary Muslim laws were also criticized on the ground of being anti-women as the husband can obtain the divorce without any substantial reason.

State, however, decided not to intervene in the personal laws of the Muslim community. Though, it did not augur well for Muslim women as respect for religious freedom of Muslim community resulted in the subjection of Muslim women. To do away with this practice and to make Islamic law more women-friendly, Supreme Court in India intervened through now infamous Shah Bano case. In this case, the Court ruled in favour of Shah Bano citing Code of Criminal Procedure and said that it should apply to Muslims as well. The Court found inadequate provision for maintenance of divorced women in Muslim Personal Law (*ibid.*: 24-25). Islamic organizations, Clergies criticized judicial decisions, and they even went on to declare Judiciary as an accomplice with a majoritarian attack on their religious freedom. Union Government finally succumbed under pressure and subsequently nullified the judgement through legislative intervention. Muslim community opposed it on the ground that Constitution itself has granted them equal protection. It also justifies differential treatment for preserving the identity of religious minorities (*ibid.*: 33). Equal Protection believes in differently treating the dissimilar form of difference. Right wing group criticized this decision, and they called it Muslim appeasement by the government.

Certain cultural and educational rights have been given to minorities in India, and very often they face the brunt for getting differential treatment. However, if we look at the ground realities as to whether the Muslim community has benefitted from this special weightage, then the picture looks more bleak and murkier. In India, effort to accommodate diversity in legal and Constitutional structure has been made, but policy measures have fallen short of expectation.[11] Sacchar Commission in its report has highlighted that conditions of Muslims in Independent India is far worse than Dalits, and it suggested that they may be given more weightage. So, what we are witnessing today is that affirmative policies favouring minorities are labelled as appeasement/pseudo-secularism and ironically little improvement is seen in their socio-economic conditions despite such measures.

Despite its weaknesses, the non-coercive, non-regulative behaviour of the Indian state towards Muslims has worked to their advantage. State in India has not indulged in aggressive policies of forced assimilation and pursued even-handed accommodationist policies by granting considerable autonomy to minorities. It has also tried to deal with the complex issue of integrating diversities without resorting to violence (*ibid.*).

Group rights may be beneficial to minorities, but the way it is implemented, it has hardly been able to address the problem of the community as a whole. For example, Andhra Pradesh Government thrice granted above limit quota to Muslims and it was quashed by the Judiciary. It clearly reflects that the way political safeguards are being introduced in India is doing more harm than good to the Muslim community and also keep refuelling belligerent animosity among minority and majority community. In extreme cases, it leads to communal riots as well. The motive behind extending group rights in India was to bridge the gap between minority and majority. Instead, it has further widened the rift between them and has brought about intra-community bonding. Prof. Gurpreet Mahajan has explained it in her scholarly works that communal violence has promoted intra-community bond rather than inter-community bonding and given birth to traditional and more Orthodox leadership that is extremely hostile to differences within the community.[12]

Lord Bhikhu Parikh while locating the fault line argues that in India, Constitution takes a very protective view of minorities. It denies the same opportunity to Majority community. Constitution thought of Hindus as majority community, and minority too feared majority. Constitution allows ample scope for the Muslim community to do many things. In that sense, there is a built-in asymmetry in the Constitution that minority communities are free to engage in collective self-expression. Their institutions, customs are untouched, but whereas majorities are concerned, state interfere with Hindu temples, Hindu Code Bill etc. Therefore, demand is made that state must be fair to all communities. On many occasions, the state goes to the absurd level to extend protection that further refuels hatred amongst majority and minority community against each other. For example, in Uttar Pradesh, ruling Samajwadi Party has announced to pay compensation to the victims belonging to the Muslim community in Muzaffarnagar. It not only further charged the atmosphere, but was also sharply criticized on the ground that principle of fair justice is applied, and all those who suffered during riots must be given compensation. Similarly, Uttar Pradesh government announced that Muslim youths are falsely implicated in terror acts and they be freed. The court, however, intervened and said that it should not be done in an arbitrary manner and due legal procedure be followed. Therefore, over politicization of genuine concerns of minorities ultimately leads them nowhere and therefore the state will have to adopt a healthy approach to addressing the minority issues while keeping the majority apprehension at bay. It requires collective rights for vulnerable communities who have been victims of discrimination. They may also be granted safeguards to preserve their diverse culture against homogenization by the nation-state, and it must not be confused with, policies of appeasement of minorities. In other words, minorities need to be accommodated within larger society without being asked to compromise with their distinct identity and policies should be so devised that concern of each group gets accommodated.

## Group Rights and Other Marginalized Groups

In India, even though minorities and other excluded groups have been given weightage, but this issue is not yet fully settled, and it keeps resurfacing. Recently, the Brihannmumbai Municipal Corporation (BMC) has banned sale of meat for four days, i.e. September 10, 13, 17 and 18 during the Jain festival of *Paryusan*.[13] It was turned down by the Supreme Court on the ground that every order of prohibition has to honour the spirit of tolerance and take into account the sensibilities of the people.[14] The judgement by the court is an eye opener. Such issues cannot be settled by imposing it on others. A cooperative effort to address such sensitive issues is required. It should not be enforced *via* government machinery as it encroaches upon individual's freedom and can be best addressed through mutual co-operation only.

In India, though, there are numerous minorities, but except Muslims none other minority groups had existential threats such as Parsis, Anglo-Indians, Jains, Buddhists and Sikhs. It may be because other minority groups are numerically insignificant in comparison to Muslims and therefore, this issue remains unresolved concerning Muslims.

It has been observed that minorities around the world demand group rights as they fear that their identity would be in danger of majoritarian state. This fear syndrome motivates them to ask for exclusive rights. The advocates of group rights in India justify it on the ground that in the last six decades, it has brought about a tremendous change in the politico-economic life of the Scheduled Caste and Scheduled Tribe. It is also a positive step towards establishing an inclusive society. They defend it on the ground that access to political power would enable the economic and social advancement of these groups. Dr. Ambedkar, while justifying group rights in the context of Dalits tried to reinterpret liberal thought. He recognizes the individual merit that is negated by the Hindu social order and justified affirmative action programmes to protect the oppressed groups from the majoritarian hegemony (Keshavkumar 2013). In fact, affirmative action has produced substantial redistributive effect although; redistribution is not evenly spread among groups and regions (Hasan 2000:92-93). It can be easily located in case of tribal community as their condition has not improved much. Sense of dejection and despair still prevails among them which forced them to lose faith in democracy, and they have resorted to violent tactics.

In the post-Independence India, along with protecting their distinct identity, efforts were made to grant them special weightage to address the problem associated with their isolation. North-east and other cut-off regions were declared 'excluded' and 'partially excluded' so that their cultural identities/differences could be safeguarded, and entry of outsiders was banned in those areas. The state also ensured that they should not remain entirely segregated and, therefore, separate representation for them has also been granted by it.[15] It has helped in safeguarding the cultural identities of the tribal people and also checked the influx of non-tribal's in the tribal region considerably. However, tribal's living in mainland still feel neglected and marginalized. Development induced displacement is going on in the tribal belt on a massive scale as large-scale mining and other projects have started in their areas. They are being forced to move out of their habitat where they have been living since ages. They are neither adequately compensated nor get a job as they are illiterate as well as unskilled. It has led to the sense of dejection and despair among them. This is a primary reason for their large-scale involvement in Naxalite movement. So, on the one hand, policies of state have been substantially successful in accommodating one group of tribal's it has failed to co-opt others. Therefore, the urgent requirement is not only to have group-specific rights but also "intra-group specific rights".

Similarly, Women who constitute around one-half of our population remained stigmatized and marginalized throughout the world. Almost all cultures place them in a subordinate position and granting cultural community rights can be a source of unfair treatment to women and other vulnerable groups. Hence, along with accommodating group rights, it is essential to see that it goes in hand with hand with equal rights for all its citizens (*ibid.*: 119). Therefore, scholars like Anne Philips have asked for special consideration for women and not cultural communities as protecting culture is likely to disadvantage women (*ibid.*: 6). In India, our Constitution prohibits discrimination on the basis of sex, but women continue to suffer entrenched cultural bias that values sons more than the daughters. They do not get opportunities and many other privileges in the name of customs and traditions and their right to lead a dignified life as a citizen gets violated in the name of group rights. In the name of protecting minority culture, minority rights based on religious freedom should not translate into a defence of the iniquitous treatment of women (Hasan 2000:99).

Similarly, on the question of gay rights those who support it, justify it on the ground that since gays are different, they should be recognized as a group. Their justification is that they are women trapped in the body of male and their differential identity be known, and they be allowed to have a same-sex partner.[16] However, in our country, both society and state humiliate Gays and lesbians as they are the miniscule minority and cannot have a decisive impact on electoral politics, and therefore nobody takes care of their plight. Our Constitution has granted safeguards to various other deprived groups. However, no Constitutional safeguard is being provided to Gays and Lesbians. Therefore, protest movement is going on in their support across the country. It seems that along with our state, even Judiciary seems confused on this issue as it has no definite position on this matter so far. Gay rights supporters have argued that in a liberal democracy like India, individuals must have freedom to choose their partner even if it is from the same sex, and it was upheld by the Delhi High Court. However, Supreme Court turned it down on the ground that it is unnatural.

Confusion also prevails among multicultural theorist concerning group rights of homosexual groups. Scholars like Kymlica believe in differentiating between different minorities and their claims. He does not believe in all kind of diversities but with those only who had a distinct "Societal Culture" which leaves out homosexual groups. However, Iris Marion Young is in favour of granting special representation to all oppressed minorities including homosexuals (Mahajan 2011:14). It amply demonstrates that confusion concerning the group rights of homosexuals prevails globally and not confined to India only.

Along with socially constructed handicaps, there are certain natural obstacles, the victims of which face social discrimination and for them, different policies are required to deal with their problems. Transsexual and homosexuals, physically disabled, mentally challenged people, elderly citizens, AIDs patient, etc. belongs to this category. Supreme Court recently pronounced its judgement in favour of transgender for granting them reservation in education and employment.[17] It has been observed that people belonging to these categories are ill-treated. Similarly, those suffering from AIDs are treated worst than untouchables. Even though, it is a non-communicable disease but social prejudices are there. Many times even hospitals do not allow them entry. It is also a kind of untouchability. Likewise, in the case of elderly people who also constitute a group and belong to the naturally handicapped category are stigmatized. Though, the government came out of its deep slumber to formulate National Policy of Older Persons only in 1993. Still, we do not have comprehensive policies to ensure graceful aging.

In India, state attitude towards newly developed groups like AIDs, patient, Gays and Lesbians, physically disabled, Elderly citizens look very casual and indifferent.

In India, group rights can be categorized in three distinct categories:

1. Certain groups had Constitutional safeguards and implemented: Scheduled Caste, Scheduled Tribe, Women, and Minority.
2. Certain groups have Constitutional guarantees and not actually implemented: Aged Citizens.
3. Certain newly emerged groups for whom no protection is available: Gays and Lesbians, AIDs patient, etc.

It seems that political motivation is there behind supporting some groups and not others, and demands of those groups are taken up on a priority basis that is numerically significant. Group rights, therefore, should not be homogenized as each group has specific character/ problem, and it should be dealt with accordingly.

## Concluding Remarks

In the end, it can be concluded that individual and collective rights should not be understood and explained as something pitted against one another. Both have their merits and demerits and instead of thinking in terms of abolishing group rights or elevating them above individual rights will weaken the cause that it has to serve. The rationale behind introducing group rights in India was to end discriminatory practices and bring all groups at par with each other. It was essential to realize the ideals enshrined in the Preamble to the Constitution. It was also supposed to bring democracy closer to the ideals of substantive democracy where those who are on the margin can be the part of the mainstream. Since, different groups had different problems, the accommodative measures also varied and after extensive debate and discussion within the Constituent Assembly safeguards were provided to various groups. However, the issue is not yet settled. Very often pro, and anti-reservation movement, communal riots, protests by homosexual groups, women groups, etc. erupts. It clearly reflects that group right may have benefitted the disadvantaged groups, but it has also left an indelible scar among others. It has, instead of doing away with the prevailing social schism, further consolidated/ entrenched it. Therefore, revisiting of group rights is required so that this issue gets amicably resolved.

## Notes

1. Wanchoo, Rohit in Gurpreet Mahajan (ed.) (2011), *Accommodating Diversity*, Oxford University Press, New Delhi, p. 207.
2. *Ibid.*
3. Rochana Bajpayi has interpreted it differently by stating that Britishers by granting political safeguards tried to adjust the balance between different communities in representative bodies, public services and also tried to improve the socio-economic conditions of disadvantaged groups. However, in nationalist vocabulary there was no such plan for balancing the number of different communities in public institutions *per se*. Political safeguards were considered acceptable only for tackling 'backwardness' which was associated with lower castes and tribes, but not religious minorities. Bajpai, Rochana in Rajeev Bhargava ed. (2010) *Politics and Ethics of the Indian Constitution*, Oxford University Press, Delhi, p. 380.
4. Bajpai, Rochana in Rajeev Bhargava ed. (2010) *Politics and Ethics of the Indian Constitution*, Oxford University Press, Delhi, p. 359.
5. *Ibid.*, p. 360.
6. The members of the Constituent Assembly, such as Mohamed Ismail

Saheb alongwith B. Pocker Sahib were in favour of inclusion of right to one's personal laws in the fundamental right to religion. They believed that right to follow personal law is part of the way of life of those people who are following such laws; it is part of their religion as well as culture.

7. Mahajan, Gurpreet, "Negotiating Cultural Diversity and Minority Rights in India", *International Idea, www.idea.int/publications/dchs/upload/dchs_vol. 2_sec 3_4.pdf.*
8. *Op. cit.,* p. 193.
9. "Alpsankhyako per Meherbani", S. Sankar, *Dainik Jagran*, Lucknow, 25.1.2014.
10. Alam, Anwar, "Liberal States and Muslim Minorities", *Seminar*, 621, May 2011.
11. Mahajan, Gurpreet, "Negotiating Cultural Diversity and Minority Rights in India", *International Idea,* p. 121, www.idea.int/publications/dchs/upload/dchs_vol2_sec 3_4.pd.f
12. Gurpreet Mahajan (December 1999), "*Seminar*, 484, New Delhi.
13. *The Indian Express*, September 8, 2015.
14. *The Indian Express*, September 18, 2015.
15. Mahajan, Gurpreet, "Negotiating Cultural Diversity and Minority Rights in India", *International Idea,* p. 121, www.idea.int/publications/dchs/upload/dchs_vol2_sec 3_4.pdf.
16. In Europe and America, more than 20 countries have national laws allowing Gays and Lesbians to marry.
17. "Supreme Court recognizes transgenders as third Gender", TOI, April 15, 2014.

## References

Acharya, Ashok (2010): "Constitutionalising Difference: The Indian Experiment", in Achin Vanaik and Rajeev Bhargava (eds.): *Understanding Contemporary India: Critical Perspectives,* (New Delhi: Orient Blackswan), p. 51.

Bajpai, Rochana "Minority Representation and the Making of the Indian Constitution", in Rajeev Bhargava (2008) (ed.), *Politics and Ethics of the Indian Constitution*, Oxford University Press, New Delhi, p. 358.

Balkrishnan, K.G. (2009): Individual Rights in India: A Perspective from the Supreme Court, paper Presented at Round Table Conference, University of Georgia, 3-6 April.

Bhargava, Rajeev (ed.) (2008): *Politics and Ethics of the Indian Constitution* (New Delhi: Oxford University Press), p. 10.

Bhargava, Rajeev (2010): *Political Theory* (New Delhi:Oxford University Press), p. 107.

Bhargava, Rajeev (2010): "India's Secular Constitution", in Achin Vanaik and Rajeev Bhargava (eds.), *Understanding Contemporary India: Critical Perspectives* (New Delhi: Orient Blackswan), p. 32.

Chandoke, Neera (2011): "Recontextualizing Liberalism," *Economic and Political Weekly*, Vol. XLVI, No. 43.

Hasan, Zoya (2000), "More Equal but Still Not Equal? State and Inter-Group Equality in Contemporary India", in Imtiaz Ahmad, Partha, S. Ghosh and Helmut Reifeld (eds.): *Pluralism and Equality,* (New Delhi: Sage Publication), pp. 92-93.

Hasan, Joya (2009), *Politics of Inclusion*, (New Delhi: Oxford University Press), p. 5.

Jayal, Niraja Gopal (2011): "A False Dichotomy? The Unresolved Tension between Universal and Differentiated Citizenship in India" (London: Oxford Development Studies), p. 185.

Jha, Shefali (2010): "Rights *versus* Representation: Defending Minority Interests in the Constituent Assembly", in Rajeev Bhargava (ed.), *Politics and Ethics of the Indian Constitution* (New Delhi: Oxford University Press), p. 340.

Jovanovic, Miodrag, A. (2005): "Recognizing Minority Identity Through Collective Rights", *Human Rights Quarterly,* Vol. 27, No. 2, The John Hopkins University Press, U.S.A., pp. 625-651.

Keshavkumar, P. (2013): "Liberal Democracy and Kymlika's Conception of Minority Rights: Towards a Perspective of *Dalit* Rights," rountablemedia.co.in, dated 30 June.

Kymlica, Will (2002): *Contemporary Political Philosophy* (New York: Oxford University Press), pp. 239-243.

Kymlicka and Norman, Wayne ed. (2000): *Citizenship in Diverse Societies*, (New York: Oxford University Press), pp. 34-35.

Mahajan, Gurpreet (ed.) (2011): *Accommodating Diversity* (New Delhi: Oxford University Press), p. 7.

Mansfield, John H., "The Personal Laws or a Uniform Civil Code?" In Baird, (ed.) *Religion and Law in Independent India*, pp. 207-246.

Mantra, Rajeev and Harsha Gupta (2013): "One *versus* Group," *The Indian Express,* 13th February.

Mookherjee, Monica (2008): "Multiculturalism," in Catriona McKinnon (ed.), *Issues in Political Theory*, Oxford University Press, New Delhi, pp. 223, 227-228.

Oestreich, Joel, E. (1999): "Liberal Theory and Minority Group Rights", *Human Rights Quarterly*, Vol. 21, The John Hopkins University Press, U.S.A., pp. 108-132.

Rodrigues, Valerian (2008): "Citizenship and the Indian Constitution", in Rajeev Bhargava (ed.), *Politics and Ethics of the Indian Constitution*, (New Delhi:Oxford University Press), p. 180.

Tharoor, Shashi, (Winter 1999/2000): "Are Human Rights Universal," *World Policy Journal*, Winter, Vol. XVI, No. 4, New York, USA.

Young, I.M. (1989/1995): "Polity and Group Difference: A critic of the ideal of Universal Citizenship," in R. Beiner (ed.) *Theorizing Citizenship* (Albany: State University of New York Press).

# 6
# Does Economic Inequality Lead to Political Conflict? A Critical Reflection on Indian Reforms

*Sarabjit Kaur*

## Introduction

Political conflicts require the mobilization of rebel forces. Why citizens choose to leave their homes abandoning their families and livelihoods to join armed rebellion—an activity associated with potentially enormous risks to personal safety has long been a central question in the conflict literature. In the early conflict literature, participation was the self-evident mechanism connecting various independent variables such as economic inequality to conflict. Since, then little has changed. The connection between economic inequality and violence has long been at the centre of conflict studies and is of immense importance to the policy-makers and of perennial interests to political scientists. However, it must be mentioned at the outset that the nexus that exists between the two variables is not a simple and straight forward one but is a subject of great deal of debate and discussion. While political and economic grievances have been repeatedly linked to conflict processes in the qualitative literature on conflicts, the plethora of quantitative studies found no robust relationship between economic inequality and conflict. Yet, in this chapter, an effort has been made to put the existing literature on the relationship between the two variables under three broad categories. The first category includes the viewpoints of those scholars who consider the occurrence of political conflicts as a function of economic inequalities and thus have established a positive linear relationship between the two variables. Under this category, one can incorporate the ideas of scholars like Aristotle, Karl Marx, Samuel P. Huntington and Bruce M. Russett. Besides, some of the psychological theories of revolution have also been incorporated for a better understanding of the direct nexus between the two variables. The second category includes the viewpoints of those theorists like Edward J. Mitchell and Mark Irving Lichbach, who do not consider the existence of economic inequalities as a necessary precondition for the outbreak of political conflicts. In the third category is included the viewpoint of a scholar, Jack Nagel, who has regarded the occurrence of political conflicts at the intermediate level of economic inequality. The relationship between the two variables therefore varies from situation to situation. In some situations the prevailing inequalities create a fertile ground for the outbreak of political conflicts. This is well seen in the case of developing countries like Nigeria and Pakistan. In Nigeria, the prevailing inequalities in the society has posed serious challenges to mention a few like the civil war (1967-70), when the notion of Biafra was put forth and the Niger Delta Crisis which was the outcome of economic deprivation that was experienced by more than 20 minority tribes which reside in the oil rich Niger Delta region. The region is the mainstay of the Nigerian economy for about 90 per cent of the nation's foreign exchange and revenue is produced here. But for the people of the region, oil has been more of a curse than a blessing. Despite so many years of oil production and hundreds of billions of dollars of oil revenue, the local people remain in abject poverty without even the most basic amenities such as water and electricity. The benefits of the oil revenue earned have not trickled down to the masses. A large section of society lives on less than 1 dollar a day. The vast oil revenues earned benefit only 1 per cent of the population. The economic deprivations has created ground for the emergence of armed militant groups willing to kill as part of their campaign for greater share of the regions oil wealth. In 2006, the large foreign oil companies operating in the Niger Delta region were targeted. Besides this, the militants known as the Movement for the Emancipation of the Niger Delta kidnapped four Shell employees, blew up pipelines, killed Nigerian soldiers and kidnapped and ransomed more than 50 oil workers (Kaur 2013: 208). Similarly in the case of Pakistan, economic disparities prevailing at inter-personal level led to demonstrations that continued for 132 days, i.e., from

November 1968 to March 1969 against the Ayub Khan government, ultimately leading to the collapse of his regime (Sayeed 1968: 103). Besides, inter-personal inequalities, the inter-regional inequalities prevailing in Pakistan generated ground for the emergence of a political party in the 1960s—the Awami league. This party gained ample mass support when its principle leader Sheikh Mujihur Rehman formulated a six point demand for near independence for East wing from Pakistan. The political struggle which took the form of civil war finally gave birth to an Independent state of Bangladesh (Brass *et al.,* 1973:259).

While in other situations severe economic inequalities prevail but do not generate political conflicts of the magnitude that would lead to the breakdown of the political system. The latter can well be seen in the case of India where economic inequalities have existed in the past and are continuing to exist even in the present times. These inequalities over a period of time with the process of globalization have further taken a concrete shape. These inequalities have from time to time posed some challenge before the political system like farmers suicide and that of Naxalism.

Since, 1997, more than 1,00,000 farmers, in the absence of financial assistance have taken their lives. The economic reforms have not led to crop insurance, land irrigation or enough bank loans. The reforms opened Indian farmers to global competition such as with United States and United Kingdom, who receive over 18 billion dollars a year in subsidies. For farmers in India such foreign subsidies have driven down the prices of crops in the global market. The economic miseries experienced have forced them to commit suicide. On an average there has been one farmer's suicide every 32 minutes since 2002. These suicides, as pointed out by agricultural economist, Vandana Shiva, are especially taking place on a very large scale in the cotton belt. Besides the farmer's suicide, another major threat before the Indian political system is that posed by Naxalism. The Naxalites are actors in approximately 40 per cent of India's geographical area. From the period, 2006-2010 alone, there were nearly 9,000 incidents with Naxalites, with over 3000 civilians killed. They have been attacking police establishments and infrastructures such as public transportation causing insecurity and instability to the area. These challenges before the Indian political system however are still not of the magnitude which has been experienced by countries like Nigeria and Pakistan and recently by the countries belonging to the Arab world. This therefore provokes one to identify reasons as to why the economic inequalities prevailing in India have not led to tumultuous change or a major challenge before the political system. But before identifying these reasons and examining theoretically the nexus between economic inequalities and political conflict, it becomes pertinent to have a conceptual understanding of the two terms, i.e. economic inequalities and political conflict. The chapter thus is divided into two sections—Section I which deals with the conceptual understanding of economic inequality and political conflict as well as with the theoretical perspectives examining the relationship between the two terms. Section II provides an insight into the prevailing inequalities in India and also identifies the factors which have prevented these inequalities from posing serious challenge before the political system in India.

## SECTION I: MEANING OF ECONOMIC INEQUALITY

The concept of economic inequality is a matter of great deal of disagreement amongst scholars. This is further complicated by the fact that the very concept has undergone change in interpretation over a period of time. According to Amartya Sen, the concept of inequity or economic inequality depends on the tolerance or intolerance of the people of the stratification and differentiation in the society. Thus, the Athenian intellectuals did not consider the issue of slavery in the discussion on equity, though in present times, the very idea of slavery would be considered obnoxious in any system of economic equality. But he notes that is important to recognize that the perception of equity is crucial to relate inequalities with the "possibilities of actual rebellion" in the society (Sen 1989: Preface). To have a perception of inequality, the comment by A.B. Atkinson is very pertinent. According to him, the concept of economic inequality basically refers to inequality that exists in terms of wealth and income (Atkinson 1983: 3). Either of these criteria has been used by the theorists. Among the scholars who have understood inequality in terms of wealth are Euripides, James Madison, Alexis de Tocqueville and Karl Marx. There are other scholars who have focused on more concrete form of wealth, i.e., land. Thus, by using land as a criterion, S.P. Huntington, Merle Kling, Bruce M. Russett, Edward J. Mitchell and Jack Nagel have studied the relationship between economic inequalities and political conflict. On the other hand, there are theorists like Raymond Tanter, Manus I. Midlarsky, M. Parvin and Edward N. Muller who have studied inequalities in terms of income.

The existing inequalities further get aggravated by events like economic development, urbanization, modernization and social change.

The other concept that needs to be understood properly is political conflict. "Political conflict is a contention among collective actors over the structures, incumbents or policies of a political regime and is a ubiquitous of a political regime feature of political life." (Lichbach and Gurr 1981: 4). Though scholars like Ted Robert Gurr have pointed in his work that there is no exact distinction in the social sciences generally or in conflict research specifically between the political and the non-political forms of conflict (Gurr 1980: 2) yet there does exist certain distinguishing characteristics which enables one to differentiate between social conflicts and political conflicts.

In any society, conflict will arise as individuals or groups having their goals interact with one another; many of these conflicts do not become political for some of them may be either unimportant and tend to fade away or they can be solved through the non-political channels. But, only those conflicts which enter the political process are the ones that acquire the form of political conflict (Conn 1971: 63). Thus, political conflicts involve the state either as a party to the conflict or as the object of people's demands and perceptions (Gurr 1980:2). These conflicts can occur at the national (internal) or the international level. In this work, the focus is on internal conflicts.

Political scientists and economists define conflict in a given country as an internal conflict that concerns at least two parties (government being among them) with a use of armed forces resulting in human deaths. A conflict is categorized as a civil war if there are over 1000 deaths per year and as a civil conflict if there are between 25-999 deaths per year (Couttenier and Soubeyran 2013: 6). Besides civil war, other forms are-armed attacks, riots and revolutions. Some scholars like Rudolf J. Rummel and Raymond Tanter have on the basis of their empirical studies put forward a typology of civil strife events. The general categories and "sub-categories" are:

(i) *Turmoil*: This includes unstructured mass strives which are relatively spontaneous events like demonstrations, political strikes, riots, political clashes and localized rebellions.
(ii) *Conspiracy*: This category of civil strife is characterized by

high degree of organization and takes place on a small scale. It includes events like political assassinations, coups, mutinies, plots and purges.

(iii) *Internal War*: This form of civil strife is characterized by high degree of organization and by its operation on a large scale. Under this category are included events which are accompanied by extensive violence like large scale revolts (Gurr 1968:1107).

## Theoretical Perspectives on the Nexus Between Economic Inequality and Political Conflict

The links between economic inequality and political conflict are among the oldest concerns in political economy. It is almost a universal assumption that an inequitable distribution of resources and wealth will provoke violent rebellion. And yet it is just as obvious and historically established that sharply skewed income and wealth distribution does not always or even usually lead to rebellion. The relationship that exists between economic inequality and political conflict is thus not a simple and straight forward one but is a subject that has generated tremendous controversy. Yet in this paper, an effort is made to put the existing literature into 3 broad categories. Each of the perspective is briefly discussed:

The first category includes the viewpoints of those scholars who consider the occurrence of political conflicts as a function of economic inequalities and thus have established a positive linear relationship between the two variables. Under this category, one can include the ideas of scholars like Aristotle, Karl Marx, Samuel P. Huntington, Merle Kling and Bruce M. Russett.

Aristotle in his work, *The Politics* has regarded the existence of inequality in terms of inherited virtue and wealth as an important factor that leads to the emergence of divisions in the society (Aristotle 1981: 297). According to him; it is the desire to overcome economic inequality that men resort to political conflict.

The existence of a direct link between economic inequality and political conflict has also been postulated by eminent political philosophers like Karl Heinrich Marx. His ideas on revolution can well be understood by linking it with the existence of economic inequalities prevalent in the society. The chief instrument that has been regarded by him as the basis of economic divisions in the society is the institution of private property (Oakley 1984:80).

Some scholars like Samuel P. Huntington, Merle Kling and Bruce M. Russett by making use of land as an indicator have established a direct link between economic inequality and political conflict. According to Samuel P. Huntington in situations where landownership is equitable and the peasants living conditions are viable, revolutions are unlikely. But in situations, where the peasant lives in poverty and the land is unequally distributed, chances of occurrence of political violence are likely (Mueller and Seligson 1987:425). Similar views were expressed by Merle Kling and Bruce M. Russett.

Another eminent scholar who has made use of psychological factor and thus established a direct link between economic inequalities and political conflict is Ted Robert Gurr. Gurr has expressed his ideas in his work *Why Men Rebel.* According to Gurr, the necessary precondition for the occurrence of violent civil conflict is "relative deprivation" which implies "actors" perceptions of discrepancy between their value expectations and their value capabilities (Gurr 1970:24). Value expectations generally stands for the goods and conditions of life to which people believe they are rightfully entitled to whereas value capabilities refer to those goods and conditions of life which they think they are capable of getting and keeping. The discrepancy between expectation and capabilities can emerge in relation to any collectively sought value, which can be economic, psychological or political and thus giving rise to the feeling of relative deprivation

The second category includes the viewpoints of those theorists like—Edward J. Mitchell, Mark Irving Lichbach, who do not consider the existence of economic inequalities as a necessary precondition for the outbreak of political conflict.

Edward J. Mitchell on the basis of a statistical study of South Vietnam came to the conclusion that the relationship between economic inequality and political conflict is not a direct one. According to Mitchell, in South Vietnam there existed inequality in terms of ownership of land, sizes of farms and lack of redistribution of large estates. This inequality that existed in terms of ownership of land did not generate a situation for the emergence of insurgency. Instead inequality provided for greater security. This according to Mitchell is mainly because of the fact that inequality of land distribution in Vietnam is directly associated with governmental control (Mitchell 1968:422). The other reasons which have been put forward by Mitchell to provide an explanation for the absence of linear relationship between inequality and political conflict are:

Firstly, the poor peasant has low aspirations and is of docile nature.

Secondly, the relationship between the peasant and the landlord is not merely economic but it is social as well as political (Mitchell 1968:422).

Thus, Mitchell on the basis of his study of South Vietnam came to the conclusion that existence of economic inequality is not always the accelerating force for the occurrence of political conflict.

A viewpoint similar to the above has also been expressed by Mark Irving Lichbach. According to him, the economically well off use social, economic and political power in such a way that inspite of the existence of economic inequalities political dissent does not arise (Lichbach 1989: 438).

The third category is included the viewpoints of scholars like Jack Nagel who has regarded the occurrence of political conflicts at the intermediate level of economic inequality. According to him, the relationship between inequality and discontent is *ceteris paribus*, begins at zero in a perfectly egalitarian system, increases with inequality, reaching a maximum at some intermediate level of inequality and then decreases as complete inequality is approached. Thus, the shape of the curve is a parabola (Nagel 1974:472).

The study of various perspectives however point to the fact that there are basically two perspectives on the link between economic inequalities and political conflict—one that regards that political conflicts are the outcome of economic inequalities and on the other hand, the second perspective that maintains that economic inequalities have no role to play in the outbreak of political conflicts. However, it should be emphasized that both the perspectives points towards the fact that these two variables—economic inequalities and political conflict, coexist but the issue is whether there is a relationship between the two variables or not.

The issue can be formulated as follows—for economic inequalities to lead to political conflict there ought to be certain conditions that exist in the society that facilitate the link. In other contexts, economic inequalities may exist without leading to political conflict and occurrence of political conflict is entirely due to other factors that have no link with economic inequalities. This points out that the issue of the relationship between economic inequalities and political conflict is context specific. Thus in societies where the following conditions existed, direct nexus existed between economic inequalities and political conflict. These conditions are—

I. When economic inequalities prevailing in the society are in a position to generate awareness amongst the have-nots that they have been deprived of certain economic opportunities and that they are accruing to only few in the society. This consciousness comes when they start making a comparison between their own economic positions with that of those people who are experiencing upward economic mobility. This leads to the emergence of a feeling of relative deprivation. This can emerge at two levels-inter-personal and inter-regional. The emergence of a feeling of relative deprivation can therefore be regarded as an essential condition for the establishment of a connection between economic inequalities and political conflict.

II. The generation of the feeling of relative deprivation should enable the have-nots to come together and put forward a united challenge against the political system. This organization is made possible and given a strong shape by—(a) by the ability of the deprived section to overcome various social barriers; (b) by the deprived sections calculations of what economic benefits they are going to derive by becoming a part of such an organization.

III. When the functioning of political system is such that it does not contribute to the economic betterment of the deprived population. This can happen when—
   (a) The political system is unresponsive to the prevailing economic inequalities in the society.
   (b) If it responds by undertaking some measures, these measures ultimately benefit the already affluent group rather than lead to the improvement in the economic conditions of the have-nots.
   (c) Sometimes the political leaders themselves pursue such kind of policies that does not give importance to the idea of equity.

As a result of the above mentioned ideas in (a), (b) and (c), the large majority of the deprived people lose their faith in the functioning of the political system. This alienation contributes to the erosion of the political system's legitimacy. To establish its legitimacy, in other words, to seek the support of the large number of have-nots, the political machinery lacks adequate means in the forms of institutions or structures. Owing to this weakness of the political system, the have-nots are made to indulge in actions which take various forms of political conflict. This poses not only a challenge before the political system, but also enables the have-nots to release their frustration which had been built by the economic inequalities. In the context where conditions—(I), (II), and (III) are absent economic inequalities do not lead to political conflicts but if present, then direct relationship is established between the two variables.

After briefly discussing the various perspectives, let us now have an understanding of the Indian scenario.

## SECTION II: EXAMINING THE NEXUS BETWEEN ECONOMIC INEQUALITY AND POLITICAL CONFLICT IN INDIA

The existence of economic inequalities in India has a long history. During the Mughal India, a few hundred families of *Mansabdar* (military officer) rank had access to one third of the groups produce of the land, This persisted in the early years of British India. However, during the first period of globalization (1780-1914), inequality did not show an increase or decrease.

India gained its Independence from British colonial rule in 1947. In 1952, the new government began to implement significant reforms to improve the lives of its people and to foster development, India's first Prime-Minister, Jawaharlal Nehru, led many of the reforms in the republics early history. Nehru was a staunch socialist, who distained capitalism and profit. Nehru and his economic advisors sought to improve India through state sponsored industrialization and by keeping the economy largely closed off from global trade. While the Nehru administration was responsible for implementing many pro-poor and pro-worker reforms including: the elimination of taxation for Indian farmer's minimum wage and benefits for blue-collar workers and the nationalization of heavy industries. These policies continued after Nehru's death in 1964 and saw periods of considerable fluctuation in economic growth. As a result of the nationalistic approach, by the late 1980s stagnation had set in and

India was in serious peril after depleting nearly all of its foreign exchange reserves. It was during 1991, the then Finance Minister, Manmohan Singh was able to usher in major reforms with the help of Prime Minister. These reforms led to globalization.

Globalization has resulted into huge economic progress in some countries. As a result of this economic progress, the distribution of income has increased to wider portion of the society resulting in the decreasing income inequalities in various societies to some extent. But some theories and research has been advocating that globalization has increased inequalities in societies and countries. For example, according to Stiglitz (2003), the practice of globalization has resulted into making poor societies more unequal rather than less unequal. Inequality in 2010 in India has significantly increased from the level of 1991. The Gini coefficient has increased from 30 in 1991 to 34 in 2010. This clearly shows that inequality has increased during this period while during the same period influence of globalization in the country has increased significantly. If we take the period 1991 to 2010, we find that the income share held by highest 10 per cent and 20 per cent increased during this period but there is no change in income share held by lowest 10 per cent and 20 per cent. This signifies that distribution of income in India after the globalization has tilted in favour of the rich. It is clear that globalization has yielded many results, some of them are positive and some are negative. Globalization has increased GDP growth rate, but at the same time results into increased concentration of resources into few hands (Upadhyay 2015). This has been upheld by numerous studies that have undertaken an in depth analysis of economic inequality in India.

Normally, when economists discuss about economic inequality, they take into account the distribution of income across households or individuals. In India, however, the inequality data collected most frequently and most systematically—by the National Sample Survey—involve the distribution of expenditure on consumption rather than income (Weisskopf 2011:45).

If one studies inequality in consumption in rural and urban India from the late 1950s to the mid-2000s then one finds that the rural consumption declined from the late 1950s through the early 1970s, then risen. In the early 1980s, then declined to reach a low point in the early 1990s- and finally risen again through the mid-2000s. It has been higher in the post-reform period since 1991 than in the two previous decades (*ibid.*: 46). Studies undertaken by Sen and Himanshu

(2004) found a slow decline in rural consumption inequality from the late 1970s to the early 1990s, followed by a sharp rise in the early 2000s. Looking at the rate of growth of real consumer expenditure in the 1990s by the poorest 40 per cent of consumers, they found that per capita consumption by the rural poor increased only one-fifth as much as the average increase in national consumption. Sarkar and Mehta (2010), comparing growth rates of consumer expenditure before and after the 1991 reforms, estimated that in the pre-reform period the poor fractile groups registered a faster rate of growth than the richer fractile groups, whereas in the post-reform period consumption growth rates were significantly higher for the top 20 per cent than for the rest of the rural population (*ibid.*).

The Gini coefficient of inequality in urban consumption has averaged about 35 per cent over the whole five-decade period-reflecting a significantly higher degree of inequality than in the rural sector. It appears to have declined a bit from the late 1950s through the mid-1970s and then risen noticeably through the mid-2000s. As in the rural sector, urban inequality has been higher in the post-reform period than in the two decades prior to 1991. Sen and Himanshu (2004) found that in the 1990s, per capita consumption by the urban poor increased only half as much as the per capita national average rate of growth of consumer expenditure (*ibid.*). Sarkar and Mehta (2010), comparing growth rates of real consumer expenditure for the decade before and the decade after the liberalizing reforms of the early 1990s, estimated that the average rate of growth for all urban consumers was 0.75 per cent in the pre-reform period and 1.77 per cent in the post-reform period. Comparing patterns of growth of consumer expenditure across fractile groups before and after 1991, they found that the pro-rich bias in the post-reform period was even more striking in the urban than in in the rural sector (*ibid.*).

Banerjee and Piketty also highlighted disproportionately large income/consumption gains by the upper tail of the population. Based on income tax reports, they found that in the 1990s, the real incomes of the top 1 per cent of income earners in India increased by about 50 per cent. Furthermore, among this top one per cent, the richest one percentage increased their real incomes by more than three times during the 1990s. While the socialist policies of the early part of the planning period shrank, the income share of the top earners very substantially until the mid 1980s, more open and pro-market policies have since allowed the ultra-rich to increase their share substantially (Pal and Ghosh 2007:5).

If one takes consumption inequality in India as a whole then one finds that Gini coefficient averaged about 32 per cent from the early 1980s through the early 1990s and then increased significantly in the post-reform period to a level of at least 35 per cent (Weisskopf 2011 : 46). Revallion (2000) calculated decile shares of consumption in India from 1983 to 1997. He found that over this period the share of the poorest two deciles remained quite flat, the share of the middle deciles fluctuated around a slight downward trend, and the share of the richest two deciles showed a clear upward trend; within the 1990s the upward trend of the latter was even more marked. These findings were supported by Tapalova (2008) who concluded that overall inequality in the 1990s increased particularly in urban areas. During this period, the top of the population enjoyed a substantially larger share of the gains from economic growth compared to the previous decade (Weisskopf 2011: 46).

Besides focusing on income, one can also understand economic inequality by taking into consideration the distribution of wealth. Data on wealth distribution in India—as elsewhere—is subject to more shortcomings than data on income and consumption. Not only rich tend to be under sampled in surveys, but even when surveyed they have every incentive to under report their assets and to hide illegitimately acquired acquired wealth. According to a study by Jayadev *et al.,* (2007) the Gini coefficient for all-India per capita total asset ownership in 1991-1992 was 64 per cent and 65 per cent in 2002-2003 (Weisskopf 2011:47). In both the years, the wealthiest 10 per cent of wealth-holders held roughly 50 per cent of total assets and 0.2 per cent of net worth. Land is the single most important asset for most Indian wealth-holders and it is more unequally distributed than wealth as whole—with a Gini coefficient of 73 per cent in both years. The ownership of financial assets is even more concentrated with an estimated Gini coeffeicient of 99 per cent in both years; 5 per cent of Indians participates in the stock market and almost all financial wealth is held by just a fraction of 1 per cent of the population (*ibid.*).

Overall one can say that in the present times, one can talk of two Indias: the India that shines with its rich neighbourhoods, corporate houses, glittering shopping malls and high-tech flyovers over which flow a procession of new-model cars. This is the globalized India which is entering the first world. And then there is the other India

(Bhaduri 2009:47), where more than a third of the Indian population lives in sub-human poverty. Nearly 42 per cent of the Indian population is absolutely poor by international standards with income less than 1 US dollar in purchasing power. More than three-fourths of the population has a daily purchasing power of less than Rs. 20 a day; nearly half the children are undernourished and in the last two decades, food deprivation has not decreased (*ibid.*: 30). "This is not just a matter of the growing, relative inequality between the two Indias. Amore brutal process is at work, with the connivance of governments at the Central and the State level, which is not only widening this divide between the two Indias, but is consciously deepening the Other India's absolute poverty, misery and rage" (*ibid.*:48). The gap between the two Indias is widened with the high economic growth.

The economic disparities prevailing certainly have had its impact. More than a hundred thousand farmers have committed suicide over the last decade or so. According to National Crime Records Bureau Report "Accidental Deaths and Suicide Report-2007", since 1997 a total of 182.936 farmers have committed suicide. The five worst affected States—Maharashtra, Andhra Pradesh, Karnataka, Madhya Pradesh and Chhattisgarh account for two-third of all such suicides. In 2006, a UN Report "Extent of Chronic Hunger and Malnutrition" criticised the Indian Government for the rising number of farmer suicides. The report said that economic growth through the 1990s had made India a more market oriented economy but had failed to benefit all Indians equally (*The Hindu* 2008). Farmers suicides are the most tragic and dramatic symptom of the crisis of survival faced by Indian peasants. Rapid increase in indebtness was at the root of farmers taking their lives. Debt is a reflection of a negative economy, a loosing economy. Two factors have transformed the positive economy of agriculture into a negative economy for peasants—the rising costs of production and the falling prices of farm commodities. Both these factors are rooted in the policies of trade, liberalization and corporate globalization.

Besides the farmers suicide another major issue which is really a matter of concern for the Indian Government is that of Naxalism. According to Government estimates, some 125 districts-spread over 12 States and covering more than a quarter of the land mass, mostly in Central India, which comprise the "Red Corridor"—are affected by extremist Naxalite activities (Bhaduri 2009:29-30). About 10,000 people have been killed in the expanding civil war since 1980. In

April 2010 in Chhattisgarh, 76 paramilitary troops were killed. On May 25, 2013 Maoist insurgents in the same State again wiped out almost the entire leadership of the Congress Party in that State killing 28 of its members in an ambush. Sonia Gandhi, the Congress Party leader was "aghast" at the Maoist assault on her party members and then Prime Minister Manmohan Singh has called the insurgents "the single biggest internal security challenge ever faced by our country" (Ismi 2013: 1). The increase in the intensity of the Naxal movement can be traced to the objective conditions of life of the tribals and to the deep seated frustrations of the people with the existing social, economic and political order, its institutions and practices and the notions of development, participation and governance which they challenge and seek to change. The tribals and *dalits* of the Naxal affected areas are among the poorest of the poor and the most socially marginalized sections of the society. At the national as well as the State level in the Naxalite belt, they are at the bottom of the ladder. The incidence of poverty is higher than 50 per cent among the tribals in Orissa (73%), Jharkhand including Bihar (59%), Madhya Pradesh including Chhattisgarh (57%) and between 35-50 per cent in West Bengal, Maharashtra, Assam and Uttar Pradesh including Uttarakhand. The social conditions of the dalits and the tribes are deeply conditioned by the agarian and social structure. The agarian structure is determined by the pattern of landholding, access to land and other productive assets and social relations evolved on that basis. The social structure is embedded in the caste based Hindu social order in the case of Dalits and the hegemonic relations between the culturally distinct tribals and the predominant non-tribal population in the case of tribes which influence all facets of their lives. The two structures combined produce oppressive conditions for these groups and reinforce each other. In this process, the landholding pattern is highly skewed and the dalits constitute the largest percentage of landless persons. A significant percentage among them does not even have secure homestead land. The tribals who at one time were privileged to own some land have recorded the fastest pace of landlessness among different social groups in recent times. The *dalits* in the absence of opportunities for wage employment elsewhere are dependent upon the landowners for providing them avenues of livelihood in the rural areas. These include payment of very low wages, long hours of work, debt bondage control over produce from owned land, if any, humiliating treatment and physical assault in the case of non-compliance of employer's orders. Their condition has further worsened by the opening of the Indian economy to trade and investment, the entry of mining companies in Odisha and Chhattisgarh poses a threat to the livelihoods of tribals and their way of life. Since 1991, the tribals thus risk losing everything they have ever known. In 2005-06, the Chhattisgarh Government signed contracts for 1.6 billon dollars with power industries. This move coincided with the start of the Salwa Judum, when tribals were forcefully evicted from their villages. One hundred Memorandums of Understanding have been signed with mostly private parties who will reap huge profits at the cost of the local people and environment. The Government industry Nexus shows up in deals like Vedanta where a Memorandum of Understanding was signed with maximum benefits to the company, with the tribals losing out (Chenoy and Chenoy 2010:119-20). This problem has further increased with the impact of globalization. Several multinational companies have started making their in roads in the tribal areas owing to their resource richness. These resources are exploited and the benefits occurring are not passed on to the tribals.

If this is the plight of the deprived masses then the question that comes in one's mind is why these people, who have totally been sidelined by the so-called developmental processes, not directed their efforts in bringing a total change in the prevailing political system?

The answer can be found in the way the democratic system has operated.

Firstly if one has a look of the Constitution then one finds that there are certain mechanisms prevailing within the Constitution, which have given the economically deprived a sense of satisfaction. The framers of the Constitution were well aware of the serious repercussions that inequality would have on the political system. Dr. B.R. Ambedkar while addressing the Constituent Assembly in 1949 expressed the following ideas—

> "...On the economic plane, we have a society in which there are some who have immense wealth as against many who live in abject poverty. On the 26th of January, 1950, we are going to enter into a life of contradictions. In politics, we will have equality and in social and economic life we will have inequality.... How long shall we continue to live this life of contradictions? How long shall we continue to deny equality in our social and economic life? If we continue to

> deny it for long, we will do so only by putting our political democracy in peril. We must remove these contradictions at the earliest possible moment or else those who suffer from inequality will blow up the structure of political democracy which this Assembly has so laboriously built up" (Sinha 2005:2).
>
> Understanding the seriousness of the issue of inequality, while committing himself completely to political democracy, he clearly saw the need for social and economic democracy if at all the Indian nation was to survive. He therefore understood the significance of the Directive Principles of State Policy. He summed up his views in the following words—"But who ever captures power will not be free to do what he likes with it. In the exercise of it he will have to respect these instruments of instructions which are called Directive Principles. He cannot ignore them. He may not have to answer for their breach in a Court of law. But he will certainly have to answer for them before the electorate at election time" (*ibid.*: 27).

Other factor which has prevented the deprived not to challenge the political system is the large scale participation of poor people in the electoral process (*ibid.*: 2). This generates a feeling of satisfaction, a feeling that they are the part of the political process. This contentment therefore prevents them to wage a revolution against the political system.

The other political factor which one can identify in the continuance of the democratic political system is the measures undertaken from time to time by the political leaders. In the fifties efforts were made to put an end to inequalities existing in the agricultural sector by undertaking land reforms.

In the early seventies the slogan '*Garibi Hatao*' by Mrs. Gandhi, all served as rhetorics to reach every household and makes families live by hope.

Besides the political factors, economic and social factors also have prevented the deprived to pose a challenge before the political system.

What is seen in the context of India is that there is an absence of feeling of class consciousness. Llyod and Susanne Rudolph have argued in their work that class politics is marginal (Gopal and Mehta 2010:130). The Rudolphs point out, Fairly enough, that "organized labour as a potential actor in class politics [in India] must contend with formidable obstacles" (*ibid.*: 142). Large majority of Indian labour force is in the informal employment, unprotected by labour legislation and with very little access to social security. Barbara Harris-White estimates that "approximately 83 per cent of the population works wholly in the informal sector" (*ibid.*). Other study conducted by Rina Agarwala calculates that only 7 per cent of the labour force as a whole or 18 per cent of the non-agricultural labour force is in formal protected employment. According to her, 45 per cent of India's non-agricultural labour force is constituted by those who are self-employed or are micro-entrepreneurs and another 38 per cent are part of the 'informal proletariat'—casual workers and regular workers—in informal enterprises (*ibid.*). And one of the consequences of economic liberalization in India, as elsewhere in the world has been to encourage the informalization of labour, so that the share of organized, formal employment in the labour force as a whole has been declining. This development has prevented the emergence of a feeling of common political consciousness amongst the working class. As a result of this it becomes extremely difficult to pose a challenge to the structural power of capital.

Even the ability of the formal sector working class who constitute nearly 7 per cent of the Indian labour force is limited for it is incorporated into competing political parties. They therefore get divided by party political allegiances (*ibid.*). The organized working class was co-opted by the Congress in the period after Independence through the formation of the Indian National Trade Union Congress which was sworn to uphold Congress policy in industrial matters.

Besides the political and economic factors, social factor, i.e. caste has also contributed in maintaining the continuance of the political system. In the Indian scenario the overlapping that exists between caste and class makes people contented with the condition in which they are living. The inequalities existing in society therefore get justified. Besides, caste, the other factor which makes the people contented and enables them to continue is the theory of *karma*. Thus, religion also has its contribution in making people satisfied and hence prevents them to challenge the political system.

Thus, one can say that the political, economic and social factors have operated in such a way that it has facilitated the functioning of the political system without any kind of threat from the economically deprived. Thus, the universal assumption that an inequitable distribution of resources and wealth will provoke violent rebellion has not proved true in the Indian context. The inequalities existing are legitimized in one way or another, that the inequality comes with a degree of power and repression that are simply too great to overcome or that there are various obstacles preventing collective action.

## References

Aristotle (1981): *The Politics,* Translated by T.A. Sanders, (Middlesex: Penguin Books Limited).

Atkinson, A.B. (1983): *The Economics of Inequality* (Oxford: Clarendron Press).

Bhaduri, Amit (2009): *The Face You Were Afraid To See: Essays on the Indian Economy* (New Delhi:Penguin Books).

Brass, Paul, R. and Marcus, F. Franda, (eds.) (1973): *Radical Policy and the Emergence of Bangladesh* (Cambridge: The MIT Press).

Chenoy, A.M. and K.M. Chenoy (2010): *Maoist and Other Armed Conflicts* (New Delhi: Penguin Books Limited).

Conn, Paul, H. (1971): *Conflict and Decision-Making: An Introduction to Political Science* (New York: Harper and Row Publishers).

Couttenier, M. and R. Soubeyran (2013): *An Overview of the Roots of Civil Wars: Natural Factors and Economic Conditions* G-MonD Policy Paper, Paris School of Economics, January.

Davies, J.C. ed. (1971): *When Men Revolt and Why: A Reader in Political Violence and Revolution* (London: MacMillan Limited).

Gurr, Ted Robert (1970): *Why Men Rebel* (Princeton: Princeton University Press).

Gurr, T.R. (1980): *Handbook of Political Conflict: Theory and Research* (New York: The Free Press).

Gurr, Ted (1968): "A Casual Model of Civil Strife: A Comparative Analysis using New Indices", *The American Political Science Review* (Washington D.C.), Vol. LXII, No. 4, December, pp. 1104-24.

Ismi, Asad (2013): "Maoist Insurgency Spreads to over 40 per cent of India, Mass Poverty and Delhi's Embrace of Corporate Neoliberalism Fuels Social Uprising," *Global Research* (December 20).

Jayal, Niraja Gopal and Pratap Bhanu Mehta (eds.) (2010): *The Oxford Companion To Politics in India* (New Delhi: Oxford University Press).

Kaur, S. (2013): *Economic Inequalities and Political Conflict: A Study with Reference to Pakistan and Niger* (New Delhi: Har-Anand Publications Pvt. Limited).

Lichbach, M.I. (1989): "An Evaluation of Does Economic Inequality Breed Political Conflict? Studies", *World Politic*, Vol. XLI, No. 4, July, pp. 431-70.

Lichbach, M.I. and Ted Robert Gurr (1981): "The Conflict Process: A Formal Model", *Journal of Conflict Resolution* (London), Vol. XXV, No. 1, March, pp. 3-29.

Marx, Karl and Frederick Engels (1975): *Manifesto of the Communist Party* (Moscow; Progress Publisher).

Mitchell, E.J. (1968): "Inequality and Insurgency: A Statistical Study of South Vietnam," *World Politics,* Vol. XX, No. 3, April, pp. 421-38.

Mueller, Edward N. and M.A. Seligson (1987): "Inequality and Insurgency", *The American Political Science Review,* Vol. 81, No. 2, June, pp. 425-51.

Nagel, J. (1974): "Inequality and Discontent: A Nonlinear Hypothesis," *World Politics*, Vol. XXVI, No. 4, July, pp. 453-72.

Oakley, Allen (1984): *Marx's Critique of Political Economy: Intellectual Sources and Evolution,* Vol. I: 1844 to 1860 (London: Routledge and Regan Paul).

Pal, P. and Jayati Ghosh (2007): "Inequality in India: A Survey of Recent Trends", *UN/DESA Working Paper no. 45,* July, New York.

Sayeed, K.B. (1968): "Pakistan: New Challenges to the Political System", *Asian Survey* (Berkeley), Vol. VIII, No. 2 (February 1968), pp. 97-104.

Sen, Amartya (1989): "*On Economic Inequality*" (Delhi: Oxford University Press).

Sinha, A. (2005): *Indian Democracy and Well Being: An Inquiry into the Poverty in a Dynamic Democrac* (Delhi: Gyan Books Pvt. Ltd.).

Stiglitz, J. (2003): *The Waring 90s: A New History of the World's most Prosperous Decade* (New York: W.W. Norton and Company).

*The Hindu* (2008) 12 December.

Tucker, R.C. (1970): *The Marxian Revolutionary Idea* (London: George Allen & Unwin Limited).

Upadhyay, R.K. (2015): "Impact of Globalization on Distribution of Income, Poverty and Inequality in India", *Abhinav National Monthly (Delhi),* Vol. 4, No. 2, online-ISSN-2277-1166.

Weisskopf, Thomas (2011): "Why Worry about Inequality in the booming Indian Economy", *Economic and Political Weekly* (Mumbai), Vol. 46, No. 47, pp. 41-51.

## Websites

http://www.indiafutureofchange.com/featureEssay_D0012.htm
www.un.org/esa/sustdev/csd/csd16/PF/presentations/farmers_relief.pdf
(www.un.org/esa/sustdev/csd/csd16/PF/presentations/farmers_relief.pdf).
(http://www.indiafutureofchange.com/featureEssay_D0012.htm).

# SECTION III
## Politics and Civil Society

# 7

# Rural Politics in India

## Its Gendered Spaces and Social Change

*Swarnamayee Tripathy*

### Introduction

Development of a nation is designed based on the aspirations and desires of its people. As India lives in its villages, rural development is a vital constituent of its development or progress. The main objective of this developmental process is to empower the disempowered such as women, Dalits and other such marginalised groups. Politics in such a society is informed by such development agenda. The main thrust of Planning in India has been the development of rural areas. All our development programmes and welfare administration are geared towards that. Since, nineties Non-Governmental Organizations (NGOs), Panchayati Raj Institutions (PRIs), Self-Help Groups (SHGs) are playing a major role as catalysts in the administration of Rural Development. They are considered as 'motivators of public' and complementary to each other. PRIs are the State Actors whereas NGOs and SHGs are the Non-State Actors in the dynamic process of rural development. Therefore, nature of rural politics and its changing dimensions need to be studied in such an environment.

India is undergoing a rapid transformation. The dynamics of social and political change cannot be understood unless we bring clarity to our understanding of the concept 'politics'. It will provide us with the analytical tool or the framework to understand dynamics of rural politics in India and its changing dimensions. The significance of such effort would help us to locate and identify the change in the social structures as well as processes, in individuals, groups and institutions. We shall be able to answer the research question, "why some are not represented in the decision-making bodies, some interests are not represented in decisions taken, and some are denied a 'public space'."

The concept of 'space' is integral to social change, and changing the social and political status of groups. 'Space' is different from the concept of 'capability' as evolved by the Economist Amartya Sen and later developed by Martha Nussbaum. 'Capability' signifies qualities within human beings which if deprived, do not allow for a human or human existence. 'Space', on the other hand, allows an individual to move, manoeuvre and negotiate, to develop capabilities.[1] Opportunities for social mobility enable groups and individuals to negotiate 'new space' in society. Social Groups or individuals acquire 'public space' depending on their representation in decision-making bodies meant for making choices that affect their lives. Even being out of these bodies, some try to influence the decision-making process as members of a 'collective'. In fully democratic societies, 'political space' is an area where unconstrained articulation and organization can occur and where political authority using structures of the state cannot arbitrarily control or inhibit the will of the people. Socio-cultural practices do not allow some sections of the population such as women and Dalits to enter into this 'space'. My effort is to locate and identify the gendered spaces in rural societies of India and analyse the nature of such 'spaces'.

The conventional wisdom that was fathered by Aristotle, the Greek political philosopher assumes that politics is associated with the structure of state and organization of government. It refers to the operation of a Constitutional system of government and publicly defined institutions and procedures. Aristotle regards, "Politics brings together, under the aegis of government, different groups each with their specific interests so that they can speak freely and thereby achieve order". He regards politics as natural but not spontaneous, as depends on deliberate individual activity. In contrast to this, the modern view, after much deliberation, states that the ambit of politics is related to issues of state power, and its distribution of "Who Gets What, and When and How?" In other words, politics is the practice and theory of influencing public policy-making by influencing others. Modern writers have emphasized on the reconciliation of conflict through law and representative institutions of the state and periodic elections. They argue that politics is the study or practice of the distribution of power and resources. They have not answered to the research question that if socio-cultural constraints do not create space for the democracy for certain specific groups what will be the solution. Feminist epistemology goes further and emphatically puts forward the argument that 'Personal is Political'.[2] Politics is not confined to the public sphere, but also exists in the private domain. Private space gets defined by the nature of politics in a society. The state draws the boundaries for 'Private Space'. Through this understanding, feminists have been able to explain women's exclusion from the 'public space' even in socially and economically advanced countries. They have justified 'alternate politics' which believes in informal ways of showing protest. They argue that 'informal politics is everyday politics, hence the idea that 'politics is everywhere'.

Further, in rural societies in India people live in various social groups where caste, religion and patriarchal practices are major forms of community life of most of the people. Therefore, the study of post-colonial rural India necessitated a greater interaction between the sociologists' understanding of a larger society and the social anthropologists' dealing with small rural communities. The insights gained from the macro-level study can be used for micro-level research. Macro-study and micro-study are not contradictory, but complementary to each other, and both are equally important to explore socio-political reality in the contemporary rural society of India. Contextual specificities, as well as community centred particularities, need to be factored to produce an adequately nuanced generalized description of rural reality.

Therefore, in order to understand the changing dimension of politics in rural India, we need to examine changes visible in social structures, political processes, forms of conflict resolution, methods of distribution of resources, opportunities available for access to resources and designated 'spaces' to influence the decision-making process.

In this chapter, I have tried to identify and locate the 'Gendered Space' in rural India through history. My research question is, "Is there any possible ways to expand this 'Space' for women?" If not, what are the roadblocks ahead before us? How could we clear this blockade? Further, it will also explore the question, "have women been successful in changing the power configuration in rural society of our country?" Do these developments will ultimately result in a proactive civil society and give 'voice' to the 'silenced ones'. This study has adopted empirical approach to arrive at the findings.

My observation given in this chapter is based on my visit to six districts of the State of Odisha. Odisha, an eastern region state of India is one of the backward states receiving BRGF (Backward Region Grant Fund) from the Government of India. Odisha is a peasant society largely dominated by small and medium farmers. Demographically, 40 per cent of its population belong to Scheduled Castes (16%) and Scheduled Tribes (22%). More than 80 per cent of the STs live in the forested tracts of Odisha, which happen to be the mining belt, let us say the 'Zone of Extraction'. So, when land is acquired for mega projects—be it a Missile Test Range, mining or steel plants—and resistances to those take place, the small and marginal peasants, Dalits and Adivasis, and most naturally women from these segments, are seen to be at the front.[3]

The first part of the chapter has focused on changing socio-political dimensions of rural India. The second part has tried to identify and locate the 'gendered spaces' in rural Odisha. This part of the study has been conducted, and women's space has been located in the social power structure of rural India according to our understanding arrived at in the former paragraphs. The third part of the chapter has addressed the main research question by which the gender dimension of politics in rural India has been analysed.

## Changing Makeover of the Village Society

Rural India is into a constant state of experimentation. In exact terms, nearly 72 per cent of India's women population live in rural areas. 833.5 million rural people are responding to the rapidly changing economic scenario, extended educational opportunities and state intervention through affirmative action. The gap between literacy rate in urban and rural areas is steadily declining in every census. The gender gap in literacy rate is steadily declining in every census. In Census 2011, the gap stands at 16.3 points. Female literacy in rural India is improving at the rate of one per cent per annum. Trust, empathy, aspiration and empowerment all these together have brought this change in the villages. On other hand, Work Participation Rate of females in rural areas are either declining or stagnant. Reasons are obvious. Due to increase in disposable income of the rural households, women are hesitant to work outside. Secondly, casualization among female workers is high and is on the rise. 46 per cent of female workers in the country are marginal workers. 90 per cent of women workers are dependent on agriculture, whereas 98 per cent of rural women workers are participating in the unorganized sector.[4]

There has been much progress in rural India during the last three decades—socially, economically as well as politically. Though there are pockets of stark poverty, the countryside has modernized itself to some extent. As a result of globalized market forces, rural India is flooded with Fast Moving Consumer Goods. Secondly, India has shown leadership in promoting gender equity within its political and legislative frameworks, and its efforts have laid a foundation for women to play a more important role in the social and political development of the country. Our Nation had embarked on the ambitious decentralization initiatives in 1992 *via* a couple of landmark amendments to the Constitution, namely, 73rd and 74th Constitution Amendment Act, to reinforce local democracy by empowering people and local self-governing institutions, both in urban and rural areas. The most important component of this development is the Constitutional arrangement to transfer power to women through quota-based political reservations for women in rural areas with the objective to promote gender equality in human development by making rural service provision and local governance inclusive and responsive to the needs of women. Recent evidence shows that reservation policies for women (1) stimulate the political participation of women in rural areas; (2) shift rural service provision to public goods that reflect gender preferences; and (3) improve the access to and the quality of public services.[5] (4) It has also brought a transformation in the nature of leadership in rural society. Despite the suggested positive effects of women's reservation policies on service provision and local governance, the gender bias in human development is still pronounced. This casts doubt on the effectiveness of reservation policies as an instrument for making rural service provision and local governance more gender equitable and raises questions about the nature and direction of the major constraints.

Coterminous with this political change is an administrative change that led to the growth of Self-Help Group Movement in India. SHGs in India are small, informal and homogenous groups of not more than 20 members. These are micro-credit groups formed to empower the poor economically. However, the Indian experience is that more than 80 per cent of the SHGs are exclusively Women SHGs. "Experiencing this development; Indian state had linked these SHG movements to Nationalized Banks for credit purposes since 1992. This has helped women to initiate income-generating activities and gathered strength as a collective".

The adage that "India lives in its villages" are as close to reality today as it was in the pre-independence period. In rural areas, it is agriculture and allied activities which still provide employment and income to a substantial segment of the rural workforce. During the post-Independence period, rural India had absorbed the impact of institutional, structural, and technological improvements leading to multifaceted changes and transformations. As a result, there have been changes in the relative asset-holding positions of castes and classes, broadening of their perspectives due to the expansion of contacts and communications, and growth and diversification of infrastructural facilities.

Forces of change and transformation affecting rural economies and societies emanated bcth from within and outside the villages. However, the resultant growth and development in rural areas across states, regions, castes, and classes have been uneven for historical and contemporary socio-political factors. Faster economic growth takes place in states and regions that are relatively more advanced than others. Asset-holding families, castes and classes would have the greater facility to register faster economic growth than those with fewer assets. On the other hand, affirmative actions by public authorities have equipped and enhanced the capacities and capabilities of socially backward categories to move forward and lessen the economic distance between them and the most advanced segments of society. All these have opened up new vistas for women to make progress.

During the last three decades, this progress in rural India, socially, politically as well as economically has created a 'new politics of class' in the countryside. The large *zamindars*, *talukdars* in Uttar Pradesh, the 'big landlords' of Bihar, Haryana and Odisha who were 'lords of the whole village' have gone. The new rich derive wealth from increasingly efficient and productive farming and 'mediation'.[6] The right-based approach of the government to ensure subsistence employment and self-employment has brought relative improvement in the socio-economic condition of the poor and the middle class in the villages.

Castes in Indian villages continue to exist, but caste system has ceased to be. James Manor in his recent writings has argued that the caste system has substantially ceased to be in rural India. In some villages it was generally the case in mid-twentieth century India that a particular jati exercised dominance locally—over land and labour, society and politics (it was the 'dominant caste', according to M.N. Srinivas' classic description)—such local power has been substantially reduced in the arena of local politics and in mediating the relations between village people and the state in globalized India.[7]

They have stepped in an army of local-level political entrepreneurs—small-time political "fixers" or "*naya netas*" (new leaders).' Political identities have in general become more fluid than they were earlier. At the same time, caste may have increased its importance in the public sphere in all sorts of ways, including in electoral politics.

In India, the Constitution (73rd Amendment Act), enacted in 1992, mandated the reservation of a minimum of one-third of seats for women (both as members and as chairpersons) within rural India's locally elected governance bodies commonly referred to as Panchayati Raj Institutions (PRIs). The Amendment also entrusted Panchayats with the responsibility of furthering the agenda of economic development and social justice. Such opportunity was extended Scheduled areas where tribal are in the majority, under PESA Act, 1996.

The Constitutional reforms have created space for women in rural politics. The Self-Help Group Movement, whose actors are mainly women has grown in lips and bounds. A possible synergy is developing between women in Self-Help Groups and Panchayats.

## Gendered Spaces in Rural India

Rural India of pre-Independent days was known for its traditional rigidity. Society was confining women to her private sphere. Women were not allowed to participate in public sphere of the society, though few women with specific family background had participated in nationalist movement. Even they were not allowed to attend schools considering the institution as the public domain. Women were not allowed to work outside the home. Indian historiography did not record the revolutionary activities of women in the nationalist movement. For example, the names of leaders like Malati Choudhury could not receive due place in Odisha history. In post-Independent India women are enjoying equal civil and political rights along with men. However, research studies state that women's presence in legislative politics varies from only 8 per cent to 10 per cent. Women's participation in grassroots politics was negligible till the end of twentieth century.

The most important component of the Constitutional development in 1992 is the Constitutional arrangement to transfer power to women by changing the social arrangement in Indian society. It is envisaged that by mandating not less than one-third of the seats for women in local government bodies, the governance process at the local level will reflect the voices of women and the concerns and issues that confront them. Consequently, it has brought around 1.2 million women at village, block and district level to the governance network. In some States like Odisha, Andhra Pradesh, Gujarat, Kerala, etc. it is mandatory that 50 per cent of *panchayat* representatives should be women. This has resulted in bringing a revolutionary transformation in the nature of leadership.

Further, these provisions extend to Scheduled areas where tribals are a majority, by the provisions of Panchayat Extension to Schedule Area (PESA) Act 1996. According to Panchayati Raj Department, Government of Odisha records, 24,734 Wards out of 87,542 Wards, 1,966 office of Sarpanch out of 6,234, 1965 office of Panchayat Samiti Member out of 6,233 and 256 Members of Zilla Parishad out of 854 come under the PESA Act. Election to these offices was conducted as per the provisions of the PESA Act. Under this Act, tribal women have got the opportunity to occupy the 'public space'.

In my research I observed the following facts:

> Fifty per cent reservation for women in *panchayats* has brought many first timers to the election fray in 2012 *panchayat* elections. Most of the elected women representatives have been elected unanimously. It seems the village community prefers to elect the first timers through mutual accommodation among the members of the community. This is indicative of the fact that there is proper power redistribution among the influential families in the community.

More than 50 per cent (53% approx. in the 2012 *panchayat* election) women have got elected as panchayat representatives. Most of them are relatively young. Their age varies between 22 to 35.

The women Sarpanches have secondary and higher secondary level of education in most cases. They belong to the lower middle-class families of the village community.

Elected women representatives in our study area have presided over Palli Sabha meetings and successfully conducted Palli Sabha meetings, taken decisions regarding MGNREGA work, Social Security benefits, names of beneficiaries were finalised in Palli Sabha meetings. Resolution for sanitation and construction of *pucca* latrines were taken in the Palli Sabha. They have also attended *Gram Sabha* meetings. The unique achievements of the tribal women are that they have raised issues of misuse of funds for development of the village in Panchayat meetings. Issues like late payments of wages under MGNREGA, Land under FRA, IAY in the name of women, pensions, construction of irrigation facilities, PDS and drinking water for the villages have been taken up by the SWORA members. They have regularised the Gaon Kalyan Samiti meetings and extended support for high-risk pregnant mothers and malaria affected persons. Women Councillors have also demanded for the separate rest room and toilet for themselves in Panchayat and Panchayat Samiti office.

In contrast to all these positive notes for women managing to acquire 'public space', in rural societies, research on local governance in India has arrived at conclusions that democratic decentralization has not been able to trigger dramatic social change in rural society. The process of decentralization has ensured representation but does not necessarily lead to adequate participation. While it is relatively easy to legislate representation, it is more difficult to create a conducive environment for participation. Experiences over the last two decades have demonstrated that the implementation of the 73rd Amendment in rural India has been plagued by many problems and shortcomings. One of them is the lack of capability of elected members of rural local bodies. The incapability is more crucial in case of women. They still face many challenges for their active engagement in the political sphere. Deeply entrenched socio-cultural constraints relegate women to the 'domestic space' restricting their engagement in public affairs, an area largely dominated by men. Lack of exposure of women themselves to politics and the absence of any experience in exercising their political responsibilities, low literacy levels, inadequate education, lack of economic independence, burden of productive and reproductive roles; all together result in lack of confidence in women. Consequently, many women are unable to comprehend the true spirit of decentralization and recognize the opportunities that the legislation for participatory democracy provides them.

Further, it reflects and reproduces existing power relations and patterns of inequality though at times facilitate their gradual erosion. If seen at the outset it appears that Adivasis often comprise substantial majorities in *panchayats*, have a substantial influence on the local council that ease their exclusion from the public sphere. On the other hand, Dalit men since long have had seats reserved for them in all types of public institutions. This has enabled them to get rid of utter exclusion from the public sphere though many of them failed to influence the process of power-sharing in these bodies. However, their exclusion appears to be less severe than those faced by women in local councils. James Manor in his writings have stated, "I was told by hundreds of non-Dalit male villagers in seven quite varied Indian states that they view reservation for women in *panchayats* as far more shocking and objectionable than reservations for Dalits." There are two explanations for this. In most villages women outnumber all reserved categories; so, if they become a coherent force, they pose a greater threat to the prevailing power structure. Secondly, the power of patriarchy has declined less; therefore, women have often remained excluded from the public sphere.

Our observation in the six-district study in Odisha has indicated that male councillors frequently conspire with village *panchayat* secretaries—who are overwhelmingly male, to deny women members information. Many a times they change the Palli Sabha Resolution submitted by a woman councillor. Women councillors can not fight out the odds as they are not with a photo copy of the Palli Sabha Resolution. The *panchayat* secretaries often prevent them from speaking in *Gram Sabha*. In some other studies conducted by Nirmala Buch and Sushila Kaushik, it has been mentioned that *panchayat* secretaries sometimes have conspired with bureaucrats who work at the block level to deny women members information. They often refuse to listen or respond to them off the meetings.

Women councillors often face scornful laughter, abuse and even sexual violence from male residents of their locality for having shown the courage to occupy space in public life. A 23-year-old women councillor in our study said if given chance she would not contest for the second time for the above reasons. Evidently, patriarchy is at its work. A young tribal women Sarpanch, who is enthusiastic to bring home wellbeing in coordination with the other women councillors, was harassed by male members of the locality in front of us.

Further impediments arise from institutional arrangements. Constituencies reserved for women change-rotate at each election and so do the chairpersons' posts in *panchayats*. Consequently, women elected once to a reserved seat have little or no chance of being re-elected, since it is highly unusual for women to win unreserved seats. Our observation in some *panchayats* reveals that though cent per cent seats belong to women, the common understanding in all *panchayats* is that only half of the seats belong to women. It is because some of the administrators have interpreted the law accordingly.

The civil society organizations in rural India in a many great ways have made efforts to enhance the political capacity of women *panchayat* representatives by providing them with crucial information, training and connections beyond the village. These associations are small community-based organizations operating at local level or sub-regional organizations with state-wide or inter-state impact. However, the reach of these organizations is somewhat limited. They usually fail to engage with more than a minority of women at the village level. Rural women have not made large gains out of it.

## The Silver Lines in the Clouds

The impediments discussed above have not deterred women to play a proactive role in creating a safe environment with a credible place for themselves. Undoubtedly, their number is few. The arrogance, corruption and bad habits of male leaders have evolved a 'zone of acceptance' for women leaders. Change has occurred at a painfully slow rate. The following significant changes have been noticed in our study that in a slow but steady way would bring 'silent revolution' in power relations.

### *(i) Networking by Women Panchayat Representatives*

Women representatives in the districts I visited have formed networks to enhance their strength, increase their awareness and negotiate collectively with the authorities in particular and society at large. State Women Panchayat Representatives' Association (SWORA), the first ever women Panchayat representatives' Association in Odisha, was born taking female elected representatives from 25 districts in a state level convention held on 27th and 28th March, 2012 after the 2012 *panchayat* elections. It was an offshoot of the six regional conventions organised by NAWO, a civil society. Each one of them has become a SWORA member by paying Rs. 10/- as a membership fee. The main aim was to create an enabling environment for EWPRs to share each others' administrative experiences as well as to create civil society space for political action. It was understood that a systematic experience sharing among the members of SWORA would strengthen their administrative capacity.

It was a new beginning for women's political empowerment as women *panchayat* representatives did not have an appropriate forum to discuss issues that are relevant to them. SWORA is a micro-initiative towards the formation of networks and associations of EWPRs. It is an innovative use of civil society space for political action. This is rooted in the concrete experiences and pragmatic strategies developed by EWPRs and civil society groups supporting them, to equip themselves to better perform their constitutionally mandated role in an adverse environment that is both patriarchal and largely anti-decentralisation.

However, only half of the representatives have become members of the Network organization in six districts that I visited. Regular meetings of SWORA have enabled the members to comprehend the process of stakeholder's participation in planning for women's development as well as village development. It has equipped them with functional skills required for engaging in micro-level planning for gender equity and social justice. The training has helped them to learn and contextualize the dream vision of their village. They have inspected MGNREGA work in the village, Anganwadi centres and village schools as they are members of school management committee. They have made an all out effort along with women in Self-Help Groups to free the village environment from alcoholism. SWORA members have highlighted women issues at Panchayat level and put these questions in front of the community.

Besides, the SWORA members have focused on two issues for advocacy purposes, such as having separate resting room and toilets for women representatives in *panchayat* and Panchayat Samiti Offices and to repeal the two child norm as election conditionality. Women through their discussions have become aware of the fact that the two child norm as an election conditionality is a reflection of state violence to keep women at bay from the 'public space' as women have very little reproductive choices. Barriers to women's participation in political and public life by the Two Child Norm tend to undermine women's quota in Panchayati Raj Institutions (PRIs). The norm does not allow women and men with more than two children to contest in elections. SWORA has been working as a pressure group at the state level to fight against this legislation.

### *(ii) Reordering Social Relations*

There is clear evidence that some male relatives or husbands of women councillors accompany them to the Panchayat office or the offices of bureaucrats. They also manage at the home front when required and extend physical and moral support to them in public. It is because they believe that women's roles in panchayats have enhanced the social status of their families.

### *(iii) Engendering Rural Society through SHG*

SHGs or Self-Help Groups are playing a major role in reshaping rural society in our country. They are designed to stand on two pillars—micro-credit (capacity building) and social reform (social position). It aims to mobilise people to make them financially sound to some extent, give them some voice and build people's organizations that will overcome barriers to participation and empowerment in rural societies. Precisely speaking, central to the ideal of 'self-help' is group-formation, the concept of community and the development of egalitarian relations among members of a village. The poor in India, however, seldom organize themselves. It is an assisted self-help process where the State, the financial institutions, and the NGOs play an important role in mobilizing and assisting the poor and needy. The Indian experience is distinctive in the sense that the SHGs are mostly formed by women through grass root mobilization with the help of NGOs and are engaged in poverty alleviation and empowerment activities. Undoubtedly, Self-help groups, as a strategy for women's development have emerged out of the perceived problem of women's lack of access to resources both at the household and the village level. It is a mechanism for women's development to bring in individual and collective empowerment through improvement in both 'condition' and 'position' of women. This would bring a gradual transformation in the gender and power relations in the society. This inspires women 'to think big' and unite them on a certain platform. From a feminist perspective, in this group-model of development, individual entrepreneurship is based on women's solidarity, the perception of common interest and fellow-feeling. Being a member of a 'collective', a woman struggles hard to create some 'space' for herself in the family as well as in the society. Empowerment in India has developed as a dynamic concept by addressing multi-dimensional issues affecting women's development. The concept of 'Self-Help Group' is a product of such empowerment approach. Development of Self-Help Groups in India is coterminous with liberalization and globalization. Both the phenomena have a history of two decades. Globalization exposed us to a vibrant market economy of a world-wide scale. Self-Help Group is a tiny effort to create a 'space' for oneself as a group in such a globalized market economy.

The reasons for women being in SHGs are the seasonal migration of their men for livelihood. Women with migrant husbands, divorcees, and women, whose husbands no longer lived with them, often had the responsibility of rearing their children. Without sufficient work their cash inflows are low and they have serious problems meeting family needs. Obviously, they take an interest in being a member of a Self-Help Group. The spread of SHGs in India has been phenomenal. It has grown from 255 groups in 1992 to some 79, 60,349 groups in 2012 that have taken loans from the banks. About 103 million poor households have gained access to the banking system.

The SHG movement in India has evolved entrepreneurship in rural women through the scheme "Swarnajayanti Gram Swarozgar Yojana". This new programme launched since April 1999 is a holistic programme covering all aspects of self-employment such as organization of poor into self-help groups, training, credit, technology transfer, infrastructure-building and marketing. Each villager who comes under this programme is called a '*swarozgari*'. The main aim of the programme is to enhance the skills and capabilities of the poor and marginalized and make their development sustainable. In 2012, 26.7 per cent of Self-Help Groups had been covered under this SGSY scheme.

In addition to this, some State Governments in India have used Self-help Groups as administrative mechanisms for executing development programmes for women and children. These informal groups are used to supervise Mid-day meal scheme, public distribution system and the execution of national rural employment guarantee scheme under 'Mission Shakti' programme in Odisha. It provides rural women with space and support necessary for them to take effective steps towards achieving greater control in their lives. Women played an active role in resolving conflicts in the community, handling cases of domestic violence or infidelity. However, women in Self-Help Groups have raised their voice against the liquor trade in the villages.

However, viewed from the perspective of women's empowerment, it can be said, through the SHGs, women are coming together for credit and other benefits and seek to promote self-reliance for themselves and ensure development. In the words of American Senator Hillary Clinton, "Microenterprise programmes work. They lift women and families out of poverty. It's called 'micro', but its impact is macro". As a community development tool, micro-lending is ideologically compatible with independence, individualism, and self-reliance. But it is a difficult process to attain the goal of empowerment. If a synergy is developed among all the shareholders of rural development like NGOs, SHGs and PRIs, rural India will take a different shape and colour, every disempowered Indian will be empowered to exercise choice and control over their lives.

### *(iv) Moments of Self-Actualization for Women*

In recent years, rural India has been the hub of rural struggles. The emergence of issue-based politics does appear as a step forward in rural politics in globalized India. While many of these struggles are explicitly linked with the development-induced displacement issues initiated by neo-liberal competition, some of them are struggles against the liquor policy of the state. In all these movements, women play a critical role. Consequently, rural India is becoming more and more politicized.

In anti-displacement protest movements, women and children are seen in front of the rallies without any fear or fervour. In Odisha, we have been witnessing continuously the valiant resistance of people in the regions of Kashipur, Kalinga-Nagar, Lanjigarh/Niyamgiri, Narayan-patna, and Jagatsinghpur. Women are in the forefront as their livelihood is affected by the development agenda of the Indian state.

Secondly, Green Revolution in Punjab, Haryana and other northern states, the impact of globalization in India has brought an increase in disposable income to rural households. This income, instead of being ploughed back into infrastructure development, was frittered away in alcohol consumption, leading to major domestic problems all over the State. Feminist research has found that wife beating and alcoholism seem to be inseparable. Unchecked flow of liquors and narcotics have started wrecking havoc with the people of rural and urban areas of different districts and following this anti-social activities has gone up in rural areas. Drunkards and drug addicts have been harassing common people in nights and create a nuisance. Police in many areas seem to have turned a blind eye to this illicit trade as many places liquor is sold not far off from the police station.

An anti-alcohol movement, spearheaded by women, has taken roots in almost all villages of the country. These women are primarily SHG members who unitedly take decisions to counter illicit liquor trade. These women adopt methods like peaceful picketing, closing down of liquor shops, gheraoing the police station and road blockade in case the authorities do not take any action against the liquor trader.

These movements are spontaneous in nature and cuts across caste and class lines. The aim of this movement is to protect women and children from the negative impact of alcoholism. Women in this movement take interest not for the sake of personal interest rather for having empathy for women and children in particular. 'Self-actualization'[8] is the highest need of human beings which get fulfilled by being a part of such movement. Women of all age groups participate in it. Even bystanders during a rally do not hesitate to join it. On such occasions women SHG members, women activists, students and civil society organization come together to express solidarity with the protesters.

This has enhanced self-confidence in women individually and collectively. At times, women have complained before National Human Rights Commission against police atrocities.[9]

Rural India is in a state of rapid transformation, so also its politics, society and economy. The rapid increase in the development funds made available to Blocks and *panchayats* bears testimony to this fact. A new set of younger, more educated and non-caste based political entrepreneurs are democratizing politics at the village level and negotiating space for themselves. Village women are no exception to this. They are trying to create new 'idioms' of politics. The evolving self-confidence in women is also influencing social relations and the status of women within the family. It seems; the 'gendered space' in rural politics is gradually expanding. Therefore, keeping track of the changing nature of rural politics will help our understanding of society and politics in the countryside.

## Notes

1. The concept of 'space' is usually understood as 'social space' as directly lived through its associated images and symbols. Feminist literature divides the social space for women into two types—one is private space or 'personal space', the other is 'public space'. It states that patriarchal society has very narrow 'gendered space'. For a healthy and prosperous society, we need to expand the gendered spaces in any society. 'Space', on the other hand, allows an individual to move, manoeuvre and negotiate, to develop capabilities. Thus, societies can empower its women by engendering societies.
2. Feminist research state that patriarchy confines women to private space or the household by politicizing it to overpower women. Therefore, in the sixties and seventies of twentieth century feminists evolved a statement, i.e. "Personal is Political", or the private is political. It is a political argument used as a rallying slogan by second wave feminists who were primarily radicals. It differentiated the second-wave feminism of the 1960s and 1970s from the early feminism of the 1920s, which was concerned with achieving the right to vote for women. The phrase was popularized by the publication of a 1969 essay by feminist Carol Hanisch under the title "*The Personal is Political*" in 1970.
3. Ranjana Padhi and Pramodini Pradhan has argued that women's participation in resistance movements against displacement is primarily a voice against the State and Capital.
4. The given data has been generated by National Institute of Rural Development, Hyderabad based on 2011 Census.
5. The effects of political reservations for women on local., https://ideas.repec.org/p/fpr/ifprid/878.html (accessed October 07, 2015).
6. Anirudha Krishna in one of his articles on 'Local Politics' has written that for most Indians state is distant in both physical and cognitive terms. The illiterate rural Indian was ill-equipped to negotiate his way through the State bureaucracy. The law and its procedures that ordinary people everyday encountered was hard to understand. Therefore, the members of the 'dominant caste' mediated between the ordinary Indian and the Indian state after Independence and

worked as 'intermediaries'. They utilized this opportunity to become '*netas*' in the constitutional arrangement. Significant changes have occurred in the last seventy years, and educational opportunity has risen enormously, particularly over the last twenty-five years. The recent upsurge in rural education has resulted in evolving new leadership and new intermediaries who worked for their social group replacing the high caste. The nature of rural politics has changed.

7. John Harris, Reflections on caste and class, http://www.india-seminar.com/2012/633/633_john_harriss.htm (accessed October 07, 2015).
8. Abraham Maslow, the American psychologist, has said, every individual has five needs—physical needs, security needs, love needs, self-esteem needs and self-actualization needs. Individuals get satisfaction by fulfilling their self-actualization needs which mean by working for others.
9. The NHRC has ordered action against Odisha Police Officials responsible for firing on villagers protesting against a liquor shop in Kendrapada district in March 2013.

## References

Bandyopadhyay, D., B.N. Yugandhar and Amitav Mukherjee (2002): "Convergence of Programmes by Empowering SHGs and PRIs", *Economic and Political Weekly*, Vol. 37, No. 26.

Buch, N. (1999): *From Oppression to Assertion: A Study of Panchayats and Women in Madhya Pradesh, Rajasthan, and Uttar Pradesh,* (New Delhi: Centre for Women's Development Studies).

Kannabiran, V. and Kalpana Kannabiran (1997): "From Social Action to Political Action: Women and the 81st Amendment", *Economic and Political Weekly*, Vol. XXXII, No. 5, pp. 196-97.

Kaushik, S. (1998): *Participation of Women in Panchayati Raj in India: A Stock Taking*, (New Delhi: National Commission for Women).

Krishna, A. (2010): "Local Politics" in Niraja Gopal Jayal and Pratap Bhanu Mehta (eds.) *The Oxford Companion to Politics in India* (New Delhi: Oxford University Press).

Manor, J. (2010): "Local Governance" in Niraja Gopal Jayal and Pratap Bhanu Mehta (eds.) *The Oxford Companion to Politics in India* (New Delhi; Oxford University Press).

Mohanty, Bidyut and Shashi Narayana, (eds.) (2001): *Women and Political*

*Empowerment,* Women's Political Empowerment Day Celebrations, Panchayats and Women's Economic Empowerment (New Delhi: Institute of Social Sciences).

Nussbaum Martha C. (1995): "Human Capabilities, Female Human Beings" in Martha C. Nussbaum and Jonathan Glover (eds.) *Women, Culture, and Development—A Study of Human Capabilities* (Oxford: Clarendon Press).

Padhi, Ranjana and Pramodini Pradhan (2013): "Women in Resistance Struggles in Odisha", *Mainstream*, Vol. LI, No. 33.

Phillips, Ann (1996): *The Politics of Presence* (Oxford: Oxford University Press).

Roy, Dayabati (2013): "Rural Politics in India: Political Stratification and Governance in West Bengal" (New York:Cambridge University Press).

Swain, Ashok (2010): *Struggle Against the State: Social Network and Protest Mobilization in India.* (England: Ashgate).

http://www.orissadiary.com/Jajpur/ShowDistrictNews.asp?id=36921#sthash.YB07Nz6Y.dpf

# 8
# What Suicides Tell us About a Polity:
## A Case of India?

*Sudhir Kumar Suthar*

### Introduction

There have been numerous explanation of farmers suicides in India. However, there have not been attempts to explain how various political processes other than agricultural policy or the policies on rural development has an impact upon people's psychology. Hence, the question which chapter attempts to raise—is there a linkage between politics as a social activity and its relationship with appearance or disappearance of various political emotions? The chapter is also based upon the assumption that politics is not always a rational activity, as the scholars of rational choice theory or theorists of development economics would argue. Rather, it is more to do with people's emotions, aspirations and individual's associational life. In other words, politics is more like a social activity where questions of 'common good' are deliberated and discussed.

Political emotions are being taken up an intervening variable which in fact gets impacted or transformed by the political processes and institutions. This in return produces significant behavioural changes. Sometimes, these changes are positive as they generate trust, confidence and love. A political system can also generate negative behavioural tendencies including stress situations, alienation, and newer forms of oppression. This chapter shows in case of Indian polity that how it has produced various negative political emotions.

Findings of this study are based upon few regular field visits to selected parts of India which has witnessed a significant number of people (especially farmers') committing suicide. These areas are located in Uttar Pradesh, Madhya Pradesh, Rajasthan, and Punjab States of India. The basic objective of the field study was to understand how political factors are impacting individual behaviour. However, the present analysis is more of an interpretation of individual responses than not based upon the quantification and mathematical calculation of the larger findings.

## Nature of Polity and Political Emotions

Norms, values or ethics are the guiding principles of a polity. Constitution of various institutions, their functioning and the larger political processes are always based on a political system's commitment to certain norms and ethics, like representation, equality, justice, freedom, liberty and so on. In terms of its impacts on a society usually a polity is measured on the parameters of its successes and failures in achieving some of these commonly accepted norms.

These norms or ethics have significant impact on the macro as well as micro level, i.e. larger social as well as individual behaviours. In other words, the norms of a polity do have a significant role to play in shaping people's political behaviour or their political psychology. However, these impacts may not be desirable or intended always. Sometimes, a regime or polity may produce psychological effects which are against the very ideals which it promises to promote or preserve. For example, inspite of a state's commitment to secularism the polity may produce communal tensions, social group conflicts etc.

An authoritarian system or non-participatory or military regime has been analyzed in comparative politics and political theory as a system which produces large scale destructive patterns in human behaviour (Arendt 1949, Habermass 1979). Various means of governing like surveillance, excessive use of coercive force, a centralized and non-participatory process of policy-making and implementation, rigid bureaucratic structures to enforce various decisions, suppression of dissent voices, suppression of freedom of expression are few such examples. These methods in return gradually generate a sense of fear, alienation and psychological unrest amongst the people. A democratic polity or participatory regime on the other hand is expected to guarantee various individual rights and liberties and allow individuals to freely take a rational decision in the realm of a competitive political society (Dahl 1989, Prezorwski 1991, Sartori 1989). Through various institutions and political processes a democratic polity generates confidence, promotes equality and also cultivates a sense of honour amongst individuals as it respects the principle of "one person, one vote and one vote one value". Besides, it encourages people to keep a check on the political system in order to ensure that so that the state does not turn out to be an authoritarian state.

However, one crucial question has been largely ignored in the existing analysis of the process of evolution of a political system. The existing analysis does not explain how both types of political system produces different kinds of political emotions. An authoritarian system is more likely to produce emotions like fear, threat, suspicion, jealousy and injustice (Arendt 1973). On the contrary, a democratic regime is more likely to foster emotions like freedom, justice, sense of honour, creativity and so on (Nussbaum 1993). A democratic regime also attempts to, ideally speaking, create a liberal and tolerant society.

It is difficult to empirically prove any such compartmentalization of effects of each of the political systems. An authoritarian system may also produce political emotions which are seen as closely associated with a democratic regime, though the possibilities are very remote. Similarly, a democratic polity may also generate political emotions which are more close to an authoritarian regime than a democratic regime, e.g. a democratic polity can also promote a culture of surveillance, suspicion and fear or marginalization of weaker sections etc. However, what distinguishes a democratic regime from the authoritairian regime is the means to achieve these ends. The primary medium or agents of production of such behavioural trends in case of an authoritarian polity is the agencies which have coercive powers like, police or army, and the bureaucracy.

On the contrary, in case of a democratic polity, the carriers of these political emotions are various democratic agencies like political parties, civil society organizations and political leaders which work at various levels of a polity. Political parties through their diverse strategies of political mobilization tend to generate varieties of political emotions. In fact, quite contrary to the authoritarian regimes where the state agencies are not of much hope for people in terms of their emotions, political players in a democratic regime are far more influential and closely attached to the people and their psychological requirements. Similarly, existence of political leaders is also dependent upon their regular and close levels of interactions with the people in their respective constituencies. In other words, the ability of a democratic polity and its agencies to produce psychological impacts is far more than the capacity of these agencies in an authoritarian system.

Emotions are defined in a variety of ways and there is no commonly accepted definition. For the purpose of this study, a popular definition of emotions by Peter Goldie has been chosen. For Goldie emotions is "typically *complex, episodic, dynamic and structured* (emphasis in original). An emotion is complex in that it will typically involve many different elements; it involves episodes of emotional experience, including perceptions, thoughts, and feelings of various kinds, and bodily changes of various kinds and it involves dispositions, including dispositions to experience further emotional episodes, to have further thoughts and feelings, and to behave in certain ways" (Goldie, 2000: 12-13).

What makes Goldie's work interesting for the purpose of this study is how he explains that emotions are dynamic and they keep changing in different circumstances. Emotions are not static and they come and go. Though his primary work is on variety of emotions especially on *jealousy*, this study touches upon various kinds of political emotions.

Martha Nussbaum's work is a classical example of how emotions are required for public life or what she calls as "political cultivation of emotions". For her there are two tasks of political cultivation of emotions; "one to engender and sustain commitment to worthy projects that require effort and sacrifice" and two, is to "keep at bay forces that lurk in all societies and, ultimately, in all of us: tendencies to protect the fragile self by denigrating and subordinating others" (Nussbaum, 2013: 3). According to Nussbaum political emotions are needed in every kind of society—liberal as well as fascist or aggressive. Though the common perception is that the aggressive societies survive by focusing on the emotions of the people, but even the liberal societies require equal amount of emotion. She argues how various political leaders did play a crucial role in cultivating varieties of political emotions amongst the people.

Hence, in order to understand policy successes and failures or survival or demise of various political institutions it is required to go beyond the traditionally existing categories of political analysis. What are the processes or features of functioning of institutions which provide psychological support and facilitates production of political emotions, e.g. a sense of confidence and mutual trust in judiciary in case of India for justice? How through creation of spaces where individuals can express their support or grievances towards the polity, can be incorporated in understanding democracies, in general, and in India, in particular. These are some of the questions which can be addressed more effectively if a linkage between creation and expansion of political emotions can be explained.

With the ongoing political, economic and social transformation in India, there is a gradual decline of certain kinds of political emotions. These emotions, which were (are!) closely linked with social emotions like a communitarian way of life, politics as a means to achieve certain benefits for the community or people related to a family. Political association with political parties or leaders was considered as a strong psychological support to various social and economic sections.

These emotions have undergone a significant change in different periods of Indian polity. Although in every phase a dominant political emotion, which largely determined people's level of interaction with the politics, can be identified, there were multiple emotions were at work. Few were the dominant ones whereas other emotions were in making simultaneously. In the pre-Independence period nationalism and patriotism were the dominant political emotions. During the period of Indira Gandhi various programmes of poverty eradication and upliftment of weaker sections of the society were major reasons behind people's attachment with political parties and leaders. Loyalty and obligation for the political leaders were major political emotions. The decades of 1980s and 90s were dominated by the questions of identity. Hence, emotions of dignity and honour were dominant forms of political emotions. Late 1990s onwards, question of development emerged as a major cause of creation of political emotions.

In each of these phases one kind of political emotion gradually declined whereas other emotions emerged as the dominant emotions. However, in both the cases political emotions played a crucial role in determining various social emotions like community feelings, norms of governing cultural realm, redefining rules for management of community resources, generating or resolving conflicts over questions of identity, control over the state resources etc. These emotions decline due to the emergence of 'materialist era,' contrary to Ingelhart's argument that the present values represent a 'post-materialist' era. With this change in the political emotions in favour of more materialist values that sense of support also disappears which these emotions used to ensure or guarantee. These political emotions provided various means and public spheres for various types of community and economic supports. Although it is necessary to mention here that this support in the form of political emotions during the initial phase of independent India came in the form of ideological affiliations or a commitment to certain values. In the later phases this support came from utilization or misutilization of state resources in favour of certain social or economic groups or communities.

In the initial phases change in the nature of political emotions did not result into disastrous psychological implications. One major reason of this was that the psychological support structures in the form of various political emotions, which the deepening and widening of democracy in India generated, did not collapse. Thought these emotions were gradually declined but also survived in the form of political spaces, associations and attachments. However, the psychological implications got manifested in its worst forms in the last decades of twentieth century. Increasing number of suicides in various parts of the country is one significant indicator of this. The next section deals with this emerging challenge before the Indian democracy in more detail.

## Suicides in India

Suicides have become a major cause of mortality not only in India but also worldwide. According to the World Health Organization, suicide is amongst the top ten causes of death worldwide. Around 8,00,000 people die every year due to suicide. Every 40th second one person dies due to suicide globally. In the last 45 years the global death rate due to suicides has gone up by 60 per cent.

India is also amongst the most affected country by this problem. In 1988, approximately 64,270 people committed suicide. This figure has doubled by 2013 and went up to 1,32,790. An average growth in the number of suicide cases is 11 per cent per year (See table 8.1). A majority of these cases are being reported in the age group of 30 years and above.

The government records related to suicides also show profile of victim in terms of profession, gender and education. Around 60 per cent of those who committed suicides were male. Besides, majority of the victims were also involved in working in the unorganized sector. After this, highest numbers of suicides are being reported amongst the farmers and students.

**Table 8.1:** Incidence of Suicides by Sex and Age Group in India (1995 to 2012)

| *Year* | *By Sex All Age Group* | | *By Age Group* | | | | |
|---|---|---|---|---|---|---|---|
| | *Male* | *Female* | *Upto 14 Years* | *15-29 Years* | *30-44 Years* | *45-59 years* | *Above 60 Years* |
| 1995 | 52357 | 36821 | 3194 | 36478 | 29084 | 14943 | 5499 |
| 1996 | 51206 | 37035 | 3404 | 33925 | 29138 | 15393 | 6381 |
| 1997 | 56281 | 39548 | 3019 | 35998 | 32376 | 17475 | 6961 |
| 1998 | 61686 | 43027 | 3262 | 39366 | 35181 | 19361 | 7543 |
| 1999 | 65488 | 45099 | 3575 | 40710 | 37826 | 20552 | 7924 |
| 2000 | 66032 | 42561 | 3324 | 38711 | 36739 | 21326 | 8493 |
| 2001 | 66314 | 42192 | 3007 | 38910 | 36448 | 21579 | 8562 |
| 2002 | 69332 | 41085 | 2880 | 39288 | 37515 | 21857 | 8880 |
| 2003 | 70221 | 40630 | 2576 | 39828 | 37017 | 22332 | 9098 |
| 2004 | 72651 | 41046 | 2913 | 40136 | 38296 | 23139 | 9213 |
| 2001 | 66314 | 42192 | 3007 | 38910 | 36448 | 21579 | 8562 |
| 2002 | 69332 | 41085 | 2880 | 39288 | 37515 | 21857 | 8880 |
| 2003 | 70221 | 40630 | 2576 | 39828 | 37017 | 22332 | 9098 |
| 2004 | 72651 | 41046 | 2913 | 40136 | 38296 | 23139 | 9213 |
| 2005 | 72916 | 40998 | 2555 | 40234 | 38183 | 23625 | 9317 |
| 2006 | 75702 | 42410 | 2464 | 42216 | 40699 | 23606 | 9127 |
| 2007 | 79295 | 43342 | 2479 | 43160 | 41832 | 25571 | 9595 |
| 2008 | 80544 | 44473 | 2381 | 44652 | 43562 | 25192 | 9230 |
| 2009 | 81471 | 45680 | 2951 | 43920 | 43488 | 26603 | 10189 |
| 2010 | 87180 | 47419 | 3130 | 47625 | 44846 | 27889 | 11109 |
| 2011 | 87839 | 47746 | 3035 | 48014 | 46215 | 27536 | 10785 |
| 2012 | 88453 | 46992 | 2738 | 46635 | 46160 | 28499 | 11413 |

*Source*: National Crime Records Bureau (visit www.ncrb.nic.in).

In case of India, suicides have been explained in variety of ways. Broadly, these studies can be divided into three categories. Firstly are those which trace the causes of increasing suicides in the economic problems of various sections. These studies reflect upon the problems related to availability of sources of livelihood, lack of adequate regular income to sustain various cash requirements etc. as the root causes of increasing psychological burden (Patnaik 2002, Sainath 2000,

Mishra 2002, Asaadi 2003). Studies which have come from economists largely focus upon this aspect of psychological burdens. Such studies also relate this to the neo-liberal policies of state in various fields, withdrawal of state from providing various essential goods and services has adversely impacted upon the rural sections which were heavily dependent upon these support systems.

Sociological analysis of suicides on the other hand largely focus upon changing nature of rural social structures, changing nature of aspirations of rural populations and increasing demands for modern amenities, empowerment of weaker sections, urbanization of rural lives and so on. Jodhka (2005) discusses how 'ruralities' in India have undergone a significant change in the last three decades. Mohanti on the other hand shown how traditional rural hierarchies have undergone a significant alteration due to increasing level of education, transportation facilities, communication technologies and so on (Mohanti, 2008).

However, there are scholars who look at variety of other factors as well and try to analyze their psychological implications. Vasavi for example looks at changing nature of individual psychologies due to factors like modernization, green revolution, urbanization and so on. She also argues how people's perceptions of crisis situations have changed resulting into psychologically vulnerable individuals.

Scholars have also analyzed changing nature of political situations, its impact upon policies related to various groups and gradual impact upon people's sense of community support. This is more applicable in case of society which is more prone to natural disasters.

In order to establish a link between suicides and politics, a definition of politics which is not confined to the logic of rational choice will be useful. In this context, the relevant question which deserves attention here is which political emotions we are referring here. Are we talking about the notions of justice, equality, nationalism etc in the form of psychological behavioural patterns that influence individual psychology? Or there are different kinds of emotions that can be identified? Next section deals with these questions in a detailed manner in the context of Indian polity.

## Political Emotions and Political Mobilization in India

Every society has its own peculiar emotional ways which individuals express or attach or get engaged with their fellow beings like how individuals feel happy, or angry about their community members or how and when do they feel jealous. There are regional or society level variations in these emotions. Similarly, various processes generate or influence these emotions in a variety of ways. For instance, political process impacts upon these emotions differently than social emotions. Similarly, political sphere will also have its own set of emotions. These emotions may vary from each other. However, despite these variations certain commonalities can also be identified. In fact, some of the emotions, like justice, love etc. is recognized as 'global' in nature.

An analysis of how individuals are guided or influenced by these political emotions can be extremely useful in explaining political behaviour of individuals. For example, what makes the agenda of nationalism so pertinent at some point of time in the history that people are ready to sacrifice their lives whereas the same society refuses to react to the similar issues at some other point of time? Other good example can be cited from a community's reaction to the state led welfare programmes (or public policies). For the purpose of this, it is necessary to understand these specific emotions and their changing nature. In case of India, the policy of reservation has received a lot of emotional reactions from the society, surprisingly including those who were to be benefited from the scheme.

This process of generation or cultivation of political emotions becomes more crucial in the societies undergoing transformation. Few examples of such political emotions can be individual's attachment with any political party, social movement or love or affection with its leader, association with programme of any political party or level of interaction with any political outfit, and so on. An attachment with a particular political party may increase the emotions of aggression and violence whereas affiliation with another political party can result into more peaceful ways of resistance. One set of emotions can create a different kind of political life than the others. Political violence can be extremely common in one part of the country against a particular community whereas a similar community might not feel the same sense of fear in another state.

Such emotions are its peak in case of an ideology driven political environment where all political emotions are closely related to the type of political ideology a political society follows. A major impact of such political emotions can be seen in case of a decline or change of political system (or regime change in case of studying a state system). For example, decline of Indian National Congress had impacted upon a large number of people who used to approach the state structures, bureaucracy or even various public forums as an activist or member of INC. Gradual decline in its political significance in some parts of the country does have an impact on such supporters. Similarly, old age persons feel very differently about Communist rule in the Soviet Union as compare to the youths of Russia. This happens more in case of the societies where such political outfits are an outcome of a long political struggle. A large number of individuals do identify with the ideals and objectives for which a particular party or movement stood for.

Gradual decline of such political structures or demise of political leaders have serious psychological implications. Decline here does not simply mean a loss in the elections or decline in numerical support base. There are always opportunities for a political party to revive in case of such upheavals. Rather, decline here is explained in more qualitative or substantive terms, i.e. a large scale organizational collapse of a political party or social movement. For instance, how INC has lost its organizational effective presence in Bihar, Uttar Pradesh and Madhya Pradesh. This has happened more in case of some regional parties.

Psychological implications can be explained in a variety of ways. Declining faith in political institutions, sudden fall in voter turnout, tendencies of depoliticization, changing political behaviour of a particular socio-economic group, development of depression tendencies amongst political leaders, increasing faith in religious activities or superstitious activities etc. can be cited as few such impacts. In some cases, increasing number of suicides can also happen. A worst form of this is increasing number of group suicides. An extreme form of this psychological stress is a society turning into a stress society (Suthar *upcoming).* Indian case can be placed in this category.

While talking to farmers' in the above mentioned regions of India it was felt that the farmers' are deeply disappointed with their profession, the village life and their future. What was more shocking was declining self-esteem amongst farmers just because they belong to farming profession or they live in the rural areas.

Many farmers' especially the elder ones highlighted that there was a time when they had an access to the people's representatives' including members of Legislative Assembly (MLA), Members of

Parliament (MP) and the *panchayat* members (Sarpanch and Zila Pramukh etc.). People's representatives used to join them in marriages, birth ceremony or on the occasion of a death festival. With the changing passage of time now they have no access to them. There are only very few political leaders whom they can think of approaching in case of an emergency. In case of Haryana and Rajasthan people identified caste bonding as a strong factor for accessibility to the centre of power. This scenario has undergone a serious change now. In case of Punjab, religion played a crucial role. One could easily feel people's close attachment with the INC during Indira Gandhi's Prime Ministership especially her *garibi hatao* programme. People believed that no such programmes were implemented after that with so much of commitment. Farmers also expressed their deep sense of dissatisfaction with currently running welfare programmes like MNREGA though they did appreciate the effort.

Psychological implications of political emotions vary in terms of the age group of the supporters. Those who are in the middle age group (30-45 say for Indian context) are more likely to be impacted by such decline as compared to the young supporters (18-30) or older people (above 45). Those who had developed a social status around being a political party's activist and do not have any other political affiliation or possibilities are more likely to be impacted by decline of a political party or leader. The youth, on the other hand, can easily switch over to newer political outfits.

In case of India it is also necessary to mention caste as a relevant factor. The social assertion of many groups is quite closely linked with their political assertion. Though this has been highlighted more in case of marginalized groups, but this is equally applicable in case of historically stronger section as well. This consciousness gets reflected in the consolidation of various caste group votes in the form of a unified vote ban or their support to a particular political party. Hence, any decline of such political party or parties or decline in the political stature of their leaders is quite likely to have significant impact on their political and social status (Mohanty). This is also closely related to their individual psyche as well. Bahujan Samaj Party in case of Madhya Pradesh, Uttar Pradesh or Punjab or Republican Party in case of Maharashtra can be cited as good examples for explaining this phenomenon (Pai 2007, Narayan 2010, Pandey 2005).

Similarly, those social groups or economic classes which are more closely associated with the political change are more likely to be impacted by the political emotions which were associated to the politics before change. For example, farmers are more likely to be affected directly by the political change and changing character of political emotions thereby. Farmers' in Bundelkhand discussed how Lal Bahadur Shastri's solgan *Jai Jawan, Jai Kisan* used to make them feel proud about their profession. Farmers' in Punjab shared their disillusionment with the left movement along with their sense of attachment with its political symbol which had a crop cutter.

Since, Indian economy is still having an agrarian character and a majority of its population still depends upon agriculture and related activities, electoral politics is also closely linked with it. A large number of voters come from rural areas and also from agrarian background. With the adoption of a mixed economy model where state played a crucial role in promoting and protecting the agricultural sector after Independence, a mix of poitical and economic interests occurred between the farmers and politicians (Vasavi 2012, Mohanty 2013, Varshney 2014, Patnaik 2007).

Economic interests of farmers were closely linked with the political processes in India. Subsidies, availability of seeds, fertilizers and timely availability of formal credit facility and many other such benefits from the state to farmers or to the people residing in the rural areas came through political networks (Mishra 2009). In many states of India a strong network of party's supporters was created through political clientalism. People living in rural areas especially those who were involved in agricultural activities or who owned the land were provided varieties of benefits by political parties in return of their political support. A large number of regional (or state based) political parties emerged in India on the basis of emergence of such networks.

This not only helped in distribution or redistribution of material resources coming from the state or being controlled by the state (like land which was under the control of *Panchayats*), but it also provided a strong psychological support to a large number of people. The historically marginalized groups, who were not in a position to negotiate in the rural society, were given negotiating capabilities by these kinds of associations. Jats in Haryana and Rajasthan got strong political voice in the post-Independent India against the dominant Rajput and Brahmin communities only due to the strong interventions by the political leadership. Similarly, dalits in Uttar Pradesh got benefitted by emergence of Bahujan Samaj Party as a strong political force. OBC's in Uttar Pradesh and Bihar received their negotiating capabilities by emergence of Samajwadi Party and Janata Dal respectively. Emergence of all these political parties was closely associated with the question of redistribution of resources in favour of these communities.

Though these political changes were based upon political rationality of the voters but political emotions also played a very dominant role in this entire process. Promises of glory of these social groups, projection of their respected leaders as political leaders of these parties were few such steps which were initiated not only for the purpose of political rationality but also to promote a certain kinds of political emotions.

The Communist Parties in various parts of India were involved in promoting economic rationality and logics of class struggle. But in order to establish their political agenda amongst the masses they also took help of local folk songs and other cultural practices. Pride of a social group was highlighted in order to mobilize people in favour of the rationality based agenda. In other words, the backbone of political mobilization in India has been dominated by promoting political emotions, even though rationality based political agenda was highlighted in the formal literature.

However, it is also pertinent to mention here that emergence and decline of political emotions is not a mechanical process. An agenda may result into providing strong support base in one part of the same state but may not work at all in case of political mobilization in other parts of the same state.

There were various methods used in order to propagate a particular kind of political emotions ranging from evening meetings, public meetings, inviting film actors and actresses, playing patriotic songs, large size hoardings and so on. Increasing usage of religion as a medium of mobilization is also a strong way of promoting a particular kind of political emotions (Kanungao 2002, Jafferlot, Hasan, Kaur 2005). Through these means image of the leader of party is created in such a manner that gradually the voter starts identifying him/her with the party agenda very closely. This also results into spreading a party's support base in the form of cadres. This may not be stated very explicitly in the party agenda, except the left wing parties or the right wing organizations but this works as a strong mobilization strategy.

Another major strategy for political emotions is emphasizing upon the identity of the voter. Political parties project themselves more as the representatives of group interests rather than individual interests. Groups in these cases are defined on the lines of caste, religion, language, region etc. In such cases people's political orientation is shifted in favour of one party to the other by recalling their emotional attachment to various cultural practices which they have been following.

Not all groups get attached with all these activities in the same manner. Uneducated male voters are more likely to be feeling attached with the political emotions which is based upon preservation of traditional social order. Similarly, women feel more attached to a female candidate as compared to male. Youth voters are more likely to vote for the parties which emphasize on usage of modern technology driven mobilization strategies as compared to the old age voters.

This can also be explained in class terms. Middle class business person is more likely to be attached with the new political formations as compared to those who are well established in the business. In order to resolve various problems which the middle class business persons face in doing business, they look up to newer political formations which are based upon some identity related ideology. Hence, they support a particular party and its activities. Big business houses on the other hand, or well established business firms in the small and middle towns are more likely to support parties which have been their traditionality. Their historical attachment with such parties become basis for their legitimate claim for support from the party in case of any difficulty like any police case related to tax evasion. Small business persons on the other hand are very flexible and open in deciding their political loyalties. For them it's neither about their economic ambitions nor about creation of a political support base. Rather the challenge is to manage their day to day business. There political emotions are taken care of during their discussions with their fellow business community members in the market itself (Kohli 1996).

Similarly, a middle class peasant is more likely to be influenced by decline of a dominant political party in a region as compared to a big farmer. For a middle class peasant any association with a political party is a onetime life time investment. It is very difficult for him/her to switch political loyalties very quickly. Big farmers on the other hand do not feel so insecure with the decline of a political party as they have the feeling that they are going to remain significant despite any political change. One major reason behind this is their strong grip over the local bureaucracy which by and large reflects local social hierarchies only.

Regional analysis is also helpful in understanding impact of political emotions. This can also be explained in case of various regions where varieties of political movements flourished generating political emotions. Punjab witnessed a very strong left movement which developed close emotional ties with the small peasantry, industrial labour classes and student community. Karnataka's *Kshetkari Sangathan* had also led a very strong peasant movement and mobilized peasantry for protection of their interests and modernization. However, both these movements gradually declined and with them also declined the sense of community and belonging which these movements generated in the form of political emotions (Huber, Vasavi 2012, Suri 2010).

Movement in Punjab declined during early 90s with the emergence of terrorism and strengthening of right wing Sikhism. Similarly, peasant movements in Karnataka and Maharashtra declined due to internal divisions of these movement and gradual takeover of agrarian economy by big corporations and politician nexus. These movements provided very strong public spaces for discussion of various issues. They were also places for reducing intensity of individual stress situations (Gill 2008).

Emergence of market forces resulted into gradual decline of these public spaces and emergence of an individual centred society. Their decline also resulted into creation of an emotional vacuum for those social and economic sections which looked up to these movements for listening to their grievances, giving their concerns and voice and above all taking them forward to the peak of political power (Pai 2013).

Political emotions are generated by various political processes, institutions and leaders in a variety of ways. By situating different psychological problems into the context of political emotions, these situations or successes and failures of institutions can also be explained. However, there gradual decline or disappearance may result into emergence of a stress society.

## Disappearance of Political Emotions and Emergence of a Stress Society

What happens that these emotions which become a strong bondage between the political processes and the people gradually start withering away? Are they so fragile and weak that they tend to disappear so soon?

Many processes can be identified which affects existence of political emotions substantially. First is the process of depoliticization. (In this process gradually politics—the activity through which common decisions are made and people get involved on issues of common concern, is gradually taken over by a more technocratic and scientific methods of dealing with social problems. Hence, there is less scope for emotions as the scientific principle of objective decision-making is emphasized over an emotion driven collective decision-making.

Progress of science and gradual expansion of technology, what Habbermass calls as 'scientization of society', in the day-to-day lives also plays a crucial role in this exercise. All those political activities which were performed by individuals with the involvement of their fellow beings is gradually done by high technology based machines. There is no emotional attachment involved in this exercise. For example, the handmade posters and hand written pamphlets which were a strong medium of communication during the freedom movement or have been a backbone of left movement have been replaced by machine made banners and posters.

Emergence of market and its associated values like output, maximum profit, threat of survival etc. have also engulfed the public life (Vasavi 2012, Mohanty 2013, Jodhka 2012). Since, market has been realized as a strong actor along with the state and other non-state actors, its values have also become newer norms for governing these actors. This leaves very less scope for human emotions and feelings in the functioning of various public institutions. Besides, market is also overpowering state's ability to generate employment in the organized sector; its values are becoming governing norms for the new generation which is becoming a part of this system.

Along with this, market principles have also become an essential part of individual and community lives. Gradually, trust and faith based norms of collective life like sense of neighbourhood, support in the crisis times have been replaced by a dependence upon centralized institutions like state or paid facility system which are provided by market. Traditional knowledge systems are gradually dying in the hands of corporate houses or being patented by companies.

Realm of politics cannot remain untouched from these developments. Gradually, various strategies of political mobilization which had a strong component of political emotions have gradually shifted in favour of more mechanical and scientific technique based agenda like governance, performance based output, and numbers based mobilization techniques and so on (Chatterjee 2012). This has also harmed other political values which used to govern public life and institutions in India like secularism, equality and so on.

A cumulative impact of these processes is gradual disappearance of political emotions from public life. This has further resulted into withering away of the psychological support which these political emotions and their associated activities used to provide. The kinds of public presence a voter used to get from his or her attachment with a political party tend to gradually disappear when that political party or any movement in which it was a significant partner, faces threat to its survival. Apart from harming the social image of their individual, this also results into losing all those benefits (economic or non-economic) which used to come from that association.

Above all, these political spaces or 'public spheres' which were created by a political party during evolving its movement or political mobilization strategy, gradually looses their significance (Ali 2001). The places which used to attract so many people once upon a time gradually turn into abandoned spaces, be it a *chaupal*, a temple, a mosque, a community centre, a school building, or any other common place of gathering. The gatherings and meetings which were also places to release individual family related stress, gradually looks empty. In such situations there is no place for those individuals who were dependent upon the political emotions and their by-products. This gradually results into accumulation of individual tensions. Affairs of family, peer groups and above all from internal dilemma start looking like problems which can neither be shared nor be resolved. Other additional factors like economic backwardness, stress coming from increasing nature of expenditures, growing expectations from the family members make this situation unbearable making the person extremely vulnerable to a cumulative stress package.

Those who can switch their political loyalties and can also shift their political attachments can still manage their stress situations. But there are people who are not in a position to do so. This is also a reason that the number of suicides in India are higher in the categories which are deeply embedded in the political activities and therefore psychologically vulnerable e.g. middle class business persons, middle farmers, or even students who come from economically middle class family.

## Conclusion

The chapter made an attempt to explain a relationship between three factors: political processes, political emotions and emergence of a stress society. In political processes section largely the focus was on the political mobilization strategies of various political parties and the role played by political leaders. It was also discussed how these strategies result into cultivation of certain political emotions and public spheres. The chapter had also argued how these political emotions have gradually started withering away due to variety of factors like: tendencies of depoliticization, market as a dominant actor and its values gradually taking over other values of public institutions and public life, decline of community values and support system. Hence, a larger section of individuals which was dependent upon these political emotions for psychological support becomes extremely vulnerable to various stress situations. If these changes take place at a large scale in a society undergoing multiple transitions, the society might result into a stress society and witness emergence of psychological diseses or increasing number of suicides. This is what suicides tell us about a changing polity: trasnforming from an emotion based polity to rationality, governance and development based polity.

## References

Arendt, Hannah (1973): *The Origins of Totalitarianism,* New York: Harvest.

Assadi, M. (1998): "Farmers Suicides: Signs of Distress in Rural Economy", *Economic and Political Weekely*, 33 (14), pp. 747-48.

Chatterjee, Partha (2005): *Politics of the Governed: The Reflections on Popular Politics in Most of the World,* New Delhi: Permanent Black.

Dahl, Robert (1989): *Democracy and its Critics,* Yale: Yale University Press.

Gill, Anita and Lakhwinder Singh (2006): "Farmer Suicides and Responses from Public Policy: Evidence, Diagnosis and Alternative From Punjab", *Economic and Political Weekely,* 41(26), pp. 2762-68.

Goldie, Peter (2000), *The Emotions: A Philosophical Exploration,* (Oxford: Oxford University Press).

——, *Oxford Handbook of Philosophy of Emotions.*

Hassan, Zoya (2012): *Congress after Indira: Policy, Power, Political Change (1984-2009),* New Delhi: Oxford University Press.

Hollander, Nancy Caro (2004): "The Psychological Meanings of Our Current Political Culture: Views from Latin America", *Psychotherapy and Politics International,* 2(3), pp. 161-173.

Ingelhart, Ronald and Christian Welzel (2005): *Modernization, Cultural Change and Democracy,* New York: Cambridge University Press.

Jafferlot, Christopher (1998): *The Hindu Nationalist Movement in India,* New York: Columbia University Press.

Jodhka, Surinder (2012): *Village Society (Readings on thc Economy, Politics, and Society),* New Delhi: Orient Blackswan.

Kanungo, Pralay (2002): *RSS's Tryst with Politics: From Hedgewar to Sudarshan,* New Delhi: Manohar Publishers.

Kaur, Raminder (2005): *Performative Politics and the Cultures of Hinduism: Public Uses of Religion in Western India,* (New Delhi: Anthem).

Kohli, Atul (1991): *Democracy and Discontent: India's Growing Crisis of Governablity,* New York; Cambridge University Press.

Kumar, Sanjay, Praveen Rai (2013): *Measuring Voting Behaviour in India,* New Delhi: Sage.

Mishra, Srijit (2006): "Farmers' Suicides in Maharashtra", *Economic and Political Weekely,* April 22, 2006, pp. 1538-1542.

Mohanty, B.B. (2005): "We are Like the Livind Dead: Farmers' Suicides in Maharashtra, Western India", *Journal of Peasant Studies,* 32 (2), pp. 243-76.

Narayan, Badri (2009): *Fascinating Hindutva: Saffron Politics and Dalit Mobilization,* New Delhi: Sage Publications.

Nussbaum, Martha (2013): *Political Emotions: Why Love Matters for Justice* (Cambridge: The Belknap Press).

Pai, Sudha (2013): *Handbook of Politics in Indian States: Religion, Parties and Economic Reforms,* New Delhi: Oxford University Press.

Palshikar, Suhas, K.C. Suri and Yogendra Yadav (2014): *Party Competition in Indian States: Electoral Politics in Post-Congress Polity,* New Delhi: Oxford University Press.

Pandey, Gyanendra (2002): *The Ascendency of Congress in Uttar Pradesh: Class, Community and Nation in Northern India, 1920-1940,* New Delhi: Anthem Press.

Patnaik, Utsa (2007): *The Republic of Hunger and Other Essays,* New Delhi: The Merlin Press Ltd.

Przeworski, Adam (1991): *Democracy and the Market: Political and Economic Reforms in Eastern Europe and Latin America*, Cambridge: Cambridge University Press.

Sartori, Giovanni (1987): *The Theory of Democracy Revisited*, New Jersey: Chatham House Publishers.

Suri, K.C. (2006): "Political Economy of Agrarian Distress", *Economic and Political Weekely,* Vol. XLI, No. 16, pp. 1523-29.

Vasavi, A.R. (2012): *Shadow Space: Suicides and the Predicament of Rural India,* New Delhi: Three Collective.

Welch, Stephen (2013): *The Theory of Political Culture,* Oxford: Oxford University Press.

Yadav, Yogendra (1999): "Electotal Politics in the Time of Change: India's Third Electoral System, 1988-99", *Economic and Political Weekely,* Vol. 34, No. 34/35 (August 21 – September 3, 1999), pp. 2393-2399.

# 9

# Democracy and New Media

## Managing the Public Discourse in India

*Roshni Sengupta*

### Introduction

Political convulsions all across the world point towards a few unique features emerging out of democratic transitions. It takes place in countries metamorphozing from dictatorships to nascent democracies while those with established democratic processes witness the appearance of modern forms of communication and methods of political campaigning. The most prominent among these factors providing a tectonic boost to democratic movements as well as processes could be delineated as the development of forms of social networking and information sharing categorized as "New Media". The implications of the development of New Media on democracy and democratic processes particularly in the developing world assume resonance and character when viewed against the statistical wealth unearthed during recent studies on democratic movements in Middle East and North Africa. One of the key contributors to the success of the Arab Spring, for instance, was the almost complete reliance on social media platforms. Viewed against similar parameters, the emphatic success of the Bharatiya Janata Party's (BJP) social media campaign seems to have ushered in an era of free dissemination of political messages, which is distinctive, effective, and one with far-reaching consequences.

Establishment of these open spaces of communication has not occurred in isolation. The stifling of democratic dissent in former dictatorial regimes of the Middle East and North Africa (MENA) before the much feted Arab Spring led to the creation and expansion of communication spaces which came to be occupied by New Media. It is due to what the BJP claims as the "pariah status" of the party and its Prime Ministerial nominee, Mr. Narendra Modi on traditional media platforms that New Media was sought out as an alternative—a choice that worked like magic, leading to the almost complete annihilation of the Indian National Congress, which leapt onto the social media bandwagon in what could be termed as a mere afterthought. The emergence of New Media as the favoured tool of political communication in established as well as new democracies remains the major focus of this chapter. The prime example continues to be the success of the BJP's social media strategy. At the outset, the chapter would briefly delineate the various theories of communication and mass media, followed by a definition of New Media and its brief history. It would then extensively analyze the BJP's media strategy and almost complete dependence on social media platform as democratic spaces.

## Theories of Communication and Mass Media

"The medium is the message", a statement on the culture of all time to come can be attributed to Marshall McLuhan (1964). His seminal study also explained, in great detail, that the personal and social consequences of any medium—that is, of any extension of ourselves—result from the new scale that is introduced into our affairs by such extension of ourselves, or by any new technology.[1] Not only did McLuhan outline the centrality of the medium as the core of all human messages and communication, but he also dealt extensively with the fact that there existed a cultural matrix within which the medium operated.[2]

The birth of the medium of human communication in the form of long distance, mass communication could be delineated as the inimitable consequence of economic growth the world over. The discovery of electricity, according to McLuhan, was the turning point in the development of societies, excessively dependent on machines. However, "mechanization was never as vividly fragmented or sequential as in the birth of the movies, the moment that translated us beyond mechanism into the world of growth and organic interrelation" (MacLuhan 1964:12). The film, by definition, a sequence of images, beginning at a point and moving towards a logical conclusion, was responsible for the development and growth of the mass medium. It took, what was limited to paper, into a surreal world of creative configuration and structure. The message, thus of the movie medium is that of the transition from lineal connections to configurations.

Language too is a system, a construct. The meaning that a particular headline generates is the foremost variable under consideration to produce a theory of media effects. There is an effort to "fix" a certain meaning to an event that has transpired, use words to that effect and adhere then to what Derrida would term "logocentrism". Jacques Derrida (2003)[3] would deconstruct a headline to differentiate between factual discourse and "pure fiction". He presupposes the role of the media in generating and sustaining discourse and propaganda. Foucault goes a step further and defines discourse as the means by which subjects frame, classify, define and generate knowledge about themselves and the "other" (Foucault 1982).

The critique of the discourse theory, elaborated by Habermas concentrates on the concept of "balance" in the dissemination of news and the cinematic image. However, balance is also a mediation of the practices of bourgeois politics. For Marx, the media, a significant bulwark of bourgeois society plays a role designated for it within the confines of capitalism, a thought pioneered—albeit as part of the liberal school—by Benedict Anderson in his deliberation on print capitalism as a precursor to the development of communities and therefore, nation-states. The language was used, then becomes a tool in the hands of the bourgeoisie to propound and construct meanings that remain embedded in the minds of the readers leading to a social construct, a stereotype. A stereotype is the result of prolonged exposure to certain kinds of messages about certain people or communities.

Dennis McQuail characterizes the mass media as possessing highly diverse content and forms of organization and including a wide range of activities, which could have effects on society. The direction of impact towards certain sections of society, while other sections are considered to be outside the sphere of influence, finds a mention within the structural paradigm elaborated by Marxist theorists like Chomsky and Herman (1994).

One of the reasons why questions about the influence of mass communication are so difficult to answer lies in the uncertainty about the "mechanisms" by which effects are produced.[4] The foremost plausible fact that one must keep in mind while making a study of mass media in general is the primary importance of the existence of a source, a message that is generated by the source and the receiver who receives the message sent by the source. Kelman (1961:57-58) comes closer in his analysis of social influence, suggesting that three main processes are involved in opinion change—compliance, identification, and internalization. This model is criticized by Katz (1960:163-204) as one that assumes man to be an irrational being who falls prey to any form of powerful suggestion. He puts forward the "rational man" model in which people are viewed as using a calculative and logical approach to new information. Both the models, however, suffer from one major drawback, that is, none of them account for any significant change in attitudes as such.

Another important socio-psychological theory that deserves a mention here is that formulated by French and Raven (1953:67-76) which offers five main possibilities for a communicative relationship in which social power may be exercised, and influence accepted. Power based on "reward" or on "coercion", which implies some interaction between the intentions of the sender and the needs of the receiver. De Fleur (1970:45) provided certain fundamentals of media theory that have shaped and advanced knowledge globally. He formulated models such as the "simple conditioning model", the "individual differences model", and the "social categories model" for furthering his contention that different people are likely to respond differently to the same message depending on variables of social position such as life-cycle, occupation or class, religion, sex and so on. He also postulated that the audience learns about their social world and social reality from the media presentation of society. The media provide the material for responding to experience, and these accumulate over time in a long-term process of socialization.

Leading up from the preceding discussion of De Fleur's models of communications impact is Seymour-Ure's (1974:23-45) analysis of effects of the mass media on political relationships such as that between the individual and the political system; the political system and its constituent institutions rather than on individuals. The mass media will affect the individual's knowledge about and attachment to the political system as a whole, and this can happen over a long period as the structure of the media change, or it can happen more quickly by coverage of particular issues and people.

Theoretically then, the media as a whole are meant to act as impartial, objective and independent brokers of information. The press thus must act as neutral observers of the political process. Judith Lichtenberg (1990:34) elaborates on the direct role of the press or more the media as political actors themselves. Formally, the media performs a negative political act by protecting freedom of speech and enjoys a positive function by brokering information across society and setting the agenda. Through the years, the democratic role of the media has been challenged. They have been seen to perpetuate the values of the political, social and economic elites. Effectively, it, therefore, appears that the mass media reinforce the dominant ideology over the mass of citizens, performing both negative and positive functions.

Alternative perspectives of the media have thrown up contesting paradigms in terms of the relationship between politics, society and the media. While the Marxists would regard the media as an instrument of class domination and control, the liberals describe them as the pillars that keep the public space intact. The political role of the media is defined as an effective check on the government of the day by the liberal theorists. The Marxists would designate the majority of media as agencies of ciass control and capitalist in nature. The communists offer the public ownership model as the most accurate pointer towards the media system as a whole. The liberals and the neo-liberals, in particular, would favour the term "free market" to public ownership.

It would be ideal at this stage to summarize a few assumptions and arguments made by the liberal pluralist as well as the Marxist traditions. The liberal pluralists assume the media institutions, media personnel and audiences to be largely autonomous (Edgely 2000:152-153), i.e. their behaviour and decision-making patterns cannot be said to be determined by other institutions (*ibid.*). In contrast, Marxist work in the field has begun from the premise that media organizations work within and are subject to the constraints of the wider economic, political and social framework of capitalism. As this economic system significantly privileges a minority group, which might loosely be described as "owners of the means of production", then it seems logical to conclude that the ideas and messages put out by media institutions operating within this system will avoid undermining these privileges. The implicit assumption behind such a framework is that audiences are an undifferentiated mass who unproblematically "read" messages in the "required" way. In other words, messages flow in one direction from the top down.

The media is a core area in the political analysis of Noam Chomsky. He and Edward Herman in Manufacturing Consent set out a systematic framework or theory, which they call the propaganda model. It is in this context that we move on to discussing the long-standing and often self-deprecating debate in media circles and among theorists. The structural paradigm has often posed a challenge to the stranglehold of the instrumentalist model or paradigm for describing the media and its effects. Chomsky and Herman's propaganda model is a logical extension of the argument being made here. It suggests that there are certain filters through which the "raw material of news" must pass before an event is deemed newsworthy (Chomsky and Herman, *op. cit.*, 2). Three of these are structural in nature and the rest instrumentalist in content.

The propaganda model is concerned with setting out the character of ownership and control of the media within capitalist society. Herman and Chomsky thus use the hypotheses that the nature of ownership does influence media content. Media are also hierarchically structured, especially the "elite media". They have the largest circulations, so the potential for impact is large, they are also agenda setters for the smaller outlets, and the elite media becomes part of the historical record. In other words, their interpretation of events becomes history. Chomsky's propaganda model thus argues that "the combination of the endless repetitions of particular views, together with the fostering of debate strictly within permitted bounds as well as the use of questionable terminology makes for an extremely well-functioning system of propaganda which ensures that to escape its impact is remarkably difficult".

## New Media: Definition and Presence

Conventionally, distinguished from 'old' media including newspapers, magazines and even television, "New Media" is a term characteristically used to encompass the range of so-called 'digital' media which complement as well as conflict with traditional media? These media are typically informal, often primarily social and are not easily reducible to specific categorizations: much of the content is extremely diverse, and even mundane activity can harbour political content (Mejlias 2011:3-5). Essentially, New Media should be understood as a series of platforms; it encompasses a vast field of digital activity including web logs (blogs), micro-blogging (such as Twitter), social media (like Facebook), video sharing (YouTube), online reporting (by both institutions and individuals) and Rich Site

Summary (RSS) feeds (information). New Media is synonymous with digital mass peer-to-peer communication as it involves the usage of mobile devices from cell phones and smartphones to computers and laptops. The New Media revolution has evolved and exploded onto the scene with the development of "Web 2.0", the new generation of internet applications in which the content is almost entirely user-generated (Loader and Merca 2011:757-759).

New Media can offer the inclusive and open space for a conversation about dominant discourses to occur as well as the articulation of transformations in the existing discourse, outside of the hegemony of established institutions such as the government or the traditional media. This space can encourage mass participation in the conversation which can allow individuals to challenge dominant narratives and develop new, more democratic discourses concerning individual, cultural, social and political representations. With the transmission of new ideas in the networked space of New Media, which allows a vast conversation to take place, citizens can engage with one another based on an inclusive set of values. New Media offers an open and inclusive discussion space which allows expression of oppositional positions. Through discussion of these ideas, users are engaging with one another democratically. This may be crucial to the prevention of an escalation of opposition and the polarization of society.[5] New Media, as space for discussion and information dissemination, encourages mass peer-to-peer conversations, inclusive dialogue, and active participation, which are crucial components of the development of democracy.

In March 2013, the independent IRIS Knowledge Foundation carried out a study which suggested that social media usage in India was sufficient enough to influence results in the forthcoming general elections (IRIS Research Foundation 2013:1). The outcome of the research posited Facebook as a "gorilla" in the field of social peer-to-peer communication and predicted that the manner in which social media was empowering Indians to network and communicate would have serious implications for the democratic space and process. It also underscored the need for all potential candidates from various political formations to strategize keeping in mind the indomitable nature of the role that social media would play in any democratic exercise. A February 2013 report by the Internet and Mobile Association of India placed the number of social media users in urban India at 62 million at the end of December 2012 (IMAI: 2013). It could be estimated therefore that the number of urban social media users by the time elections concluded in 2014 was a whopping 80 million. The report also places considerable importance on the role of the 25-million strong NRI communities which remains hyperactive on various social media platforms.

The IMAI report also highlighted that Facebook is the leading social media website recorded across all platforms with as much as 97 per cent of the users registering a presence on the networking site. Further, apart from an email a majority of Internet users connect to the web to interact on platforms such as Facebook with Indians networking on the World Wide Web all seven days of the week. A third factor of significant relevance from the point of view of this study is the revelation in the IAMAI report that social media usage is spreading fast in areas other than the top eight Indian metros. One-third of the social media users, as the study reveals, are residents of smaller towns with the population of fewer than 5,00,000.[6] Even more significant is the fact that a quarter of social media users are residents of towns with a population less than 2,00,000.[7]

Add to this incredible mix, the role of the upwardly mobile, aspirational Indian youth—the ubiquitous demographic divided on which Indian democracy would undoubtedly like to pin its hopes. The Indian electorate has never been younger. Between 2004 and 2009, the voting population went up from 670 million to 720 million. The number to increase to 800 million by the time the country went to the polls in 2014, a greater number of voters than ever before were 25 years old or younger. In June 2012, the proportion of college students spending considerable amount of time on social networking platforms was capped at 82 per cent (about 14.9 million Indians), while the percentage of young men logging into New Media portals was 84 per cent (close to 24.2 million people (IMAI:2013).

Although the top eight metropolitan cities constituted more than a third of the entire user base, the other 66 per cent belonged to other smaller cities in urban India. Quite notably, almost a quarter (24%) of all social networking users in India belonged to small towns with population of less than 2 lakhs, while another 11 per cent were from towns with populations between 2 and 5 lakhs. Essentially, more than a third, i.e. about 35 per cent of the urban social networking base belonged to small towns having populations of up to 5 lakhs.[8] According to results from a survey conducted by I-Cube in 2012, there were about 39.7 million mobile Internet users in India. This was almost 50 per cent of the active Internet base. The figure additionally suggested that a greater proportion (82%) of active mobile Internet users logged on to the WWW as social media users, as compared to the overall general active Internet population (72%). Therefore, it can be safely assumed that the majority of active mobile Internet users access social networking sites for staying connected over time and space.

The fast and furious young India was, thus, logging in and how. It would have been tantamount to political harakiri for any media strategist to ignore the trends. Facebook was fast emerging as the primary vote bank for any political formation nudging aside caste and community considerations, at least for the time being or so it would have been assumed by parties delirious with the opportunity it presented, particularly concerning the general elections.

## Harnessing the New Vote Bank: Political Parties on Social Media Platforms

Investing heavily in the promotion and campaigning on New Media platforms was not an idea germane to electoral politics in India. The Obama campaign in 2008 which brought America's first black president to the White House had been a runaway success. The presidential election was the first even for the United States as candidates attempted to connect with Americans directly through microblogging sites like Twitter and social networking platforms such as Facebook and MySpace (Fraser and Dutta:2008). Exit polls released just before polling revealed that Obama had managed to garner 70 per cent of the votes of Americans aged under 25—the foremost users of social media platforms. Barack Obama, therefore, in many ways, was America's first Facebook President!

The Obama campaign's masterful leveraging of Web 2.0[9] platforms marked a major eruption in electoral politics—in America and elsewhere—as the methodology of campaigning moved from traditional political machines such as road shows and rallies toward the horizontal dynamics of online social networks. The Web, a perfect medium for genuine grassroots political movements, is altering the power dynamics of politics. While there are no barriers to entry on sites like Facebook and YouTube, power is diffused because participation is not limited. The Web was being leveraged not only for vote-gathering but—as the Obama campaign demonstrated—for grass-roots fundraising, too.[10]

According to a survey by the Pew Research Centre, nearly half—46 per cent—of Americans used the Web, E-mail, or text messaging for news about the presidential campaign, to contribute to the debate in whatever way they could or to mobilize others in some form. Some 35 per cent of Americans said they watched online videos gain more knowledge about the campaign and the political commitments the various candidates were making—three times as many as during the 2004 presidential election. And roughly 10 per cent said they had logged on to social networking sites like Facebook and MySpace to engage with the election process.[11] With the success of the Obama campaign in the background and the burgeoning social networking space and knowledge of the manner in which urbanizing India was communicating, the major political players in the electoral race attempted to make the world of New Media their own. According to web-based analysis based on research conducted between 15 December, 2014 and 22 January, 2014 [12] the BJP, Indian National Congress (INC) and the Aam Aadmi Party (AAP) made the most use of micro-blogging platforms like Twitter for their social media outreach campaigns (74%), followed by social networks like Facebook (25%). While the AAP made use of "Thunderclap."[13]—a crowd-speaking platform that helps people be heard by saying something together—to post messages on Facebook and Twitter handles, the BJP almost transformed Facebook into their election war room with their Ek Hi Vikalp—Modi and India 272+ campaigns. The research further concludes that the INC's social media campaign was weak and did not go beyond attempting to engage potential voters on Facebook and Twitter. The general disillusionment resulting from UPA II's dismal record of governance affected the party's social media presence in a negative manner.

The BJP garnered the largest percentile of support from social media users—an enormous 2.1 million followers; the AAP stood at 1.4 million followers while the INC could attract 1.0 million followers. Poised interestingly on its development plank with the ideological agenda taking a backseat, the BJP managed to secure the maximum exposure on Facebook. Following close on the heels of the BJP, particularly concerning presence on social media platforms, the AAP emerged as the most popular party on Twitter with 4,40,925 followers. The cataclysmic result that the Congress returned from the polling booths was reflective of the response their social media strategy reaped. While the party's Google+ circle had 3125 members, 1921 more than the BJP circle, they were far behind the AAP circle (1,41,366) members. With a mammoth 1,188,857 followers, Narendra Modi was the most popular politician on the Google+ Hangout platform.[14]

The lateral communication opportunity that social media platforms offer remains an essential contribution to the spread, use and popularity of the media—traditional and new age. Such communication, virtually impossible in the years before the telecom revolution and the advent of the Internet generation, has provided the throbbing, restless young masses a venue to voice both support and dissent, a platform previously unavailable. The development signifies the further extension of the process of democratic deepening. It is interesting to note that political strategists have identified the social media sphere as a "vote bank". Although the categorization appears negatively connoted, the tectonic shift away from the traditional vote banks of caste and community is noticeable and holds promise.

## BJP's Social Media Strategy

The rise of the BJP as a social media powerhouse could be traced back to 2004. This was the period around which Narendra Modi's name as a possible prime ministerial hopeful began to be discussed in inner-party circles. The process of building Brand Modi as a leader committed to economic development—an image far removed from the reality of 2002—subsequently, took shape. In a curious way, BJP members believe the mainstream media failed to provide the party with an adequate platform. The claim could be contested on two specific grounds. First, the discourse dominating the Indian media, particularly television has stark *Hindutva* overtones, magnified manifold by the proliferation of the imagination of the larger-than-life, united, sanskari Hindu family. Second, traces of the majoritarian discourse pervade popular film narratives as well.[15] Considering the broad reach of popular Hindi films, it would be natural for the dominant discourse to filter down to the lowest common denominator.

The BJP's objection remains confined to the space provided to the party on mainstream television news channels. With a centrist, left-liberal image and orientation, NDTV—India's first private, independent television news channel—is usually singled out by party strategists as the main culprit. Therefore, the social media onslaught could be described as reactionary in many ways. Media managers in the BJP term social media platforms like Facebook and Twitter as "campaign alternatives" to the pariah status accorded to the party, especially Mr. Modi, by the mainstream media. In fact, top BJP functionaries and spokespersons mount a scathing attack on television media channels particularly with regard to what they claim was an attempt at destabilizing the Modi campaign by raising the Shivraj Chauhan bogey, followed by the public recounting of Raman Singh's success as a Chief Minister.

It might come as a surprise, but both Chhattisgarh and Madhya Pradesh have clocked impressive growth rates in recent years, good enough to challenge Gujarat effectively in the economic arena. As per data gleaned from the Economic Survey Report (ESR) for 2013-14, the State of Chhattisgarh grew at 7.05 per cent, even though slipping from the 7.56 percentage points that the state gained in the previous year of assessment, staying eons ahead of the national growth rate. Further, Chhattisgarh's service sector grew at an impressive 9.09 per cent compared to a national average of 7 per cent. Interestingly, the state has managed to achieve remarkable levels of economic growth despite offering tax relief and subsidies to small and medium enterprises, cottage industries and small dealers to enable them to cope with the recession. If Chhattisgarh appears firmly ensconced in its growth train, its territorial neighbour and erstwhile progenitor, Madhya Pradesh—with a BJP chief minister at the helm of affairs for a second term—recently dislodged Bihar as the state with the highest rate of growth of Gross Domestic Product (GDP)—a stupendous 10 per cent (2012-13).

When compared with Gujarat the rate of growth acceleration for Madhya Pradesh was six percentage points higher in the latter half of the last decade while the north-western state remained at about three percentage points higher. Further, if the previous term of Shivraj Singh Chouhan (2004-05 to 2010-11) is taken into account, Madhya Pradesh seems to have had a sharper turnaround. Reports indicate a high level of awareness of welfare schemes like the Mukhyamantri Swasthya Bima Yojana in Chhattisgarh, which lends evidence to the State Government's accessibility and popularity among the masses. The tremendous improvement in the public distribution system of the state brought about by policy initiatives taken by the Dr. Raman Singh

Government has led to Chhattisgarh being labelled a "showcase" state concerning PDS and its working.

It is, therefore, clear that Mr. Modi's elevation as the Prime Ministerial candidate became a matter of him being the natural choice with his *swayamsewak*, and *pracharak* background blended quite well with his *Brahmachari* status. To give credit where due, it must be said that Mr. Modi very cautiously and effectively veered the intra-party opinion in his favour with help from the RSS, so much so that anti-Modi thoughts are made public only in the realm of cyberspace, if ever. The rise of Narendra Modi within the BJP's rank and file defines the inroads the RSS is making into active politics. The party, however, makes the claim that Modi was a considered choice as his victory margins in subsequent elections in Gujarat had been higher than both Shivraj Chouhan and Dr. Raman Singh.

That be so, the BJP's charge against mainstream media remains a contested issue. Meanwhile, party officials draw a timeline for their media blitzkrieg. It was for the first time in 2009 that first time voters began to be considered as a vote bank. The 2014 general elections thus provided a testing ground for their media strategists who went all out to target 10-12 crore first-time voters (between 18-24 years), also the biggest users of social networking platforms. The utility of this infinitely democratic medium began to be realized and put to use. The improvement and advancement in mobile technologies and the flooding of the market by Internet-enabled phones, particularly in 2012-13 marked the beginning of strategic targeting of the youth or the first-time voters. However, party veterans opine that interactions with the youth had started taking shape in 2007-08. By September 2013, Narendra Modi had notched up one crore followers on Twitter.

The "following", when analyzed, revealed the breaking of caste and regional boundaries although the support came mostly from among the Hindu voters with Muslims appearing few and far between. "About 17 per cent of the Yadav's voted for the BJP under the leadership of Mr. Modi. And what is more, 18 per cent-19 per cent of the *Dalits* also voted for Brand Modi," states a senior BJP youth wing leader. This, for those manning the media control rooms in the party, means a victory of their targeted social media campaign.

When seen in terms of numbers, the impact of the campaign becomes apparent. In 1998-99, 24 per cent of the young voters went to the BJP, which fell to 18 per cent in 2009 while the Congress managed a larger vote share among the youth at 28 per cent. On the contrary, in 2014 the BJP alone garnered 31.5 per cent of the vote share bolstered by the support generated from among young voters while the NDA pulled away from the Congress at 41 per cent.[16]

The party credits a tactical change in political strategy as a cause for the immense landslide. "We started considering the youth as a category, rather than emphasize on caste and communal cleavages," explains a party official. In fact, according to the official the fact that Mr. Modi mentioned his backward caste credentials in a rally on 19 January, 2014 reveals the party's careful avoidance of traditional vote bank categories. The most efficient way of getting the message across to the youth, they realized, was through social media platforms. The wide outreach of these platforms and the large user base facilitated the party's decision to adopt their now-successful media plan.

The BJP asserts a dominant position among scientists, technocrats and IT sector professionals although the claim remains unverified. A formidable presence among the technically inclined population, they opine, thrust them ahead in terms of engagement with IT and its offshoot sectors. "The efforts of two categories of people contributed to the success of the campaign—those who were part of our IT team and those who ceaselessly worked by sharing information on their social media networks," concurs a party official, adding that the "ideal state" has been achieved primarily as a result of the IT crusade.

Due to the growing popularity that the BJP and Brand Modi were garnering on social media networks, 70,000 to 80,000 young volunteers approached the party, hitherto a political pariah for the largely liberal elite groups, to join the campaign. As Modi began his promotion overdrive, the number of youth desirous of making contributions to the party rapidly amplified. Close to 5,00,000 volunteers signed up for the BJYM Campus Ambassador Programme—a voluntary programme geared towards augmenting Modi's campaign across the country. Interestingly, the programme trended in a big way on social networking platforms such as Facebook and Twitter.

"As the impact became clear and more, and more people started showing interest, we appointed district youth coordinators who made ample use of the social media to take the campaign forward," says a media strategist for the BJP. "An 'offline campaign,' therefore, turned into an 'online movement,'" he adds. In the Hamirpur parliamentary constituency in Himachal Pradesh, for example, 650 volunteers registered for the 272+ campaign, on its website and its Facebook page. These volunteers were further motivated by the party which sent Brand Modi merchandise across to their residences.

Party strategists do not also deny the success of the Aam Aadmi Party and its success on the social media. "We were inspired by AAP's social media success, and we do acknowledge it in no small measure," says Swadesh Singh, National Vice-President, Bharatiya Janata Yuva Morcha. The BJP attributes AAP's initial success to it's almost complete reliance on the technology savvy youth and the presence of NGO volunteers and professionals in its rank and file. Emulating the AAP's social media operation, claims the BJP, was not an easy task. According to a party media strategist, AAP enjoyed the advantage of having trained professionals as its active and working members who contributed in large measure to the successful campaign, a historic opportunity which the fledgling party lost out on primarily because of the desertion in Delhi.

On the other hand, the BJP had the benefit of a well-entrenched, cadre-based, and committed organization which along with the faith shown by the party in social media produced unmistakable success at the hustings. "Disillusioned by the Congress, the mainstream media supported the Aam Aadmi Party representing it as a worthy successor to the existing left-liberal political dispensation," offers a party official by way of explanation. "Till December 8, the mainstream media and the social media were both firmly in favour of Arvind Kejriwal and AAP. Then the cookie crumbled," he adds. Remarkably, for a better part of the campaign, Narendra Modi remained behind Kejriwal particularly in terms of Facebook "likes".

Mobile technology and its latent potential concerning political and electoral strategy as well as a non-sectarian, democratic medium remained a stringent ally for the BJP's media managers. In fact, the use of 3D technology emerged as an active, strident, and operational campaign tool. The BJP's first 3D rally was held at Bilaspur in Himachal Pradesh. "In a small town like Pratapgarh in Uttar Pradesh, more than 2000 people attended Modi's 3D rally," says Swadesh Singh, evidence of the impact technology was having on potential voters. The lowest common denominator was being targeted in an effective way. When quizzed about the effect of the BJP's social media blitzkrieg on the Muslim voters, a senior party official furnished the example of 2000 Muslims from Gujarat campaigning among members of the minority community in Varanasi, Modi's prestigious parliamentary constituency. "The fact that 9 per cent-10 per cent of the Muslim vote has come to the BJP-NDA proves that our message has reached the intended target," he claims.

Gradually, the party claims, private media channels (such as *Times Now*) started easing up self-imposed curbs on the BJP. According to one senior party member, the BJP's voice and the message was also heard on prime-time television news and beamed into living rooms across the country. Television news, therefore, began to augment and complement the growing discourse in favour of the BJP's brand of politics and its ostensibly developmentalist prime ministerial candidate, Narendra Modi whose political image was blotted by the 2002 carnage of Muslims in his home state of Gujarat. The surge, however, was a result of the enormous support base provided by social media platforms and the party's strategy to harness the outreach potential of information technology and its outgrowths.

The increasing dependence on New Media for political messaging and campaigning reveals an extraordinary trend—towards greater democratic deepening brought about by an enhanced reliance on technology-enabled methods. The use of technology, therefore, has promoted the extension of democratic processes to the hitherto untouched masses and social groups. As aspirations, both social and political, rise and more and more social groups become upwardly mobile, the outreach of New Media would portend a remarkable potential for subsequent political movements, electoral processes and democratic protests.

## Notes

1. McLuhan, Marshall, 1964 [2003], Understanding Media, p. 7., London/New York: Routledge.
2. *Ibid.*, p. 11.
3. Jacques Derrida, 2003. *Writing and Difference*, pp. 23-45. London and New York: Routledge (Indian reprint).
4. http://shodhganga.inflibnet.ac.in:8080/jspui/bitstream/10603/14460/10/10_chapter (accessed August 23, 2015).
5. New Media and the Development of Democracy, http://www.democraticprogress.org/wp-content/uploads/2012/10/New-Media-Paper-ENG (accessed August 23, 2015).
6. Social media may influence next general elections-CXOtoday.com, http://www.cxotoday.com/story/social-media-may-influence-next-general-elections/ (accessed August 23, 2015).

7. *Ibid.*
8. How much has social media penetrated in India? | India Social., http://www.indiasocial.in/social-media-penetration-india/ (accessed August 23, 2015).
9. Web 2.0 described World Wide Web sites that use technology beyond the static pages of earlier Web sites. The term was coined in 1999 by Darcy Di Nucci and was popularized by Tim O'Reilly at the O'Reilly Media Web 2.0 conference in late 2004. Although Web 2.0 suggests a new version of the World Wide Web, it does not refer to an update to any technical specification, but rather to cumulative changes in the way Web pages are made and used 26 Web 2.0 because of its technical advantage is used to connect instantaneously with other users on the World Wide Web through social media platforms
10. Obama's win means future elections must be fought online., http://www.theguardian.com/technology/2008/nov/07/barackobama-uselections2008 (accessed August 23, 2015)
11. Barack Obama and the Facebook Election-US News, http://www.usnews.com/opinion/articles/2008/11/19/barack-obama-and-the-facebook- (accessed August 23, 2015).
12. Analysis of Social Media Strategy: BJP *vs*. AAP *vs*. Congress. 2014. http://www.slideshare.net/Webfluenzintelsys/campaign-analysis-of-social-media-strategy-bjp-vs-aap-vs-congress
13. https://www.thunderclap.it/
14. Analysis of Social Media Strategy: BJP *vs*. AAP *vs*. Congress. 2014. http://www.slideshare.net/Webfluenzintelsys/campaign-analysis-of-social-media-strategy-bjp-vs-aap-vs-congress
15. Glamorous, well-mounted family dramas such as Hum Aapke Hain Kaun? (1994), Hum Saath Saath Hain (1999), Kabhi Khushi Kabhi Gham (2001), Vivaah (2006) and so on create the imagery of a perfect, united Hindu family which abides by sanskaras, thereby promoting a narrative of Hindu solidarity and togetherness.
16. All figures are courtesy interviews and conversations with BJP media strategists and senior officials of the Bharatiya Janata Yuva Morcha, the BJP's youth wing.

## References

Chomsky, Noam and Herman, Edward S. (1994): *Manufacturing Consent*, (London: Vintage), p. 23.

De Fleur, M. (1970): *Theories of Mass Communications*, (Philadelphia: McKay), p. 45.

Edgely, Alison (2000): *The Social and Political Thought of Noam Chomsky*, (Routledge:London and New York), pp. 152-153.

Foucault, Michel (1982). The Subject and Power In Hubert L. Dreyfus and Paul Rabinow, (eds.): *Beyond Structuralism and Hermeneutics*, (Brighton: Harvester Press).

Fraser, M. and S. Dutta (2008) "Barack Obama and the Facebook Election". US News, http://www.usnews.com/opinion/articles/2008/11/19/barack-obama-and-the-facebook-election.

French, J.R.P. and Raven, B.H. (1953): "The Bases of Social Power". In D. Cartwright and A. Zander (eds.), *Group Dynamics* (New York: Free Press), pp. 67-76.

IMAI. 2013. Social Media in India—2012. Details available at www.imai.in.

IRIS Research Foundation. 2013. *Social Media and Lok Sabha Elections*, p. 1.

Jacques Derrida. (2003): *Writing and Difference*, London and New York: (Routledge: Indian Reprint), pp. 23-45.

Katz, D. (1960): "The Functional Approach to the Study of Attitudes" *Public Opinion Quarterly* (24):163-204.

Kelman, H. (1961): "Processes of Opinion Change" *Public Opinion Quarterly* (25):57-78.

Lichtenberg, Judith. (1990): *Democracy and the Mass Media*, (New York: Cambridge University Press); p. 34.

Loader, B. and D. Mercea. (2011): "Networking Democracy?" *Information, Communication and Society* 14(6): 757-769.

McLuhan, Marshall. 1964 [2003]: *Understanding Media*, (London/New York: Routledge), p. 7 Mejlias, U. (2011): "The Twitter Revolution Must Die". *International Journal of Learning and Media*. 2 (4): 3-5, 3.

Seymour-Ure, C. (1974): *The Political Impact of Mass Media*, (London: Constable and Robinson), pp. 23-45.

# 10
# Technology and Democracy in India
## Western Perspectives and Indian Realities

*Siddhartha Mukerji*

### Introduction

Technology plays a crucial role in every sphere of human thought and action. Its ability to transform societies can be found during the industrial revolution when significant advancements in the fields of science and technology led to the creation of new class structure and modern ways of living. It promoted rapid urbanization with the large-scale migration of people from rural areas to urban centres in search of jobs created in the newly-established factories. Science and technology have not only created the modern infrastructure to provide a higher standard of living, but has produced new avenues for social and political engagement.

However, in general, terms technology has often been understood in isolation with social and political implications. In ancient Greek philosophy, technology was seen as an entity separate from human consciousness. Its potential to initiate progress was interpreted merely in physical and technical terms. For a long period, its link with culture and politics was wittingly or unwittingly not established. However, technology and science was viewed as vital ingredients for the capitalist mode of development. Much later, the post-structuralism or post-modernism questioned this apolitical nature of technology by showing how modern technology, particularly information technology, and the new knowledge industry drive the modern political culture. Many scholars who take this position believe that human beings have turned into mere instruments of technology so much so that their self is unframed, and our interests and aspirations are guided by it. In other words, post-structuralism highlights the undemocratic character of modern technology that only creates and perpetuates class interests and the concomitant divisions.

The policy-makers in Independent India realized the significance of technology for rapid development of the economy and society. New institutions of research on science and technology were established under state control. However, the technological innovations could never reach to the masses as it mainly catered to the requirement of Government departments and later the emerging private industry. Rajiv Gandhi's technocratic background had grave implications for the policy developments during his regime under which he made attempts to decentralize technology and liberalize policies to exhort private investment in the computer software industry. However, many of his visions to democratize technology were not realized. Rather new technologies that were produced and imported either fulfilled the consumerist desires of the new middle class or served the business needs of the foreign companies based in US and Europe. The initiation of E-governance programme in the recent past was the first attempt made by the Indian policy-makers to use information technology for greater participation of the masses in the developmental process. But a giant leap forward was made by social media and the internet that regenerated public consciousness and civil society activism and gave a new direction to democracy and social movements in India.

The core argument is that technology policy in India which was state-driven and based on the objectives of self-reliance and home-grown production left a little possibility for its penetration at the grass root level. Later, globalization of technology opened windows of opportunities for IT and service exports to US and Europe. It implies that the technical competencies of the fast-growing IT industry were mainly used to serve the business and information needs of the foreign client companies. In the recent past, E-governance programmes of the Government and increasing significance of cyber activism have democratized information and communication technology. Technology in this context has expanded its reach to masses and led to a form of political mobilization that was unknown in the past. Social media that became a popular mode of protest in the democratic movement in Egypt and other countries in North Africa was also used extensively during the anti-corruption movement in India in 2011. This new perception of technology and its social utility refutes the contention of Frankfurt school that hold on to the assumption that technology enframes human beings in the modern culture industry. The ensuing section locates the perceptions about technology and its socio-political dimension in the Western philosophical discourse.

## Technology and its Social Character in the Western Philosophical Discourse

The link between science and philosophy was established in the ancient Greek political thinking. The Greek notion of 'techne' referred to 'the art of making' or 'craftsmanship'. Plato viewed technology as a means of creating and perfecting material objects and was governed by certain rudimentary mathematical principles. Technology creation was primarily the work of the artisan. But, the technology was being created was not refined. Plato highlighted seven classes of technology that are: 1. First born class of things, 2. Tool, 3. Vessel, 4. Vehicle, 5. Defence, 6. Plaything, and 7. Nourishment. Beyond this, no other category of technology was thought to be possible. Plato considered technology to be external to human consciousness and, therefore, the domains of technology and society were different from each other (Arnautu, 2013: 3). Plato held a critical viewpoint towards the creation of technology stating that the emerging technology would undermine the vitality of the rich traditional literacy. Writing that was synonymous with technology would reduce the need for memory and attentive learning because it documented the thoughts in a systematic manner. Aristotle made a fundamental distinction between natural things and artifacts and attempted to establish a direct link between technology and human creation. In Physics II, he stated that natural things possess the principles of generation and motion inside while technology or artifacts are generated by outward causes namely human aims (Morrell 2012). Polis in this framework was also seen as a technique or art of governing. The ancient Greek philosophy pursued scientific investigations and understood the epistemological dimensions of technology. However, technology in the ancient Greek philosophy was only seen as a means to a desired end.

The Frankfurt School that offered a powerful critique of modern technology questioned the disconnection between technology, power relations and the ensuing social structures as well as the instrumental definition of technology being held by the Greek political thinkers. It argued that social action is not autonomous but conditioned by technology in the modern world. The technology could not just be considered as an artefact but means to condition human lives and purposes. Heidegger in his essay on "The Question Concerning Modern Technology" critiqued the impact of modern technology on human relations and society. The technology was seen to be an ontological disposition that determined our way of being in the world. It enframed human beings as it brought a new way of ordering the society. Enframing is understood as a historical mode of revealing in which every entity including human beings and nature is manipulable and, therefore, appears as resources that could be optimized. Heidegger states that, "in the full blown age of technology, the phenomena of art, politics and gods are flattened in being understood as the objects of scientific knowledge, in the light of which they become merely useful" (Weinberger 1992:113).

In line with Heidegger, others in the Frankfurt School namely Theodor Adorno, Max Horkheimer, and Herbert Marcuse interrogate technology's domination of nature in the twentieth century. Western Enlightenment that inadvertently results in domination of man by man. Herbert Marcuse understands modern technology in a broader perspective where technology is not merely seen as the functions of a technical apparatus but as a 'social process' in which human being are inseparably involved. He distinguished the conception of individual rationality that emerged in the liberal philosophical discourse of sixteenth and seventeenth century with the technological rationality of the twentieth century. Individual rationality was primarily based upon autonomous self-interest that was realized through the application of human reason. On the other hand, technological rationality refers to the rationality of domination and social control in the age of high-flown technology. Marcuse states that, "technological rationality fashions everyday life into a 'technological reality' that encloses the subject's perceptions, experiences and thoughts by projecting the world's objects and nature as a world of instrumentalities." Modern technology is totalitarian as it, what he says, not only determines social occupations, skills and attitudes but also individual needs and aspirations (Marcuse 1964: 11). It creates forms of life that seeks to reconcile the forces opposing the system. Henceforth, technical progress tends to maintain *status quo* and inhibits the possibilities of social change that is integral to democratic life. Elaborating on the dominative tendencies of a technological society Marcuse exclaims that, "As a technological universe, advanced industrial society is a political world, the latest stage in the realization of a particular historical project—namely the experience, transformation and organization of nature as the mere stuff of domination" (*Ibid.*).

Drawing from Marxist understanding of class relations in capitalism, Adorno views modern industrial technology as alienating. It fosters production relations based on power relations whereby the worker gets completely disempowered to apply her creative potential in various technical operations that have to be handled. Adorno holds a critical viewpoint about social implications of modern technology when he says that, technology is making gestures precise and brutal, and with them men. It expels from movements all hesitation, deliberation and civility. It subjects them to implacable, as it were ahistorical demands of objects (Adorno 1978:40).

Habermas in his understanding of the interface between technology and society differentiates between three types of rationalities that are found to exist in the modern world. These are scientific-technical rationality, moral-practical rationality and aesthetic-practical rationality (Owen 2002: 89). The first sphere of rationalization is considered non-social, neutral and objective as it represents universal interests and the actual world rather than any particular social interest, value system or ideology. It directly finds its application into the natural system and therefore nature becomes amenable to technological rationality. On the other hand, the second and third categories concern human relations and social interests. They influence what Habermas calls as 'lifeworld'. Therefore, the other two rationalities become relevant for society in so far as they determine human relations. A strict compartmentalization of the three rationalities is however not possible in the modern world where human lives are entirely controlled by the new technologies that surround them. Habermas himself believes that in the age of modern technology technical rationality has not merely remained as an objective piece of nature, but has brought technical considerations in the society. It has colonized the life world that was primarily the sphere where moral and aesthetic rationalities operated. This further implies that as technological consideration finds its way into the social system the three spheres of rationality do not remain entirely distinct from each other. In other words, Habermas tried to locate the interlinking between them and, therefore, the political and social contents of technology. On this count, he observes the flip side of technology show how it sometimes leads to social pathologies. In its original sphere technology is treated as neutral, but outside this sphere it causes certain social pathologies that appear to be recurrent problems of modern societies.

The post-structuralist theory, therefore, gainsays the neutral character of modern technology that was underscored by the Greek political thinkers. Technology inherently remains objectified by directly manipulating nature, but the purpose for which it is used and the outcome that it creates presupposes human behaviour and actions. Technology enframes individuals as Heidegger advocates; at the same time it gets shaped by social interests and human purposes. Overall two contrary positions could be cited regarding the understanding of technology and its implications for human world:

1. The first place is taken by Greek thinkers particularly Plato who treats techne as mere artefact.
2. The other line of argument taken by the post-structuralist thinkers finds a clear-cut linkage between technology, social interest and power in the modern age.

The difference in position lies more in the contexts in which the ideas got embedded. The post-structuralist writings emerged when the nature of technology itself had undergone a significant transformation. Technological developments in the fields of medical sciences, nuclear energy, bio-medical sciences and above all the foundation for all these different varieties of technologies namely information and communication technology brought significant change in the life and thought processes of individuals. Technology, however, became another mode of domination when it exalted the position of scientists and engineers who were working in their respective scientific fields. It created a chain of the dominance of those who created it and the ones who used it for commercial purposes. It became a symbol of power for those who created it primarily to serve either the requirements of the government agencies or the industrial capitalists who used them to enhance the quality of their products to earn generous dividends.

Technological advancement triggering rapid industrialization served as pre-requisite for economic growth, and economic growth was further considered as an essential condition for maturing democracy. Quite contrary to this assumption, technology appeared to be another source of social stratification as it became a prerogative of the elites and the rising middle class in the society. Technology is another tool of exploitation in a stratified society like ours where resources are concentrated in few hands. If state does not play its role judiciously, by making it accessible to all, there is a strong possibility that those who are in privileged position will further consolidate their position whereas poorer strata will be further marginalized. In other words, technology may be used by the privileged class to marginalize the poorer class. This is visible in the Indian case. The gap between haves and have-nots or inequality is becoming unmanageable. As per the second version, technology lacked the democratic rigour as it failed to produce conditions for equity, especially in the economic sphere.

The Indian case provides a clear-cut evidence of the second mode of thinking on technology and democracy where technology for a pretty long period remained another source of power aggrandizement and socio-economic division in the society. The core argument here is that the technological institutions that were created under the ISI (import-substitution model) model was primarily to serve the needs of the defence and attain self-reliance in space technology. The fundamental objective of the science and technology policy during the early years after independence was to achieve self-reliance in the economic arena. This meant establishing public sector monopoly in the domain of science and technology to achieve the stated goals of development. However, the purpose of creating new technologies lacked the democratic content as its use, and the end-products remained confined to either industrial hubs or Government agencies especially in the defence sector.

With the rise of new middle class especially in the 1980s, electronic goods and items assumed larger markets within the country. As the consumer base expanded, the utility of electronics and computer became broad-based. This got triggered in the 1990s with rising income levels and therefore increasing economic mobility of people into the middle-class category. In other words, growing consumerism had created a culture industry characterized by rapidly growing demand for high-tech products. Technology in this industry does not simply appear as a product of utility, but a mark of social status or identity. Those who could learn and access it felt differently placed in the society. The new class consciousness, therefore, assumed another dimension that was the ability to access new technologies and to adopt them in different ways in day-to-day life. This new class consciousness based on accessing new technologies not only presupposed an economic division between the new middle class and the poor masses but also a psychological rift between them. The PCs, iPods, laptops, mobile and internet thus appeared to be commodities that could be utilized by the middle class for utility sake but more so for enhancement of their social esteem and high regard in the society.

The industrial policies also favoured the influx of foreign products and gadgets in the Indian market through imports but more recently through the entry of multinational companies. India thus became a huge market for leading global brands like Samsung, LG, HP, Nokia, etc. But, by the year 2000 it had become apparent that the India companies in the software sector also had tremendous potential in the international market. The policies, therefore, favoured the promotion of export-oriented IT and software companies. Lately, it was realized that the potential could be harnessed for developmental purposes within the country especially to bridge the gap between urban and rural areas. E-governance, which would be elaborated in the latter part of the chapter, is a means through which the government tends to make technological benefits accessible to the common public. The idea was to democratize technology itself so that it could be brought closer to masses to improve their standards of living.

A shift is therefore observed in the technology policy of the Indian state whereby the fundamental thrust is to use technology to improve public delivery systems and democratize it by providing its access to rural masses. This new model of development administration is often referred to as e-governance the ideological thrust of which is to shed the class-based utility of technology and ascribe a democratic outlook to it. The following sections attempt to understand this shift in the context of changing contours of technological and industrial policies of the government.

## Science and Technology Policy—The Early Decades

The idea of achieving the goals of social and economic development through the promotion of education and research in the field of science and technology was mooted by the political leaders during national movement. However, it was given a concrete shape only after

Independence when Nehru and others identified the development of science and technology as a prior policy agenda of the government.

The technology discourse in post-colonial India revolved around the contradiction between Nehru's agenda of technological modernization through state-led development and Gandhian critique of Western civilization and modernity that brought in new technologies only to expand human wants and desires and kill the moral pursuits of human existence. In this regard Chakravarty points out that,

> "The discourse of technology in post-colonial India revolved around Gandhi's vision of *Swaraj* and Nehru's vision of collective interest before individual profit. In contrast to Nehru's version of Fabian socialism, which saw in the Russian revolution a model of technology-led development and progress, Gandhi emphasized manual work and a moral economy of Indian village life" (Chakravarty 2004 : 232).

Nehru like Gandhi also opposed industrialism of the West because of the inherent inequalities that it promoted. But, he considered technology as a dire necessity to build modern India. The alternative to the Western model was, therefore, a state-driven model of technological development that was both democratic and egalitarian in its objective. The fundamental purpose of this thrust was to achieve self-reliance by creating indigenous sources of technology and depend less on others. Technology infrastructure was an essential component for the overall development of the economy and therefore it needed the required push from the government. This further necessitated public sector control over science and technology infrastructure.

Given this objective, the government under the leadership of Nehru created a broad-based public-sector driven S&T establishment. To begin with, the Planning Commission was entrusted with the responsibility of formulating national plans on science and technology. One of its members was always an eminent scientist. At the next level, the CSIR that was established in 1942 by the then operative Central Legislative Assembly framed and reviewed plans for R&D in diverse fields of S&T. Finally, the scientific research was to be carried out by a chain of laboratories that were linked with CSIR and institutions of higher learning in science and technology like the IITs, ICMR, ICAR, IISc, and many others (Mascarenhas 2010: 24).

The Science Policy Resolution passed by the Parliament in 1958 highlights the objectives of a sound S&T policy and its significance in altering the life of a common man. Its democratic orientation and purpose are clearly reflected in its vision. Underscoring its relevance in triggering human progress, the resolution observes that,

> "The dominating feature of the contemporary world is the intense cultivation of science on a large scale, and its application to meet a country's requirement. It is this, which for the first time in man's history, has given to the common man in countries advanced in science, a standard of living and social and cultural amenities, which were once confined to a very small privileged minority of the population."[1] In developing countries like India, agriculture is the mainstay of rural economy and in this sector, there is tremendous scope of application of technology but the scale and pace of technological application in this area is very slow. In other words, the government should prioritise the areas where it should focus first.
>
> Elaborating on the objectives of S&T policy, the resolution states that it (S&T policy) will encourage the creative potential of men and women and individual initiative for the acquisition and dissemination of knowledge, and for the discovery of new knowledge in an atmosphere of academic freedom. The resolution clearly opens new doors of opportunity for creativity and knowledge. In the end, the policy statement also mentions the larger purpose of the intellectual pursuits in the field of S&T which would be to, "to secure for the people of the country all the benefits that could accrue from the acquisition and application of scientific knowledge."[2]

The Scientific Policy Resolution was the first official statement of the S&T policy of India. Its broad vision and outlook about science and its impact on human lives marks the optimism of the political leadership particularly Nehru towards contribution of S&T in not only modernizing the society with rapid industrialization, but also bringing in socio-economic democracy by raising the standards of living. The Resolution was, therefore, both democratic and all-inclusive in its content and purpose.

Nevertheless, the scientific developments that took place during the first two decades after independence mainly contributed towards meeting the needs of the defence sector and achieving the goals of heavy industrialization. The debacles of the Sino-India War of 1962 shifted the focus of S&T policy on strengthening defence base of the country. Around 40 laboratories itself were run by the Defence Ministry to meet its technical requirements (Rao 1985:133). The overall scientific and technological effort since the mid-1960s was directed towards strengthening the defence sector. This agenda received further impetus when the Committee of Electronics in August 1963 was constituted immediately after the Sino-India War of 1962. Homi Bhabha, the chairman of AEC (Atomic Energy Commission), was also made the chairman of the newly-established Committee. At the backdrop of the war with Pakistan in 1965 and the growing need for integration between technology and defence, the Committee was brought directly under the control of the Defence Ministry's Department of Defence Supplies. This form of institutional integration worked towards creating new technology required for producing sophisticated defence equipment. Technology that was itself not in an advanced stage of its development was far from access to the common man.

## Rajiv Gandhi's Technocratic Vision: The Transformative Era

The new thinking on technology found its way through the policy developments that took place during Rajiv Gandhi's regime. The two dominant modes of this thinking were: decentralization and liberalization. The idea of democratizing technology is closely linked with the aspect of decentralized administration. Decentralized administration meant greater participation of people in the decision-making process at the grassroots level. It also implied bringing technology at the grassroots level and connecting people with their developmental and welfare programmes. Knowledge dissemination at the grass root level can help achieve this purpose. This was possible through liberalization and promotion of competition so as to make the technological products and services available at the grassroot level.

Rajiv Gandhi's technocratic orientation was a natural outcome of his technical background. His technocratic bent of mind was clearly reflected in his professional style of functioning. It offered him a modernist and technocratic outlook that undoubtedly influenced the line of policies that he pursued during his regime. In this regard, Bhabhani Sengupta exclaims that "His (Rajiv Gandhi's) style of functioning was different from the earlier Congress leaders. It had a new orderliness, discipline and meticulousness, a new attention hitherto unknown to Congress culture. The technocratic and managerial language of Rajiv Gandhi's administration often contradicted with conservatism of the old guards within the party and therefore the young Prime Minister's innovative ideas and radical policy shifts were cited as premature and hasty by many of his colleagues and senior leaders."

The entire focus of industrial policy during this period was towards promoting technology-driven sectors like telecom and computer software. By the mid-1980s, it was realized that the technological backwardness of the Indian industry was primarily responsible for its stagnation and sickness. Therefore, the primary thrust of the industrial policy must be technological upgradation of the Indian industry. This was thought to be possible when new technical skills and innovations could be brought in through competition and greater encouragement to private investment. Henceforth, certain fast-track policy decisions were taken for quick advancements in the fields of emerging technologies particularly computer software that had immense potential not only to enhance the competitive edge of the Indian industry in the international market, but also democratize it by making it accessible to the common masses particularly those in the rural areas. In this context, in one of the speeches delivered at the inaugural session of the "National Conference on Productivity through People" in New Delhi on 29 October, 1986, the Prime Minister said that:

> "What India needs today is not just gradual growth of technology and upgradation of technology. We are now ready to take a jump. If we go through full process at each step, we will only fall behind; we will never be able to catch up; we will go through all the negative aspects that the developed countries have already gone through."[3]

The Government under the leadership of Rajiv Gandhi advanced several policies that created new avenues for private investment in technology-driven sectors electronics and computer software. The first step in this direction was the Electronics Policy of 1984 that encouraged private production of microcomputers which was initially the monopoly of ECIL (Electronics Corporation of India Ltd.), the dominant producer of electronics and computer in the domestic market. The other breakthrough in this regard was the announcement of the Computer Software Export, Development and Training Policy on 18 December, 1986. The major thrust of the policy dispensation was to encourage export-oriented software sector by removing existing restrictions on software imports. Under the new scheme, software imports were placed under the 'Open General License' category which implied that now software could be imported in any form, in any quantity and by anybody by paying 60 per cent *ad valorem* duty.

The next significant step in this direction was to revolutionize telecom by bringing communication technology to the doorsteps of rural people. It was reported that less than 1 per cent of India's 6,00,000 villages in the 1970s had access to telephones. The DoT's monopoly position in the telecom sector as a regulator, producer and service provider was held responsible for the restrictive market. Paula Chakravarthy observes that "the regulatory structure shielded the telecom bureaucracy from any form of accountability from any extremely disgruntled public. The DoT's problems were compounded by charges of petty corruption" (Chakravarty, *op. cit.*, : 235).

Rajiv Gandhi's technological thrust through policy changes was met with two contradictory responses, namely export-oriented industrialization that pushed technologically driven sectors like IT in a direction that had less to do with domestic socio-economic development and administrative decentralization a phenomenon that entailed greater mass penetration of technology. To substantiate the latter, Rajiv Gandhi made public commitments to bring technology closer to masses especially in rural areas. In one of his speeches delivered at the National Convention on Small Industry on 17th September, 1986 at New Delhi, Rajiv Gandhi said that, "we want the sophisticated computer to study the monsoon so that we can tell the farmer when to plant and what the rainfall is likely to be, more accurately."[4] This clearly indicates that Rajiv Gandhi aspired to distribute the benefits of technology to the indignant, poverty-stricken masses and to educate them in science and technology so that they could live a life of self-reliance and dignity. He found a complementarity between the technocratic approach of policy implementation and redistributive measures providing benefits of modernization on equal terms.

Rajiv Gandhi also did not find a contradiction between liberalization and democratizing technology. Rather liberalization was seen as a precondition for a free market where people could exercise their choice freely without any monopoly constrains. The public sector was seen to have failed on both counts namely, generating the required output and delivering effectively to the people.

However, the new technology and industrial policy ultimately turned out to be beneficial for the business groups and the emerging new middle class in the society. This was primarily due to two reasons: (1) A large mass of people were illiterate and would not understand modern technology; (2) The mainstay of the new liberal policy was still to promote private investment and help business entrepreneurship grow fast. Decentralization, therefore, remained meaningful in the political realm and had a little offer for the economic welfare of the marginalized groups. Even if the commitments were valid, computer technology was still not in a stage to create wonders in domestic lives. The removal of restrictions on MRTP (Monopoly Restrictive Trade Practices) and FERA (Foreign Exchange Regulation Act) was welcomed by the big companies who have been demanding for relaxation in these policy measures. The big industrialists also welcomed import liberalization as this was found necessary for technology transfer.

The other segment that came to be benefitted by the liberalization drive was the newly emerging new middle class and the rising consumerist culture within it. Atul Kohli (1992) has pointed out three modes of linkage between the middle class and the government that are as follows:

1. The new technocratic approach of the political leadership appealed to the new middle class.
2. New tax policy appeared to be particularly beneficial to the new middle class.
3. A greater impetus provided to the electronics consumer industry for the production of high-tech products like television sets, refrigerators, cars, and the computer seemed to be highly attractive. The new middle class welcomed the idea of greater engagement with foreign companies through foreign collaborations especially for the purpose of technology transfer. Access to imported goods and

technologies did not just add to the comfort but also appeared as a status-symbol for this class.

Elaborating on this score, E. Sreedharan (2004) also exclaims that, deregulation can be expected to command widespread support among middle classes, as regulation is identified with corruption and inefficiency.

The new technology and industrialization drive thus assumed a class dimension rather than a mass dimension despite a recurrent commitment made to decentralize and democratize technology. Also, it laid a solid foundation for the future growth of indigenous technological development in India by promoting the export-oriented IT industry. But, the strategy that was adopted to build the industry was first to qualify the litmus test in the international market and then orient it towards the domestic sector for various socio-economic development projects.

Rajiv Gandhi's era is often cited as a phase in India's economy history which witnesses an unprecedented breakthrough in microelectronic technology that led to the emergence of new products in the market characterized by high levels of efficiency, reliability and versatility. The convergence of electronics, computing and telecommunications also referred to as the "New Industrial Revolution" or the "Information Technology Revolution" brought about a paradigm shift in the production activities of Indian industries. Computer and information technology industry was seen to be horizontally and vertically linked with almost every sector of the economy. India's potential to compete in the global market for the new technology was immense; a future potential that was already sensed by the technocratic leadership and harnessed by the new technocratic entrepreneurship. However, putting this technology to public use and for public welfare had only touched the fringes of political and administrative thinking and was therefore far distant from its realization. Rather, the thought became obscure and faded since 1991 as the technology, and industrial policies of the government entirely focused on the globalization of the Indian industry.

## Technology Globalization Since 1991

The year 1991 marked a radical departure from the past economic policies by adopting globalization-driven private investment and opting for export-oriented industrialization strategy, especially for the emerging computer software industry. These two trends determined the growth trajectory of software and IT industry in the post-reform period. In fact, the growing salience of the technological-driven sector became so apparent that the technological and industrial policies now came to focus exclusively on its promotion in the international market.

Globalization entailed transnational mobility of capital, technology, and human resources. The technology industry in India was made to serve the global market especially the United States and the West European nations. The technology institutions in India produced world-class engineers who worked mostly in the Silicon Valley in the United States to earn better salaries and higher standards of living. In India, the previous trend of entry of imported electronic gadgets gained further momentum with the emergence of multinational companies. This meant that the technological development in India fulfilled two important purposes:

1. Serve the foreign companies particularly in US and West European companies externally.
2. Assume a class dimension internally by serving the consumerist interest of the rising middle classes.

By 1991, the competitive potential of the technology industry particularly computer software and services in the global market was well evident. SAP (Structural Adjustment Programme) that was being adopted by the government sought to facilitate liberalization for creating a business-friendly environment both for domestic and foreign companies. The policy changes like delicensing, import liberalization, relaxation of corporate tax and tariffs, foreign investment, etc. were to be pursued in a phased manner. They were meant to create avenues for private investment in the broad range of industrial sectors. However, technology-driven sectors especially computer software and services needed a special impetus for their promotion in the international market. The general changes in the policy environment were still not adequate to deal with the administrative hurdles faced in getting clearances. Above all, poor infrastructure and lack of telecommunication links appeared to be major impediments before the new technological ventures.

Given this, the government in the year 1991 introduced the STP (Software Technology Park) scheme with the objective of providing special policy benefits for the export-oriented companies. This primarily included tax exemptions and infrastructural support like provisions of continuous supply of electricity and high-speed data links. Other maintenance and technical support services offered within STPs were network design, system integration, installations, and operations and maintenance of application networks.[5] There has been a consistent rise in the number of export companies registered with STP. The Annual Report of STPI shows that the number of exporting units in STPI has increased from 4279 in 2001-02 to 5814 in 2009-10.[6]

The policy support for liberalization and export-oriented industrialization in the software sector did not directly come from the political leadership. Senior bureaucrats within DoE corroborated the innovative projects of the private software entrepreneurs. Moreover, the DoE in collaboration with some of the big software companies tried to push for investment-friendly policies. In this case, its attempt to give space for private entrepreneurship was in contrast with the position of DoT that continued with its monopoly as a service provider in the telecommunication industry. The monopoly position of DoT was a predicament for the software companies. Due to this reason, the DoE could only approach DoT for data communication links in the STPs that charged high rates and imposed strict conditionalities for providing the required facility.

The globalization of the service sector also resulted from the increasing influence of NASSCOM, the umbrella organization for software and services industry in India. It was formed in the year 1988 mainly to promote business and trade in the software and services sector. NASSCOM was a brainchild of some of the big players in the software market like TCS, Wipro, Infosys and Satyam. It has gradually evolved into a powerful organization that has worked in close collaboration with the Union Government. At present, many State Governments are working out programmes and policies for the promotion of the software and now also the IT industry. The apex organization has also taken initiatives to liaison with the global market players to enhance the brand equity of the Indian service sector in the world market (Strategic Review 2001:14). Both NASSCOM and the current Ministry of Information and Technology have jointly organized many Conferences and seminars to find ways and strategies for the

IT and software industry to compete with other countries like China, Philippines, and Israel.

The trilateral collaboration between the DoE (now the Ministry of IT), NASSCOM, and the big software companies helped in pursuing policies and schemes that were meant to support the export-oriented software firms. It exerted additional pressure on the government to make necessary interventions in this matter and formulate a comprehensive plan for institutional support to the private companies through STPs. The incentives proved to be especially beneficial for the SMEs (small and medium enterprises) that were more in need of it due to capital and infrastructural constraints. These companies were able to gain greater voice as they became members of NASSCOM and could channel their demands through it.

Telecom liberalization was achieved while the mid-1990s opened windows of opportunity for expansion of the IT and software industry. But, the major contribution it made in the technology services sector was that it helped in the rise and expansion of BPO and later KPO segment of the industry in the global market. BPOs that are often referred to as call centres provide back-office business and technical services to companies located in US or Europe through disper sed long-distance communication network. Its overall contribution to the economy is mainly two fold, namely enhancement of foreign exchange reserves through service exports and creating employment opportunities for young professionals. The liberalization policy in this sector largely supported the growth of the export-oriented IT industry, but at the same time by enhancing competition in the telecom market and the mobile revolution that followed it brought technology at the grassroots level. The mobile industry facilitated by the liberal policies of the government has been able to penetrate rural hinterlands, enhancing communication within.

While the export-oriented policies of the government raised the brand equity of Indian software and services in the global market, its utility for mass development and economic democracy that was envisioned by Rajiv Gandhi became a figment of the past. The idea and the vision were lost in the wake of globalization-oriented policies of the government. The overemphasis on export-promotion led to dereliction of the domestic market until very recently. As Mascarenhas (2010) comments, "While Indian software developers have put India on the IT world map, they have unwittingly become the target of the critics who question the undue emphasis given by the government to the export of software. The software and IT sector exhibits the distinctive character of having maximum forward and backward linkages with industry and other sectors of the economy. Consequently, it provides immense business opportunities in the domestic market. Its application in several social and economic sectors like health, education, banking, rural development and management and agriculture is particularly crucial from the standpoint of its implications for the overall development of the economy. This could be achieved by improving the public delivery system with the help of IT and software technologies a phenomenon or a process that is commonly known as E-governance.

## E-Governance—The New Mantra for Democratizing Technology

E-governance is the state led drive for technology penetration at the grassroots level that seeks to introduce the varied range of services and facilities particularly in rural areas for facilitating accessibility to public utilities. It serves as an important means of social inclusion as it helps in connecting people and regions at the periphery to the mainstream. As a result, it appears as a new *mantra* for democratizing technology by bringing it closer to masses, enhancing the common's participation in the developmental process and promising an economic life that is free of affliction and tribulations.

The E-governance programme was first adopted by the Andhra Pradesh Government in the year 1996 under the stewardship of Chandrababu Naidu before it became popularized in other states and lately the Central Government. Under its comprehensive e-governance programme several initiatives were taken like e-Seva, e-Procurement, e-Suvidha (complete application for municipalities), financial accounting system for Gram panchayats, Computer Aided Registration of Documents and Citizen Friendly Services of Transport. In order to develop state-wide networking of data, voice and video services the Andhra Pradesh Government launched the APSWAN (AP-State Wide Area Network) that seeks to connect state headquarters with 23 district headquarters and 1088 mandal headquarters. It also attempts to develop broadband connection in rural areas. For the management of administrative files and to promote paperwork administration the government has introduced the KM-ATOM system.

The Government of Andhra Pradesh has worked in collaboration with the private sector in several projects on IT-driven inclusion. In

2002, it undertook the project 'World e-Inclusion' with Hewlett-Packard at Kuppam in Chittoor district.[7] The objective of this project was to develop ICT technology and products for rural development and make extensive provisions for internet facilities in the countryside. It also initiated training programmes for the youth, women and the *panchayats*.

The Karnataka Government has been equally active in making e-governance meaningful with the introduction of several programmes. One of the most prominent software system developed by the STPI-Bangalore for its use in the Karnataka Finance Department called Khajan. The government has also established several kiosks meant for providing easy payment of the water, electricity and phone bills. A kiosk is a computer terminal designed for specialized hardware and software to access information and for its application in the delivery of public services. Karnataka Government's Bhoomi project was started in 2004 that sought to computerize 20 million land records of 6.7 million land owners in 176 taluks in the state. Under this project, kiosks were established for the farmers in getting a quick access to their land records. They were freed from the burden of going all the way to the taluk headquarters for procuring the land records. Similar kiosks have been established in rural areas by the Andhra Pradesh Government through three of its major e-governance projects namely rural e-Seva, Rural Service Delivery Points and Rajiv Internet Village Centres.

The Central Government announced the National E-governance Plan on 18 May, 2006, almost a decade after the Andhra Pradesh Government began venturing into it. The Department of Information Technology within MIT serves as the nodal agency for the implementation of the programme in a phased-wise manner. Under the scheme, the government would first provide public services at a convenient location through CSC (Common Service Centres). The next step would be to connect with State Government through state-wide electronic networks and finally priority areas of public services would be identified and covered under MMPs (Mission Mode Projects) for their speedy execution.

The most innovative programme of the Central Government and many of the State Governments under the E-governance scheme are to establish Kisan call centres country-wide. The scheme was launched by the Department of Agriculture and Cooperation, Ministry of Agriculture on 21st January, 2004 to provide extension services to the farmers. These units work in the line of BPOs and KPOs that provides all necessary information to the farmers about agricultural development and resolve the queries and qualms raised by farmers in the local language. The primary purpose of the extension service, as pointed out is that, "both technology generation and technology transfer have to focus more strongly on the themes of optimization in the management of the available resources by agricultural producers, sustainability, coping with diversity by adapting technology more specifically to agro-ecological or social circumstances and raising the economic efficiency of agriculture."[8]

Public extension programme through Kisan call centre is seen to be, "a paradigm shift from top down blanket dissemination of technological packages, towards providing producers with the knowledge and understanding with which they could solve their location-specific problems."[9] The emerging knowledge industry has therefore something new to offer by expanding the scope of democracy in the rural areas. Connecting with new technologies, accessing information through new modes of communication, and disseminating this knowledge to others helps in direct participation of people in the process of governance. Information technology not only serves as a basis to improve the functioning of public administration, but helps in democratizing the overall process of public administration by maintaining transparency and accountability in public works through people's participation. In other words, information technology democratizes the system of administration in mainly two ways:

1. Making the process people-friendly and transparent.
2. Enhancing the participation of people in their developmental programmes.

Technology has thus penetrated the system of governance in rural areas. The overall responsibility for making the best use of implementation of various rural developmental schemes lies with the Panchayats and local administration. This, however, requires adequate training in handling new technologies on the part of the local government. Due to illiteracy and ignorance the Panchayats fail to learn and adopt new technologies for the improvement of administration at the local level. Second, maintenance of computer systems and technological equipment is difficult due to the unavailability of the required support system in rural areas. The use of electronic systems also become meaningless when there is acute power shortage. In other words, the necessary infrastructure needed for the maintenance of new technology lacks in villages or even smaller towns due to which running new technologies becomes precarious.

Public access to new technologies is not only inhibited by the above-mentioned physical factors, but also socio-cultural level reasons. Rural people often feel reluctant to handle new technologies as they prefer to continue with their traditional practices. The feudal mode of thinking amongst the dominant social groups in rural settings also hinder the entry of modern technology in rural areas as it is sometimes seen to threaten the *status quo*. Modern technology is viewed with suspicion by such groups who think that it acts as a source of modern consciousness by connecting people and leading to free exchange of ideas and thoughts between them. Second, sometimes the local administrators also act as clects[10] who make use of modern methods of the organization including new technologies but retain particular goals. While, they project themselves to be modern and progressive in their practices their ideas and vision appear as profoundly undemocratic and sometimes even misleading. In fact, many innovative projects may be actively pursued at the Gram Panchayat level, but due to lack of support by the BDO (Block Development Office) that is constituted by local administrative officials the implementation may fail.

Thus, while e-governance schemes and programmes of the government has provided ample opportunities to democratize technology innovations by bringing them closer to the people and bridging the gap between urban and rural areas, the goals are far to seek due to structural and socio-psychological factors that inhibit the process of its implementation. E-governance is, however, a top-down approach to democratizing technology as it is initiated by the government in collaboration with private sector.

## Social Media, the Internet, and the Democratic Revolution

The role of electronic and digital media has emerged as an important means of social integration and democratic protests in contemporary societies. New internet sites of social networking have provided a sound basis to connect with friends, relatives, fellow colleagues and with those having common interests. The online networking serves as a social tool to connect, collaborate and organize and is commonly known as social media. To be precise, social media has been defined as, "an umbrella term that encompasses a variety of websites, services, and applications that allow users to engage in social behaviours online or on mobile phones."[11] Social media is used synonymously with other terms like a social tool, social software, social web, or social technology. Some of the common tools of social networking are websites such as Facebook, Twitter, LinkedIn, Xing and MySpace; blogs through which people communicate their messages on the web; Wiki a web page that can be edited by users; and content sharing through websites like YouTube and Flickr.

The question that arises is what additional benefit does the internet, and online networking provide. Is it a more efficient mode of communication and participation in public affairs? How does it appear to be different from traditional methods of social networking? Traditionally, newspapers or magazines served as principal sources of information to people till the recent past. With the advent of internet communication, people could not only get the information online, but also connect with others to propagate and share their ideas and thoughts. Information dissemination can be done much expeditiously through online networks. People can pass on their messages through Blogs or send them to mobile phones and request for action on the submitted applications. Therefore, in modern society, social media and the internet have appeared as new forms of social and political mobilization. In this regard, Eltantawy and Wiest point out that,

> "new communication technologies especially social media *via* the internet have become valuable resources for the mobilization of collective action and the subsequent creation, organization, and implementation of social movements around the world. The development of social media created opportunities for Web-fuelled social movements, or cyberactivism, to change the landscape of collective action" (Eltantawy and Wiest 2011:1207).

In the contemporary discourse on democracy and protest movements, the civil society has made extensive use of social networking sites to organize and mobilize people. Civil society activism in today's world has taken the form of mass movements to protest against the arbitrary and anti-people policies of the government. In some cases, such mass movements with the help of social media have overturned political regimes in the Middle East and North Africa. Social networking sites particularly Facebook and Twitter served as powerful tools to coordinate with people and organize them to lead the pro-democratic movement in these countries. In Egypt, the popular revolt was triggered as the protestors organized protest logistics; provide live updates of ground-level information and mobilizing people to connect in large numbers with the movement. Highlighting the importance of social media for the democratic movement, a researcher Era Martens has pointed out that, "in the Egyptian context, Facebook, in particular, helped accelerate the protests."[12] The process of cyber activism began in the early 2000s when a group of Egyptian bloggers became famous for addressing public issues. Later, many others joined the bandwagon and attempted to extend their reach to masses by using other communication technology modes like Facebook, Twitter, Flickr and mobile phones. The traditional modes of protest like posters, pamphlets and leaflets were substituted by social media. The public activists created Facebook groups, Twitter accounts, and personal blogs to integrate people at large with the revolution. ElBaradei, the prominent figure is this entire political exercise created his personal Facebook page and Twitter account making the best use of the communication technology (Eltantawy and Wiest 2011:1213).

The recent anti-corruption movement in India that made extensive use of social media for organizing the protest also exemplifies the cyber-activism that became popular in the democratic movement in Egypt and other North African countries. Like many other countries, the online networking sites have provided space for social movement in India. This was well evident in the 'fast unto death' protest launched by Anna Hazare in New Delhi in the year 2011. Anna holding on to Gandhi's *Satyagraha* principles became the social crusader of the movement against corruption in modern India. While the style of protest was comparable to Gandhi's civil disobedience movement, the means to link, organize and collaborate with people in the country had changed dramatically. Communication technology that was supposed to be a commodity for the big business and financial sectors in US and Europe now appeared as a means to generate public consciousness and public debate over the issue of Lok Pal Bill. The Anna Hazare movement has therefore rightly been called as the first 'real social networking' movement in India. In this movement, the social media radically altered the reach of the movement by connecting a large mass of people ever since independence serving as a powerful tool for public activism.

The anti-corruption movement organizers created a Facebook page labelled as 'India Against Corruption'. To begin with, in the first four days of the campaign a total of 1,16,000 people posted their messages on the page showing their overarching support for the cause. In due course of time, it was reported that around 1.5 million people extended online support to the movement out of which around 5,00,000 people alone sent their messages on the IAC Facebook page by 7 February, 2012. Other means of communication like mobile and smartphones were also used to link people with the movement. According to a survey maximum number of people who organized and joined the protest belonged to the age group of 18-24 (Bong and others 2012:6).

The contribution of social media and the communication technology towards lodging social protests in the recent past clearly shows the democratic essence of modern day technology. Information and communication technology has not really enframed human beings in a way that have made them cogs in the machine but has rather generated a new sense of public activism by expanding its outreach far more expeditiously than traditional modes of social integration. This is well corroborated by the contribution of social media towards energizing and invigorating the Anna Hazare movement. Its role was for a democratic cause and a democratic outcome.

Moreover, in contrast to the e-governance project of the government, cyber activism or social movements launched under the aegis of social media is a bottom-up approach to democratize technology. It is an initiative of the people who felt that information and communication technology has something new to offer to modern democracy as it appeared as a new mode of public activism and an effective means of political communication in contemporary Indian society. Information and communication technology in such movements has not only attempted to mobilize masses within the nation, but has popularized the cause worldwide by connecting people with it all across the globe. Therefore, its reach is not just local or national, but global and international.

## Concluding Remarks

India's science and technology industry has surged ahead to make a global imprint. It has accorded a superpower status to the country and lessened the economic dependence on others to overcome its economic problems. India's tcchnocratic entrepreneurs have earned international repute as their contribution to the progress of software, and computer technology is of global significance. The overall assessment from a global perspective is that India's giant leap forward in the technology realm and its attempts to achieve double-digit growth has established its position as a superpower in the contemporary world. The slogan of "India Shining" highlights this very status of India in global political economy.

Nevertheless, its superpower status in world politics has not complimented by equivalent efforts towards the contribution of science and technology for societal development. Although the e-governance scheme has been an initiation point in this regard, its implementation for enhancing mass access to technology-based services remain far to seek. As pointed, this is due to lack of education and training amongst local people and local and administration and also partly because of unwillingness to adopt such technologies at the local level.

The class-based culture industry with which technology is usually associated puts modern technology in a negative light. Technology inherently does not promote hierarchy and class consciousness in modern societies. Its creation is directly linked to human aims and intentions. Therefore, its democratic or undemocratic character primarily depends on the purpose behind its inception. Ability to use it may create social differences, but then its potential or organize and link people will lead to social integration. This is well evident in the contribution of social media and online networking in expanding the outreach of the movements carried out in Egypt and India. Technology, therefore, touches every aspect of human life is modern times. When seen in a different light, technology brings a humanitarian dimension whereby it strengthens emotional bonding between individuals and involves them in collective action to struggle for their rights and justice in modern democracies.

## Notes

1. www.dst.gov.in, Scientific Policy Resolution 1958, Department of Science and Technology, Ministry of Science and Technology, Last accessed on 13th March, 2013.

2. *Ibid.*
3. *Rajiv Gandhi's Selected Speeches and Writings: 1986*, Vol. 2, May 1989, p. 116.
4. Inaugural Speech to the "National Convention on Small Industry", New Delhi, 17th September, 1986 in *Rajiv Gandhi's Selected Speeches and Writings: 1986*, Vol. 2, May 1989, p. 102.
5. http://www.stpi.in/index1.php?langid=1&level=0&linkid=126&lid=172 (the official website of STPI).
6. http://www.stpi.in/writereaddata/links/2534218955annuarl1.pdf, Annual Report 2009-10, STPI, Government of India, last accessed on 18th March, 2013.
7. Apit.ap.gov.in, Information Technology and Communications Department, Order no. 21, 27th May, 2002, Government of Andhra Pradesh, last accessed on 11th November, 2013.
8. http://www.manage.gov.in/kcc/concept.htm, Official website of the Ministry of Agriculture, Government of India, last accessed on 13th November, 2013.
9. *Ibid.*
10. The term clect was used by F.W. Riggs in his Ecological Theory of Public Administration to refer to a group of people in the administration who make the best use of the modern technologies in organizational activities, but work towards fulfilling self-appointed goals. They have very little concern for public welfare. The Sal officer in prismatic society maintains a close relationship with clects.
11. http://*www.ukessays.com/essays/media/twitter*-becomes-surprisingly-useful-media-e, last accessed 20th August, 2015.
12. http://www.dw.de/social-media-use-evolving-in-egypt/a-16930251, last accessed on 26th November, 2013.

## References

Adorno, Theodore (1978): *Minima Moralia,* Frankfurt: Suhrkamp Verlag.

Arnautu, Robert (2013): *Early Modern Philosophy of Technology: Bacon and Descartes*, (Budapest: Central European University), p. 3.

Chakravarty, Paula (2004): "Telecom, National Development and the Indian State: A postcolonial critique", *Media, Culture, and Society*, 26 (2).

Eltantawy, Nahed and Julie B. Wiest (2006): "Social Media in the Egyptian Revolution: Reconsidering Resource Mobilization Theory", *International Journal of Communication*, 5: p. 1207.

Kohli, Atul (1992): *Democracy and Discontent: India's Growing Crisis of Governability,* (Cambridge: Cambridge University Press).

Marcuse, Herbert (1964): *One-Dimensional Man: Studies in the Ideology of Advanced Industrial Society*, (London: Routledge).

Mascarenhas, R.C. (2010): *India's Silicon Plateau: Development of Information and Communication Technology in Bangalore*, (New Delhi: Orient BlackSwan).

Morrell, Kelvin (2012): *Organization, Society, and Politics: An Aristotelian Perspective,* (New York: Palgrave MacMillan).

Nahed Eltantawy and Julie B. Wiest (2011): "Social Media in the Egyptian Revolution: Reconsidering Resource Mobilization Theory", *International Journal of Communication*, 5 (2011).

Owen, David S. (2002): *Between Reason and Progress: Habermas and the Idea of Progress*, (New York: New York Press), p. 89.

*Rajiv Gandhi's Selected Speeches and Writings: 1986*, Vol. 2, May, 1989.

Rao, J.S. "Science and Technology in India", *Science*, 12th July 1985: 229 (4709).

Sasha Bong and others, (2012): "Analyzing Social Media Momentum: India's 2011-12 Anti-Corruption Movement", Prepared for US Government Office of South Asia Policy, Workshop in International Public Affairs, Spring 2012.

*Strategic Review* 2001, New Delhi: NASSCOM.

Sreedharan, E. (2004): "The Growth and Sectoral Composition of India's Middle Classes: Its Impact on the Politics of Economic Liberalization", *India Review*, 2004, 3(4), p. 425.

Weinberger, Jerry (1992): "Politics and the Problem of Technology: An Essay on Heidegger and the Tradition of Political Philosophy", *American Political Science Review*, March 1992: 86 (1).

**Websites**

www.dst.gov.in, Scientific Policy Resolution 1958, Department of Science and Technology, Ministry of Science and Technology.

http://www.stpi.in/index1.php?langid=1&level=0&linkid=126&lid=172 (the official website of STPI).

Apit.ap.gov.in, Information Technology and Communications Department, Order no. 21, 27th May, 2002, Government of Andhra Pradesh.

http://www.manage.gov.in/kcc/concept.htm, Official website of the Ministry of Agriculture, Government of India.

# SECTION IV
## Current Economic Pathways and Its Socio-Political Implications

# 11
# India's Economic Growth and Equity
## The Search for the Missing Link

*Sanjay Gupta*

### Introduction

The major theme of the chapter revolves around the twin issues of economic growth and human development which are quintessentially interconnected. To study the impact of the economic model on social and human development, India's growth pattern needs to be examined in the post-Independence period. Generally, three phases could be identified: Phase I from 1947 to 1955, Phase II from 1955 to 1990, and Phase III from 1990 up to the present. While phase I and II are conspicuous of India's vulnerability arising out of it's socio-economic and scientific-technological backwardness coupled with western countries' attempt to fish in India's troubled waters and influence India's course of economic development, phase III heralds a new era of growing confidence, maturity, knowledge, competitiveness and entrepreneurship that has become more manifest in the twenty first century. It is this phase that witnessed far-reaching changes in India's economic policy assumes the primary focus of the current chapter. Economic reforms which gradually stabilized after a weak start during the initial years of the 1990s ushered in prosperity as well as immense challenges to human survival, particularly for the weak and the marginalized. This phase saw the worsening of human scenario amidst lop-sided, elitist growth, giving rise to popular discontentment against the economic reforms. The resentment sent out a strong message to the policy-makers that equity cannot play second fiddle to growth, that social and human development cannot be sacrificed in the name of economic growth, and those economic policies exclusivist in nature cannot usher in a genuine and harmonious democracy. The search, however, for a right developmental model suited to India's socio-economic-cultural milieu is still on that incorporates the virtues of both growth and equity.

## India's Economic Structure and the Nehru-Mahanalobis Model

The search for an economic model arose even before India's Independence, which is manifested in the debates that took place between the stalwarts of India's freedom fighters even before India's Independence. Figures like, Dadabhai Naoroji, Mahatma Gandhi, Sardar Patel and Jawaharlal Nehru presented their ideas about the type of economic model to be adopted in free India. While each of them denounced colonialism, they were not equally critical about the western model of development. Sardar Patel and C. Rajagopalachari advocated for a western model of development with private initiative and entreprenurship to be given greater priority in the economy. On the other hand, considering the massive social backwardness of people, Netaji Subhas Chandra Bose, Jai Prakash Narayan and M.N. Roy favoured a socialistic pattern of nationalization of key sectors and public sector playing a major role in the development of the society. The Gandhian philosopher, Kumarappa sought to include a greater emphasis on rural development and cottage industries to cater to the needs of rural India which then, according to him, deserved the greatest attention in terms of development and equity. Here, it is worth mentioning that before the British colonized India, it had one of the largest GDPs in the world. An estimate by Cambridge University historian Angus Madison puts India's share of the world income as 22.6 per cent in 1700, comparable to the whole of Europe's share of 23.3 per cent, which fell to an abysmally low 3.8 per cent in 1952 (Madison, 2001).

In order to revive India's economy, Nehru, the architect of modern India, however, proposed his own model of economic and social development without, however, discarding the merits of the views of his colleagues. Adopting a rather 'golden mean path', he formulated a 'mixed economy' model in which there would be co-existence of public and private sector, with public sector playing a lead role and working as 'engine of growth' and achieving 'commanding heights' of economy (Dube 1989). Nehru's adoption of a mixed economy model was also an attempt to steer clear of a purely western approach to development that, in his perception, was more akin to capitalism and an instrument of colonialism and imperialism. But he was not against liberalization provided it could lead to faster growth and development for India. To give a fillip to his ideas, Nehru initiated Five Year Plans (FYPs), and the first plan was a great success to achieving both these goals. However, Nehru's economic approach was not much likened by the west as they sought to interfere in India's affairs and dictate the kind of economic structure that the country should follow. Buoyed by the success of the first plan, Nehru initiated the second FYP in 1955 with heavy industrialization as the main objective. Together with this, he proposed a chain of medium and light industries to be set-up all across the country to provide employment to the rural people and also to give initiative to the entrepreneurs. However, the plans hit a roadblock due to the resource and technology crunch, as well as the BOP crisis which the government faced while implementing its plans (RBI, 1948).

Nehru, compelled by the circumstances, took recourse to loans from the IMF. The IMF agreed to provide economic aid subject to conditionalities that Nehru reluctantly accepted to avoid the failure of his plans. This was the first post-Independent colonial intervention which also affected Nehru's vision of development. Bhagwati and Desai (1970) observed that owing to the compelling circumstances of the 1950s and '60s, interventionist policies became a part of government's planning by the late 1960s. Though general controls on all imports and exports had been presented since 1940, import controls were relaxed through the expansion of the Open General Licensing (OGL) list in a stop-go fashion after Independence. But a foreign exchange crisis in 1956-57 put an end to this phase of liberalization and comprehensive import controls were restored and maintained until 1966. In June that year, under pressure from the World Bank, India devalued the rupee from 4.7 rupees to 7.5 rupees per dollar. The 57.5 per cent devaluation was accompanied by some liberalization of import licensing and cuts in import tariffs and export subsidies for approximately a year. But by 1968, intense domestic reaction to the devaluation led India to turn inward with a vengeance. Almost all liberalizing initiatives were reversed, and import controls tightened. This regime was consolidated and strengthened in subsequent years and remained more or less intact until the beginning of a period of phased liberalization in the late 1970s (Bhagwati and Srinivasan, 1975:153).

## Post-Nehru Western Intrusions in the Indian Economy and Crumbling of the Socialist Edifice

The post-Nehru economic scenario was not much different from before. Concerted efforts by Western capitalist forces continued to exert pressure and find a way to intervene in India's economic growth. India under the leadership of Mrs. Indira Gandhi stoutly resisted the western covert intrusions by not only resolving to continue with the Nehruvian socialist legacy, but also by crafting a new set of socio-economic policies to counter the growing western hegemony in India. This included the abolition of the British-era climb (feudal ownership of land) system, abrogating the fundamental right to property, scrapping the system of privy purses for the erstwhile princely class, nationalization of 14 major banks, initiation of land and agrarian reforms and rendering them unchallengeable by pushing them into the newly-created 9th Schedule to the Constitution of India, the enactments of MRTP (1969), Indian Patent Act (1970) and FERA (1973) Acts. Despite these social welfare enactments, certain domestic and international events greatly affected the course of India's development journey. Domestically, the declaration of emergency by Mrs. Gandhi in 1975 followed by widespread arrest and imprisonment of the politicians and social activists and the untold repression leashed by government on the masses to stifle the rising descent and opposition to the government greatly undid the government's efforts on the socio-economic front.

Coupled with this, the second and the third international oil crisis that erupted in 1973 and 1979 respectively due to the Arab oil embargo and other allied factors severely affected India as other countries. Contrary to India's expectations of receiving a favourable treatment from the Arabs due to the former's close friendly relations with the Arab states, the OPEC expressed its inability to grant concessions and to adopt a dual pricing system for India. Resultantly, India's oil import bill increased from Rs. 204 crore in 1972-73, to Rs. 560 crore in 1973-74, and further to Rs. 1157 crore in 1974-75. Apart from this the country had to resort to the import of fertilizers and foodgrains during the same period, which further aggravated the import bill.

This was around 40 per cent of its potential export earnings, and twice the amount of its existing foreign exchange reserves. The heavy drain of foreign reserves left India quite vulnerable leading to macro-economic instability (Sheriff 1998). The crisis left India extremely vulnerable and left numerous problems on the macro-economic, inflation and balance of payments fronts between 1973 and 1975 (Joshi 1964:105).

The government approached the IMF for the loan that was readily provided but with conditions. The oil crisis of 1973 and 1979 thus came in handy for the international financial institutions that compelled India to water down its socialistic policies and move towards a market economy. These events also gradually initiated the process of the crumbling of the socialist edifice in India. India's economy remained vulnerable throughout the 1970's and '80s although with short bouts of growth and recovery. Added to these developments, were the government's internal socialistic policies which though appearing attractive, were in fact marred by "extensive regulation, protectionism, public ownership of large monopolies, pervasive corruption and slow growth" (*Economic Survey of India*, 2007). The much-despised License-Permit-Quota Raj was a natural by-product of this inward-looking, state-driven system that gave little incentive to private entrepreneurship. With this system, India's share of global trade fell from 2.2 per cent in 1947 to 0.45 per cent by 1985 "but socialists viewed this as a success of self-sufficiency rather than a disastrous loss of the gains of trade, (Aiyar, 2008). Quoting statistics on economic growth and development during the years of socialism in India, Aiyar, the noted economist, observes that it is difficult to "estimate the number of "missing children," "missing literates," and "missing non-poor" resulting from delayed reform, slower economic growth, and hence, slower improvement of social indicators" (*ibid.*). Critics argue that "even this (socialist) system could have delivered more had it been better implemented. It did not have to degenerate into a 'license-permit-quota raj'" (Das 2006).

Arvind Pangarhiya, the noted Columbia-based Indian Economist, sums up the pre-1990 growth trajectory in India, saying: "the growth spurt prior to 1991 was fragile and volatile. There was a jump in the growth rate during 1977-79, massive decline in 1979-80, a jump again in 1980-82, return to the Hindu rate during 1982-88 except 1983-84, climb up again in 1988-91 and crisis in 1991-92. This volatility in the growth pattern itself raises doubts about the sustainability of a 5 per cent plus growth rate over long haul. The 1991 crisis only confirmed the fundamental weakness of the underlying forces ex-post" (Panagariya, 2004).

Shashi Tharoor, a noted think-tank of the Congress party, however, rebuffs these arguments and holds that it was the post-Independent India's socialistic policies that laid a formidable foundation of India's modern-day economic growth and development. Notwithstanding the election results, "most Indians' lives and living standards have improved in the last ten years. This was not because of doles.... but because of more generous and effective government.... the social investment carried out by Congress Governments that put more children in school and more people to work, while ensuring that their basic needs were met" (Tharoor, 2014).

### The Dawn of Globalization and India's Reluctant Entry

The third oil crisis that started unfolding with the beginning of the '80s culminated in the extreme BOP crisis by the end of the decade. The sagging Indian economy was manifested by the devaluation of the rupee, the depleting foreign exchange reserves, the slump in the trade and commerce industry, the rising inflation, and the overall worsening of India's monetary and fiscal scenario. The fear of debt trap grew, economic growth came to a halt and development no more remained on government's radar. Compelled by the circumstances, India approached the IMF for a loan to tide over the extreme crisis. The IMF obliged but not without imposing the "Structural Adjustment Programmes" (SAPs) on a reluctant India. The SAPs included policies such as, giving way to free-trade, free-market, open competition, lowering of trade and tax barriers, removal of subsidies, environmental and labour reforms, holiday concessions, reducing government expenditure on social sectors, shrinkage of governmental role, de-regulation and de-bureaucratization, amongst others.

Thus, the adoption of the IMF's SAP led to the inauguration of a new era of liberalization, globalization and privatization (LPG) in India which saw farm subsidies, public planning, protection to native industries and state expenditure on social sectors and vulnerable classes getting greatly reduced. The economic reforms brought under the leadership of then Finance Minister Manmohan Singh and P.V. Narasimha Rao succeeded in eliminating much of government controls and regulation. Economic reforms opened gateways to private sector firms and MNCs to work and invest in India. Foreign Direct Investments (FDIs) and Foreign Institutional Investments (FIIs) were encouraged. Foreign Direct Investments (FDIs) largely came in consumer durable areas and not in social and infrastructure sectors where it was required most. Nevertheless, the IMF policies enabled India to achieve a relatively higher growth in GDP something which was hovering around a meagre 3-4 per cent with an annual growth of around 5 per cent by 1990.

These reforms have been commended by many scholars and even hailed as "India's second Independence" that saw immense growth potential in the new policies. As one of them writes: "...in July 1991... with the announcement of sweeping liberalization by the minority government of P.V. Narasimha Rao... opened the economy... dismantled import controls, lowered customs duties, and devalued the currency... virtually abolished licensing controls on private investment, dropped tax rates, and broke public sector monopolies.... [W]e felt as though our second independence had arrived: we were going to be free from a rapacious and domineering state..." (Das 2000).

Working in tandem with the new circumstances, the Government formulated a New Trade Policy (2004-09) that gave a fillip to export promotion, import liberalization and integration of the trade with the economic development of the country. Pragmatism became the watchword of the new trade policy, identifying the thrust areas which had the potential for generating employment in urban and semi-urban areas. These areas were agriculture, handicrafts, handlooms, gems and jewellery, and leather and footwear.

Supporting the government's reform policies of 1991, Arvind Pangariya, counters the arguments of economists such as Desai, (1999), Pursell (1992) and Virmani (1997) who argue that it were the government's liberalization policies of the '80s that led to an increase in the growth during this decade and that the continued growth in the '90s is an outcome of those liberal policies. Virmani terms the liberalization during the 1980s and 1990s as "sub-phases" of an overall phase. He attributes the shift in the growth rate in the 1980s virtually entirely to liberalization. These scholars assert that liberalization in trade and industry of the '80s has yielded the desired dividends in the '90s as well and the credit for the renewed growth in the '90s could not be given exclusively to the reform policies of 1991. Refuting these arguments, Pangariya asserts that the liberalization in the 1980s laid down the groundwork that helped carry out systemic and systematic reforms in the 1990s. He argues that growth during the 1990s has been more robust and far less volatile. Following the June 1991 crisis, he observes, the annual growth rate quickly picked up and reached the 5.1 per cent mark in 1992-93 and never fell below 4.4 per cent subsequently. The five-year averages of growth rates during 1992-93 to 2001-02 have ranged from 5.5 to 6.7 per cent. This compares with the five-year averages of growth rates ranging from 4.8 to 6.2 per cent during 1981-91 and 3.3 to 6.2 per cent during 1977-91 (Panagariya, 2004).

## Reaping the Dividends of Globalization

Since, the economic liberalization of 1991, India's GDP has been growing at a higher rate. The following table depicts the growing this reality:

**Table 11.1 : GDP Growth in 2000-2012**

| *Year* | *Growth (Real) (%)* |
|---|---|
| 2000 | 5.6 |
| 2001 | 6.0 |
| 2002 | 4.3 |
| 2003 | 8.3 |
| 2004 | 6.2 |
| 2005 | 8.4 |
| 2006 | 9.2 |
| 2007 | 9.0 |
| 2008 | 7.4 |
| 2009 | 7.4 |
| 2010 | 10.4 |
| 2011 | 7.2 |
| 2012 | 6.5 |

*Source*: Economic Survey, 2011-2012.

The economic reforms adopted by India heralded rich gains in the form of direct and indirect investments in different sectors leading to enhanced employment and income of the people. The reforms have placed industry, trade and commerce and export promotion activities at the centre of the economic revival of the country. All sectors of economy have significantly grown but "the service sector has emerged as the fastest growing sectors in India with annual growth rate of above 9 per cent since 2001, which contributed to 57 per cent of

GDP in 2012-13" (Bhargava 2015). The country has also become a major exporter of IT and IT-enabled services, Business Process Outsourcing (BPOs) services, and software services with $167.0 billion worth of service exports in 2013-14. It is also the fastest-growing part of the economy (*Indian Economy*, 2015). It also happens to be the largest private sector employer in India (NASSCOM, 2015).

Agriculture contributes 17 per cent (2013-14) to the country's GDP although this share is declining now (*Economic Times*, 2013). The industry is another significant sector that contributes nearly one-fourth to GDP and generates employment for almost one-fifth of the total workforce (*Indian Economy*, 2015). Data further informs that the Indian auto industry is one of the largest in the world with an annual production of 21.48 million vehicles in FYP 2013-14. Besides, India has $600 billion worth of retail market in 2015 and is one of the world's fastest growing E-Commerce markets (Retail Industry, 2015).

Scholars hold that the path of growth and development has been aided by "six major drivers of the Indian economy: market size, size of the working population, knowledge and ability, financial structure, availability of information, and open competition." First, India's market size and its purchasing power has increased along with the rapidly growing middle class, from just 25 million in 1996 to more than 160 million in 2014, and which by the end of 2015, is expected to go up to 267 million (Varma, 2013). This is more than the size of the middle class of EU or USA. The second driver of the Indian economy is the size of the working population. In the next 25 years, the young population of India is slated to increase which will contribute to the productivity of the economy. This is revealed by the 2026 Census Projection report according to which the percentage of people in the age group of 15-59 (the working age) is likely to increase from 57.7 per cent of the total population in 2001 to 61 per cent in 2006 to 64.3 per cent in 2026 (Sikri, 2006). Similarly, knowledge, entrepreneurial capability and confidence of the leadership of the working population have added to the strength of the Indian economy. A sound financial structure constitutes the fourth driver of the economy. The country is gradually moving towards financial maturity and stability and this is reflected by Reserve Bank of India's (RBI) figures which say that India's total foreign exchange reserves stood at US$ 353.46 billion for the week ended July 31, 2015. This includes Foreign Currency Assets (FCAs) worth US$ 329.87 billion and gold reserves amounting to US$ 18.25 billion (*Times of India*, 2015).

India's external economic profile, as per RBI data has considerably improved as short-term debt to total external debt ratio fell to 17.8 per cent in 2014-15, the lowest in eight years. This could give boost to the Central Bank and the government in a volatile external financial situation. In 2013-14, the ratio stood at 20.5 per cent. Besides, figures of the Comptroller & Auditor General of Accounts show that the government is keeping the deficit under control. The fiscal deficit in the first two months (April-May) of the fiscal year 2015-16 stood at 37.5 per cent compared with 45.3 per cent during the same period last year. Revenue deficit was 43.8 per cent of the budgeted Rs. 3.9 trillion against 54.2 per cent during the same period last year. Concerning infrastructure building and capital expenditure, the government spending has stood at 13.6 per cent of the budgeted amount against 11.4 per cent spent during the same period a year ago (Mishra, 2015).

The growing awareness of the consumer and availability of information is India's strength of the economy. This is exhibited by the enactments of the Right to Information Act (RTI), 2005, Consumer Forums, increased consumer and human rights litigations and greater use of information and communication technology (ICT). Open competition and greater transparency in recruitments, public dealings, and businesses have further given strength to India's growth process.

Besides the above factors, economic success has also been attributed to its primary reliance on its domestic market, focus on consumption rather than investment, on services more than on industry, and on high-tech rather than low-skilled manufacturing (Das, 2006). It has been pointed out that India's growth is mainly due to increase in domestic productivity and consumption. Consumption accounts for 64 per cent of India's GDP, as opposed to 58 per cent for Europe, 55 per cent for Japan, and 42 per cent for China. This model, he maintains, has resulted in better insulation of the economy from global fluctuations, and less increase in inequality among its people (measured by Gini index on a scale of 0 to 100, putting India at 33 (with China at 45, USA at 41 and Brazil at 59). Moreover, 30-50 per cent of the GDP growth is due to rising productivity rather than increase in the amount of capital or labour, making the economy less susceptible to the fluctuations in foreign investment (*Ibid.*).

The post-liberalization era has also seen a rise in the fortunes of Indian companies. According to statistics released by Forbes 'Global 2000' list for the year 2014, there are 54 Indian companies in Forbes' annual list of the world's 2000 largest and most powerful public companies. Reliance Industries is ranked 135 on the list with a market value of 50.9 billion dollars in sales as on May 2014. Reliance is followed by State Bank of India which is ranked 155 and has a 23.6 billion dollars market value (*Ibid.,* 2014).

India's impressive economy growth in the post-1990 period following economic reforms have brought in rich tributes by various financial dailies asserting that they have led to "increased foreign competition, privatization of certain public sector industries, opened up sectors hitherto reserved for the public sector and led to an expansion in the production of fast-moving consumer goods" (*The Economist*, 2003); "private sector as increasingly coming of age, showing maturity, handling the change by squeezing costs, revamping management, focusing on designing new products and relying on low labour costs and technology" (*The Economist*, 2004).

Paying rich tributes to India's journey on the path of development since Independence, the World Bank observed: "With 1.2 billion people and the world's fourth-largest economy, India's recent growth and development has been one of the most significant achievements of our times. Over the six and half decades since Independence, the country has brought about a landmark agricultural revolution that has transformed the nation from chronic dependence on grain imports into a global agricultural powerhouse that is now a net exporter of food. Life expectancy has more than doubled, literacy rates have quadrupled, and health conditions have improved. India will soon have the largest and youngest workforce the world has ever seen" (World Bank, 2014).

Summing up, the debate on India's impressive growth since inception of liberalization policies in India in 1980s, Das observes that after three post-Independence decades of meagre progress, the country's economy grew at 6 per cent a year from 1980 to 2002 and at 7.5 per cent a year from 2002 to 2006—making it one of the world's best-performing economies for a quarter century. In the past two decades, the size of the middle class has quadrupled (to almost 250 million people), and 1 per cent of the countries poor have crossed the poverty line every year. At the same time, population growth has slowed from the historic rate of 2.2 per cent a year to 1.7 per cent today—meaning that growth has brought large per capita income gains, from $1,178 to $3,051 (in terms of purchasing-power parity) since 1980. India is now the world's fourth-largest economy. Soon it will surpass Japan to become the third-largest (Das, 2006).

**Economic Growth Sans Inclusivity?**

Post-1991 success stories of a globalized India have been in abundance. Scholars have declared this period as "a triumph of economic reforms over India's darkest economic decades" (Das, 2006). While globalization undoubtedly gave a fillip to economic growth, social and economic developments have not been commensurate. Economic reforms with emphasis on FDI, MNCs, IMF, World Bank and WTO-propelled policies of SAPs have benefited the rich, educated, skilled, trained and middle-class urban-based population. The phenomenal growth in the service sector, and to some extent in the manufacturing sector, largely came at the cost of the agricultural sector.

Scholars have praised both the progress and the poverty arising out of economic reforms. They assert that "there has been a revolution in India's economic development. Economic reforms widened the arena of the private sector.... high growth was accompanied by striking rise in income inequalities and exclusion of rural and urban poor from the growth process. Growth was constantly under pressure to comply with the expectations of international investors and frequent financial crisis have consumed more attention than efforts to ameliorate human poverty. Growth has failed to make a dent in areas of poverty, literacy, public health, sanitation, etc." (Raju, Murty and Singala, 2015:315). Not denying the progress taken place in core social sectors since the turn of the present century, scholars have, however, held that growth has been tardy and uneven, and that there is a disconnect between India's economic growth and socio-economic development.

Grim statistical figures revealed that deep divide and fault lines in terms of human and regional developments had come to stay notwithstanding the rapid economic growth of the last two decades. The unorganized, unskilled and untrained workers involved in unorganized and informal sectors have been at the receiving end. Women, children, *Dalits*, tribals and minorities who collectively constitute a major chunk of the vulnerable population have largely remained outside the domain of economic gains. If the increased GDP brought about a "Shining India", then it also created a "Suffering India" where the weak and the marginalized people had no place in India's impressive growth story. Large swathes of the population remained outside and untouched of the fruits of economic reforms in India. The following are the major areas of concern that deserve special mention:

## Lack of Basic Amenities

### *Poverty and Hunger*

In the post-reform period, several social and economic problems have continued to persist despite impressive progress made on the economic front. This is demonstrated by the fact that out of the world's 872.3 million people below the new poverty line, 179.6 million people lived in India. In other words, India with 17.5 per cent of total world's population had 20.6 per cent share of world's poorest in 2013 (World Bank, 2015). Likewise, a look at the statistics on hunger reveals a tell-tale story of the development saga in the post-economic reforms period. According to the Global Hunger Index-2011, India stands at 67th rank among the 80 nations having the worst hunger situation that is worse than nations such as North Korea or Sudan. 25 per cent of all hungry people worldwide live in India. The report states that though there have been some improvements since 1990 for children, but the proportion of hungry in the population has increased. Data says that 72 per cent of infants and 52 per cent of married women in India have anaemia, while 44 per cent of children under the age of 5 are underweight (Varma, 2013).

### *Malnourishment*

Similarly, health issues, primarily over the last decades, have become a serious cause of concern among scholars on development studies. According to a 2005 report, 60 per cent of India's children below the age of three were malnourished, which was greater than the statistics of the sub-Saharan African region of 28 per cent. One in every three malnourished children in the world lives in India. The estimates vary within the country. It is estimated that Madhya Pradesh is having the highest rate of 50 per cent and Kerala the lowest with 27 per cent

(Reiff, 2009). Although India's economy grew 55 per cent from 2001-2006, its child-malnutrition rate only dropped 1 per cent, lagging behind countries of similar growth rate (Robinson, 2008).

The situation is especially worrisome in rural India where over 68 per cent of India's total population, half of which lives below the poverty line and always struggle for better and easy access to health care and services (Census of India, 2011). Statistics reveals that rural people confront many kinds of health problems such as malaria, diabetes, cancer and quite often, these are very serious in nature leading to death. Similarly, maternal postpartum illness is quite common among poor rural women which again results in increased maternal mortality (Sutherland and Bishai, 2008). However, according to a study titled: "*Rapid Survey on Children (RSOC)*" conducted by the UN agency for children, UNICEF, and Government of India, there have been encouraging signs as the proportion of underweight children has fallen from 42.5 per cent a decade ago, to just under 30 per cent now. Similar improvements have been noticed in the incidence of malnutrition (*The Economist*, 2015).

### *Infant and Maternal Mortality Rates*

Also, there is a problem of high infant mortality rate despite health improvements during the last thirty years as a result of economic growth. More than two million children die every year from preventable infections. Casualties to early childhood diseases, inadequate newborn care, and childbirth-related causes have been occurring. Approximately 1.72 million children die each year before turning one. The under-five mortality and infant mortality rates have been declining, from 202 and 190 deaths per thousand live births respectively in 1970 to 64 and 50 deaths per thousand live births in 2009. Likewise, Maternal Mortality Rate is high. Only 15 per cent of mothers receive complete antenatal care, and only 58 per cent receive iron or folate tablets or syrup (Sharma, 2008). Economic growth has not contributed to infrastructure development like hospitals, roads, water and sanitation which are lacking in rural areas. Shortages of healthcare providers, poor intrapartum and newborn care, diarrheal diseases, and acute respiratory infections also contribute to the high infant mortality rate (Ramadoss, 2008).

Economic reforms may have brought prosperity in industrial, technological and the entrepreneurial sectors, the unprivileged classes having no access to basic amenities of having remained deprived of the fruits of economic growth. Several basic socio-economic issues which could have been solved by improved economic growth are still waiting for credible state action. India's rank of 102nd among the 132 countries on the Social Progress Index 2014 is a manifestation of this reality. Compiled by a US-non-profit group Social Progress Imperative, this index measures human well-being going beyond traditional economic measures, like per capita income or GDP. According to the Index, among the BRICS countries, only India ranked lower than the 100th position on the list of the Social Progress Index 2014 (*Indian Express*, 2014).

### *Open Defecation*

The practice of defecating in the open, particularly in rural India, in the absence of toilet or latrine at homes, has further compounded the health problem of the under-privileged classes. According to a World Bank report released on the eve of the first-ever U.N. "World Toilet Day" on November 19, 2013, over 600 million people in India or 53 per cent of Indian households (over 50% of the population) defecating in the open in the absence of toilet or latrine. It says that more than 2.5 billion people worldwide lack access to toilets, one billion people practice open defecation and 600 million in India openly defecate. Cautioning on the dangers of open defecation, the World Bank said that "open defecation lies at the root of many development challenges, as poor sanitation and lack of access to toilets impact public health, education, and the environment," said Jaehyang So, Manager of the World Bank's Water and Sanitation Project (*Hindustan Times*, 2013).

### *Literacy*

Problems abound on the literacy front too despite the growth in literacy rate from 52.2 per cent in 1991 to 74.04 per cent in 2011. However, this is still lower than the worldwide average, and the country suffers from a high dropout rate (*The Economist*, 2008). Scholars like Amartya Sen and Jean Dreze have pointed out that there are serious problems related to other aspects of education such as the quality, enrollment, and the infrastructure. Besides, literacy rates and educational opportunities vary by region, gender, urban and rural areas, and among different social groups (Dreze and Sen, 1996:960).

### *Environment*

The destructive aspects of the current economic growth have also severely impacted the environment. This is demonstrated by the ever-increasing pressure of corporate sector on forests and rich agricultural lands. The rampant urbanization and industrialization process, and the ever increasing rate of concrete jungles coming up in the form of SEZs, EEZs, food parks, multiplexes, industrial corridors, housing schemes, dams etc. at the expense of the environment is a tell-tale story of the current economic reform driven by the imperatives of globalization. India's corporate-driven development process has taken a toll on the environment which is demonstrated by the rising global warming, Greenhouse Gases and Ozone depletion. The ever-increasing environmental pollution—water, air and noise—due to increased industrial activity and automobile emission is taking a huge toll on people's health and livelihood. The increased instances of earthquakes, Tsunami, cyclones, landslides, etc. are the manifestation of unbridled economic activity at the cost of environment. Scholars hence hold that "degradation of the environment is the direct outcome of the process of capitalist development. Forests, in the ongoing development programmes, are considered just for consumption or for mining. Consequently, in the scheme of economic growth, the forest as a resource does not exist. The current development model does not consider the need to strengthen the relationship between natural capital and economic growth resulting in an acute livelihood crisis for the vast majority depending on these resources for survival (Das, 2011).

### *Land Acquisition*

Another aspect of corporate globalizationled economic growth is the issue of land acquisition. Under the pressure of MNCs and corporate/business houses, violent methods have been adopted to acquire the rich agricultural lands of farmers and evict the latter from their lands. Land acquisition purportedly being done for industrial and infrastructural projects has resulted in the head-on collision between the farmers and the state. In the process, farmers, peasants and tillers have been pushed off their lands and out of agriculture. Land acquisition under faulty schemes and unaccompanied by proper compensation and relief and rehabilitation policies have led to massive unrest and violent protest. As a result, there have been violent struggles against land acquisition in Singur, Nandigram, Haryana, Orissa, Andhra Pradesh, Madhya Pradesh and Uttar Pradesh. The Mahamumbai SEZ project of the Reliance Ltd. Company in Raigad district of Maharashtra was forced to shut down due to massive protest. The Nandigram and Singur police firing that resulted in the killings of several people in West Bengal in 2007 is still very much alive in the minds of the people. A study reveals that one of the driving factors behind resentment is that land far in excess of needs has been taken over. According to the report, about 53,000 hectares of land acquired for SEZs several years ago are still lying vacant. About a quarter of India's districts is witnessing mass protests over land acquisition issues. The study identified 252 land conflicts spread over 165 districts, spanning practically all states, in 2013-14. This is an increase of over 40 per cent over 2012 (Varma, 2015).

**The Plight of the Vulnerable Groups**

In the name of economic development, farmers, workers and tribals have been pushed out of their habitat and livelihood. A consistent pattern of violation of the basic entitlements of vulnerable groups in rural and tribal India has been witnessed ever since the introduction of economic reforms in India, particularly after the year 2000. Development-induced displacements (DIDs) and Project-induced Migration (PIM) have become the order of the day due to the increased mining, irrigation, housing and industrial projects in the rural and tribal areas. This has resulted in massive displacement and migration, especially of poor tribals. The scenario is particularly troublesome with regard to the mineral-rich states of Orissa, Jharkhand, Chhattisgarh and Madhya Pradesh where as a result of extensive mining activities carried out by MNCs, the condition of the tribals has gone from bad to worst. They have been rendered beggars and are leading pathetic and wretched lives in slums all across the country (Mohapatra, 2012).

Legislations, such as Forest Rights Act, Panchayat Extension Scheduled Areas (PESA) and the like for safeguarding the rights and livelihood of forest dwellers have been circumvented and distorted to seize the tribal lands. According to the Ministry of Tribal Affairs (MTA) nearly 85 lakh tribals were displaced (55% of the total displaced persons) up to 1990 on account of mega developmental projects like dams, mining, industries and conservation of forests etc. Lakhs of tribals have additionally been displaced since mid-1990 without proper rehabilitation (Tribal People in India, 2012). Further, no sincere attempts have been made for their proper rehabilitation and integration into the modern development processes (Meher, 2009:25,457). They have been left out of the compensation calculations because their land rights are not recognized. Also, their use of common forests is not given any value (Varma, 2015).

Farmers' suicide starting from the later part of the '90s and now several lakhs in number is another aspect of the destructive side of the globalization policies in the agricultural sphere. It is estimated that from 1995 to 2013, a total of 296,438 Indian farmers committed suicide (Sainath, 2014). Farmers' suicide rate in India has ranged to 1.4 to 1.8 per 100,000 total population, over a 10-year period through 2005 (Gruere, G. and Sengupta, 2011:316-337). Scholars like Prabhat Patnaik and Jayati Ghosh have attributed farmer's suicide to the structural changes in the macro-economic policy of the Indian Government that favoured privatization, liberalization and globalization (Patnaik, 2010). Vandana Shiva, the noted environmentalist and social activist, notes that "rapid increase in indebtedness has been at the root of farmers taking their lives... Debt is a reflection of a negative economy, a loosing economy." She observes that "the policies of trade liberalization and corporate globalization have set off a widening spiral of debt and despair initiating the process of farmers' suicide since 1997" (Shiva, 2008).

Problems abound in all areas of human development in spite of impressive economic growth. Reflecting on the scenario, Jean Dreze and Amartya Sen, thus observed "indeed, even today, after 20 years of rapid growth, India is still one of the poorest countries in the world, something that is often lost sight of, especially by those who enjoy world-class living standards thanks to the inequalities in the income distribution. According to World Development Indicators 2011, only 16 countries outside Africa had a lower "gross national income per capita" than India in 2010: Afghanistan, Bangladesh, Cambodia, Haiti, Iraq, Kyrgyzstan, Lao, Moldova, Nepal, Nicaragua, Pakistan, Papua, New Guinea, Tajikistan, Uzbekistan, Vietnam and Yemen. This is not exactly a club of economic superpowers" (Dreze and Sen, 2011).

**Inclusive Growth in India's Planning Process**

The growing exclusivity of the marginalized sections from India's rapid economic growth was acknowledged by the Planning Commission in the approach paper on the Eleventh Five Year Plan which was titled: "Towards faster and more inclusive growth". The approach chapter observed:

> ".... that economic growth has failed to be sufficiently inclusive, particularly after the mid-1990s. Agriculture lost its growth momentum from that point on and subsequently entered a near crisis situation. Jobs in the organised sector have not increased despite faster growth. The percentage of our population below the poverty line is declining but only at a modest pace. Malnutrition levels also appear to be declining, but the magnitude of the problem continues to be very high. Far too many people still lack access to basic services such as health, education, clean drinking water and sanitation facilities without which they cannot claim their share in the benefits of growth. Women have increased their participation in the labour force as individuals, but continue to face discrimination and are subject to increasing violence, one stark example of which is the declining child sex ratio." It further states that "the Eleventh FY Plan provides an opportunity to restructure policies to achieve a new vision based on faster, more broad-based and inclusive growth. It is designed to reduce poverty and focus on bridging the various divides that continue to fragment our society."

The approach chapter observed that rapid economic growth would remain meaningless if unaccompanied by a corresponding upliftment of the poor and weaker sections. However, it is to noted that an earlier version of the inclusive growth model, themed "Growth with Social Justice and Equality" was adopted in the Ninth plan along with the target of high economic growth. But the Eleventh Plan formally introduced the agenda of faster and more inclusive growth necessitated by the development-induced displacements. The Eleventh FY Plan acknowledged that high economic growth had taken place, but had failed to achieve inclusive growth and social justice for the poor and the deprived people. The Plan, therefore called for "improving the condition of the vulnerable sections, reducing poverty and inequality by adopting more broad-based policies and judging these policies by their performance and target achievements and not merely by sectoral outlays as had been happening before." The plan emphasized the need for the continuing rapid economic growth as that was essential for increasing the incomes of the people and uplifting the people out of poverty.

Realising that the private sector could contribute substantially to faster and inclusive growth, the plan called for strengthening the private sector. It also emphasized the need to remove restrictive policies, introduce reforms for greater private participation and the role of the markets, and provide incentives to the entrepreneurs, especially the Micro, Small and Medium Enterprises (MMEs) (Panning Commission, 11th FYP).

The Twelfth FY Plan (2012-17), came in the backdrop of the slowdown in the global economy as a result of the Eurozone crisis and other allied factors. The crisis affected the entire world including India, which saw the latter's annual growth rate dropping to 6.2 per cent in 2011-12 and this continued till the first year of the twelfth plan. The Plan lays great emphasis on reviving the economy and investors' sentiment together with a strong emphasis on inclusive growth. The agenda of rapid economic growth and inclusiveness of the Eleventh Plan has been carried forward with the subtitle: "Faster, Sustainable and More Inclusive Growth". Inclusiveness is sought to be achieved through poverty reduction, mainstreaming the marginalized sections, minimizing the gender disparity and regional disparity and income disparity among people. For sustainable growth, an all round human development in which literacy, educational, health, nutrition, and living standards of the deprived people are taken care of together with a sustained focus on improving and strengthening infrastructure, such as, power, transport, telecommunications, etc. Highlighting the statistics, the Plan accepts that inclusive growth has been taken place in the last few years as in the Eleventh Plan as poverty has declined, agriculture growth improved, and per capita consumption in rural areas has grown over the years since 2004-05 at the rate of 6.6 per cent per year as against a mere 1.1 per cent per year in the preceding ten years. However, people's expectations and needs have also grown in proportion to the economic growth and hence, to measure the progress in the inclusiveness of growth, the

Plan lays down 25 monitorable indicators that include the GDP, poverty and unemployment, education, healthcare, infrastructure including rural infrastructure, environment and service delivery (Planning Commission, Twelfth FYP).

## Strategies for Inclusive Growth

The issue of inclusive growth refers mainly to the inclusion of the disadvantaged groups in the development process, reducing poverty and creating employment opportunities for the poor classes. Inclusive growth implies that the fruits of rapid economic growth must reach the marginalized and the vulnerable sections. Today, economic growth, unlike the past, has come to mean that growth should not be measured simply in terms of increase in GDP but must include the social and human development of people. Pro-poor growth would be genuine only if it is equitable, i.e., the accruing wealth should be disper sed as widely as possible so as to reach the last and the least developed person of the society. As India is a country where still a huge majority of the population resides in the rural areas, and this rural population is mostly and massively poverty-stricken and steeped in illiteracy, ignorance and backwardness, it is here that economic reforms must bring in rapid economic growth which is equitable, harmonious and inclusive. Peeved at the reports of a survey that revealed that 42 per cent of the nation's children are underweight, former Prime Minister Manmohan Singh termed it as a "national shame" (Dhar, 2012). Expressing the need for revamping the whole system, he called for strengthening four most important things for ushering in inclusive growth: rural education, rural employment, rural infrastructure and a sharp increase in rural investment (Planning Commission, 2006).

To implement the goals of inclusive growth and usher in a genuinely inclusive democracy, changes have to be initiated at the policy the micro and macro levels. Planning has to be devised not solely in terms of achieving more GDP growth but also improving the physical quality index of people's lives, and this includes basic minimum wants that concerns the everyday lives of the people. The basic problems arising out of the current economic policies should be tackled along with the traditional issues that have worked at cross-purposes with demands of inclusive growth in India. However, both—past and present issues must be taken together in dealing with problems of strategies of balanced economic and social growth. Many factors go into the making of a balanced socio-economic growth, and they all collectively need urgent attention and action of policy planner and decision makers.

(a) Eliminating extreme poverty, disease, hunger and squalor.
(b) Raising public expenditure on health and nutrition.
(c) Increased investment in education, training and development of skills.
(d) Social Justice, gender equity and empowerment of weaker sections.
(e) Access to essential services and improving public delivery services.
(f) Participatory Governance and responsive administration.
(g) Introducing agriculture reforms including land reforms.
(h) Addressing Infrastructural issues- rural and urban.
(j) Generating new sources of energy with special focus on renewable energy and alternative sources of energy.
(j) Eco-friendly and sustainable environmental development and conserving natural resources.
(k) Generating employment with special focus on labour-intensive sectors.
(l) Controlling the inflation and stabilizing the price system.
(m) Combating Corruption and controlling black money.

The role of the state in minimizing extreme poverty, misery, disease and hunger is one of the most critical requirements of a balanced growth. No democracy can be successful if a large segment of its population is underfed, malnourished or starved. It is unfortunate that still a vast majority of India's population is under the scourge of these evils. Deaths occurring on account of repeated droughts in various parts of the country or crop failure leading to hunger deaths and farmers' suicide in Maharashtra, Andhra Pradesh, Telangana, Orissa and other states has led to the demeaning of inclusive growth. According to a New Delhi-based report of Centre for Equity Studies, Bihar, Jharkhand and Madhya Pradesh account for the three hungriest states of India. The people of these states suffer from the worst kind of problems that one can think of. In a book titled: "Starvation and India's Democracy", the author Dan Banik observes that the policy makers, bureaucracy and public representatives do not wish to be held accountable for high-levels of malnutrition, and even hunger deaths on the ground that a developing country has to pass through these pangs before it achieves stability and self-reliance (Banik, 2007:246).

However, the tenth, eleventh and the current twelfth plans have started giving more attention to these problems on an urgent basis. The Centre has committed to putting in more resources and efforts to deal with these crucial problems. Apart from overcoming these critical challenges, increased efforts are needed to address the health, housing, nutrition and living standard of people. The affirmative action of the governments can undo the deprivation suffered by the people.

Inclusive and equitable growth is incumbent on a vibrant educational sector that provides quality education and offers cutting-edge research opportunities. Unfortunately, the entire educational sector abounds with shortcomings, with all three sectors—primary, secondary and tertiary—performing poorly. Quality education is fundamental to the growth of the economy and the society. The poor quality of education makes our student unworthy of the job market and renders them unemployable. Great efforts are needed to reform the educational sector so as to build the productivity and capacity of the students. There is a need to ensure the continued supply of skilled manpower for the industrial and technological growth of the nation. Inexpensive and skilled manpower is the need of the hour and this can be fulfilled only quality education but also through a sustained process of training and skill development programmes which is ready to be absorbed in the manufacturing and service sectors of the economy. At the same time, it is to be ensured that the surplus population working in the agricultural sector needs to be diverted and absorbed in non-agricultural pursuits, and the nation's economy has to create this additional space for them. It is here that the role of education and skill development becomes a critical factor in ensuring a smooth passage for the surplus population engaged in rural and agricultural sectors which are quite slow growing, less productive and less employment oriented. Thus, more government investment and support is needed in the sphere of public education. If this could be done, the 'demographic dividend' which India is passing through can be of great significance for the nation's rise to eminence and equitable growth.

Inclusive growth demands humane treatment of the weaker and marginalized sections. However, this has not happened as the post-reform measures have led to 'iniquitous growth', 'growth without employment', 'growth without job' or jobless growth and 'growth without a humane face'. The negative effects of globalization have played out and brought miseries to the vulnerable populace. Questions have been raised as to what is the cost of this economic growth? Who are the beneficiaries of this growth? Do the marginalized and uprooted people have any place in this growth process and growth model? Thus, ensuring 'development with a humane face' or in other words, a social justice-led growth that fulfils the basic requirements of the vulnerable and creates space for their dignified living and progress constitutes an important strategy of inclusive growth.

The incorporation of social justice and gender-equity and empowerment policies is vital to justify rapid economic growth. Unless the marginalized people are involved in the decision-making process, the task of economic growth and society building can never be achieved. But unfortunately, the schemes of social justice, social security, empowerment and participatory development have remained hollow promises. Instead, corporate and business houses have largely influenced government policies and social legislation to their advantage leading to widespread unrest among the masses (Jain, 2015). This kind of developmental model pursued by India over the last few decades has resulted in the increased alienation of the weak and vulnerable masses from the national mainstream giving rise to conflict and violence between the state and the masses. Thus, it is imperative that the powerless and the voiceless get a voice and a share in decision making so fulfilling the basic requirements of social justice and empowerment.

India's another major handicap has been the lack of proper infrastructure in the form of better roads, power, communication and transport facilities. This has adversely affected the public delivery of essential services—food, water, housing, medicine and education—in the rural and remote areas where the country's majority of the poor population resides. The poor delivery mechanism for essential services and the public distribution system has accentuated the poverty in the rural areas and has obstructed the fight of the state against poverty. Thus, infrastructural growth needs urgent attention of the policy makers for it is associated with the access to basic services by the deprived masses. Meaningful progress in this direction would lead to a just and inclusive growth.

A responsive and a sensitized administration wedded to the notions of transparency and commitment to the people's cause is a milestone in building a harmonious and equitable society.

Unfortunately, the lack luster performance of the bureaucracy in implementing public policies has crippled the essence of democracy as essential services are still out of the reach of poor masses. In addition, the administration's role, is also crucial to combating corruption and unearthing black money. Corruption and black money together have undone the meaning of justice to an economically weak person who is not in a position to please the corrupt officials for accessing the basic services of the state. Reports have incessantly poured in disclosing the endemic corruption prevailing in India. A 2005 Transparency International Report states that "more than 62 per cent of Indians had first-hand experience of paying bribes or influence peddling to get jobs done in public offices successfully (Transparency International, 2005). Another report by the same organization for the year 2008 revealed that about 40 per cent of Indians had first-hand experience of paying bribes or using a contact to get a job done in public office (Transparency International, 2008).

Environmental protection also needs immediate attention from the policy-makers as economic growth cannot remain detached from environmental concerns. A safe environment is integral to sustainable economic and inclusive growth. However, India's growth over the last two decades has less than been environment-friendly as natural resources—forests, water, minerals have been indiscriminately exploited. Vast swathes of forests have been cut down to make way for the growing population. The disappearance of forests and green cover has led to the extinction of endangered species and exposed the tribals to hostile conditions, forcing them out of their natural habitat and leading them to begging and living in slums in urban areas. According to a survey conducted by the World Health Organization (WHO), environmental degradation costs India $80 billion per year or 5.7 per cent of its economy. In a survey of 178 countries, India ranked 155th overall and almost last in air pollution exposure. The survey also concluded that India's environmental quality is far below all BRICS countries [China (118), Brazil (77), Russia (73), and South Africa (72)]. Thus, green growth strategies have been recommended for sustainable development as that is "affordable, desirable and measurable" (WHO, 2014).

Inclusive and justifiable growth of agriculture, which employs almost 50 per cent of the country's workforce with a share of almost 17 per cent of GDP, demands widespread reforms. Unless financial and infrastructural reforms are introduced, the goal of poverty reduction cannot be achieved. Financial reforms involve the increased state support in the form of enhanced investments, fair and justifiable Minimum Support Price, crop insurance against crop failures. The infrastructural aspect refers to better irrigation facilities, cold storage facilities, increased availability of electricity and water, better transport system for reaching agriculture produce to urban markets, better agriculture technology, improving soil health, easy availability of chemicals and fertilizers, minimizing dependence on agricultural activities and creating options for non-agricultural activities. Urgent attention is required for improving the basic amenities of the farmers in the form of food, clothing, shelter, health, education and training. Special attention needs to be given to enhancing their education, skills and training enabling to take up employment in organized sectors. Special programme for their skill development should be initiated both in agriculture and non-agriculture activities. An undeveloped, unnourished and illiterate farmer can neither contribute to the agriculture growth nor cater to his personal growth.

Employment generation is indicative of a vibrant economy. A democracy in which youths remained unemployed or under-employed can never become an inclusive and a stable one. The beginning of the liberalization and globalization in India has opened new vistas of employment for the youths despite the global economic crisis of 2007. Data reveals that India is passing through a 'demographic dividend' implying that while the population growth is slowing, the number of young people joining the labour market is expanding. The young demographic profile of India should be harnessed to the maximum so that it contributes to the growth process of the nation. Allied with this is the need to expand the employment avenues both qualitatively and quantitatively so that both the highly qualified, talented and skilled professionals, as well as the unskilled or semi-skilled workers, are able to seek employment in the market. It is to be remembered that over the years, the agriculture share in the GDP is declining, and more agricultural workers or labourers are moving to non-agricultural sectors. Hence, creating sufficient employment for the new entrants—migrating from rural to urban areas and from agricultural to non-agricultural activities should be a key priority to addressing the employment challenge. Key areas of employment generation need to be identified in the services and manufacturing sectors. The contribution of the latter in the economy, which currently stands at around 26 per cent much lesser than the services sector (56%) can be enhanced substantially by identifying labour-intensive industries in small, micro and medium scale industries which have the potential to absorb unskilled or semi-skilled labourers. Special training programmes should be devised for the workers of the targeted groups such as weavers, artisans and craftsmen. This will contribute both to the inclusiveness and rapidity of the growth of the economy. Several training and skill development programmes, as well as, employment generation scheme have been initiated during the Tenth and the ongoing Twelfth FY Plans.

**A Critical Appraisal: Can Growth and Equity Go Together?**

As development debate goes on, a simultaneous debate too goes on whether the neo-liberal policies can bring about growth with equity? Whether growth should be given precedence over redistributive policies or *vice-versa*? Whether the market represented by private actors in the form of business houses and corporate groups can take care of the interest of the deprived masses? Whether the demands of social justice can be met along with the rapid growth of economy? Whether capital would be attracted to non-profitable areas of social development? Whether a retreating state in a globalized world be able to safeguard the rights and interests of vulnerable sections? Scholars are divided over these issues. The noted economists Amartya Sen and Jean Dreze assert "that though economic growth is necessary for ensuring development, it would be a mistake to "sit back" and rely on economic growth *per se* to transform the living conditions of the unprivileged." He cautions against the dangers of "unaimed opulence"—the indiscriminate pursuit of economic expansion, without paying much attention to how it is shared or how it affects people's lives?" (Dreze and Sen 2011). Amartya Sen rejects the "conventional wisdom" of economics that considers development in terms of growth, a growth that believes in maximizing the profits. He says the market economists who consider the purpose of development as guaranteeing growth and who consider this freedom as most important that paves way for other freedoms are mistaken. Calling their demand of growth to be allowed unrestricted as "madness", he observes that this way of considering growth would make "socially useful members of society such as school teachers and health workers feel more threatened by conservative economic policies that do army generals" (Sen 1999:366). Sen regards that the welfare of human beings should occupy the centre-stage and developing their capabilities would lead them to freedom. Therefore, "development should be seen as a process of expanding freedoms". To achieve development, he calls for "removing poverty, tyranny, lack of economic opportunities, social deprivation, neglect of public services and the machinery of repression." He cites examples of how the per capita income does not necessarily lead to greater life expectancy. Instead of searching for answers in accumulating profits, he argues for strengthening the accessibility of public services by the poor (Sen, *ibid.*).

In sharp contrast, Jagdish Bhagwati and Arvind Pangariya, Columbia University economists forcefully argue for economic growth supported by the market economy and liberal state policies to meet the challenges of poverty alleviation in India. Both economists argue that market-induced economic reforms initiated in the early 1990s set India on a path of higher growth and this process should be continued with further reforms to successfully overcome the poverty challenge. Emphasizing on the need of promoting trade liberalization and minimizing government interference in growth process, they call for making the best use of democracy and rule of law which is well saddled in India (Bhagwati and Panagariya, 2013). They disapprove of the 'mixed economy strategy, that India adopted after the Independence attributing it as the prime reason for India's slow growth while the newly industrialized nations of East Asian took another path of development. On the issue of redistributive policies, while Sen believes that redistributive justice supported by the desired institutional reform should take precedence and this would drive growth. Bhagwati disapproves this contention and asserts that "redistribution, as distinct from growth, cannot be the answer to removing poverty." However, Bhagwati and Panagarihya are not totally at variance with Sen and Dreze as both argue for adopting redistributive policies "designed to ease the plight of society's most impoverished members" (Sambandhan, 2013).

In addition to the above debate, there are scholars who do not hold that the state can provide inclusive growth with a focus on vulnerable groups given the compulsions in the era of globalization. Atul Kohli argues that the modern state though has progressed in terms of economic growth, is on the roll back and cannot perform the social welfare functions which is used to play during the era of socialism in India before the decade of 1980. According to him, the earlier India state was essentially a socialist state caring for the welfare of the people and despised capitalism. But now capitalism, not socialism has become the dominant language of the state. He holds that the contemporary state caters more to the requirements of the corporate sector than anybody else and therefore, the political elites are least interested in the state's redistributive policies in education, land reform, employment and the health sectors. He attributes the falling standards and dismal efforts of the state to the growing apathy and inefficiency of the state because of which even popular government programmes such as MNREGA have largely failed. The growing collusion between the state and corporate elites is undoing the welfare character and the policies of the state. Though not totally pessimistic, he calls for building up popular pressure and creating a suitable electoral environment wherein political elites could be compelled for taking up social interest issues and reviving social democratic politics (Nagraj, 2012:238).

Vivek Chibber arguing almost on the same lines, too holds that in a post-liberalized India, the social security paraphernalia whatever little that was too has ceased to exist "as the space for labouring classes has narrowed, as their political muscle has waned, and their presence in the policy apparatus has been more precarious." He asserts that in the aftermath of the economic reforms, the political support for the social welfare has declined. The hold of the 'dominant groups', implying capitalists, has increased over the economic and political systems resulting in falling wages, strikes and lockouts at public sector units (*ibid.*).

Popular perceptions about a balance between growth and equity are not particularly encouraging given the nature of growth over the last two decades of economic reforms in India. The growing constriction of the Indian state as a result of the economic reforms brought under the influence of structural adjustment policies of IMF and World Bank has led to a debate whether rapid economic growth achieved with the greater involvement of private capital can contribute to justice and equity? The state is increasingly withdrawing from core social sectors paving the way for industrial and corporate houses to invest in profitable areas and reap rich economic gains. The poor have been left at the mercy of the market to fend for themselves with little relief coming from the state. Though impressive economic growth has been achieved at the cost of the growing vulnerability between and among states, regions and people. The rise in the GDP has not translated into an inclusive and equitable growth in the real sense as terms like 'jobless growth', 'employment-hostile growth', and 'job-destroying growth' have been used to define the post-1990 economic growth in India (Gandhi, 2008:206-284).

Scholars are skeptical about equity and justice becoming a part of a capitalist growth system because of the inherent contradiction between profit and charity (social service). Markets are never interested in equity, charity, inclusivity or poverty reduction, their guiding principle only being growth and profit. They argue that economic reforms have largely skipped equitable and inclusivity in the growth process and this is evident by huge disparity among people where "the richest 1 per cent of Indians own nearly half (49%) of India's personal wealth. The rest 99 per cent are left to share the remainder among ourselves. And that too is very unequally shared. The top 10 per cent Indians own nearly three-quarters (74%) of the country's personal wealth. The remaining 90 per cent share a meagre quarter. At the other end of the spectrum, of the world's poorest 20 per cent people, nearly one in four are Indians" (Shah 2015).

Critics argue that in a globalised world, the state has become the savior of market and private capital and less concerned with the social welfare issues confronting people. This is the new *avatar* of a neo-liberal state which is marked by under-investment in critical social sectors and where "growth does not allow trickling down" (Subramanian, 2012). In its new form, the state has emerged as a mediator or a regulator that manages the essential services and the relationship between business-doing private firms and the common masses. As the current state is more interested in bagging business contracts and inviting foreign investments, it is giving way to the demands of the MNCs. The state, as a result, cannot afford to annoy the private players for the fear of losing capital and thus the fight for vulnerable masses and their interests get weakened. During the last twenty years, the state (both the Central and State Governments) is increasingly withdrawing from social welfare activities leaving the poor and the marginalized sections at the mercy of the market and private players. The later is getting active at the cost of the inactivity and apathy of the former. The selling of the public sector units (PSUs), the downgrading of social security cover to the workers, and the increased retrenchment in the labourer sector are some of the manifestations of growth with inequity wherein business activities flourish, capital gets concentrated in the educated elite urban classes and the vulnerable masses are push to the margins of the society struggling for their survival. Many scholars have attributed the growing misery of people to the neo-liberal political-economy and hold that unless the state is "brought back", there can be no equity, justice and a balanced social and human development despite rapid economic growth.

**Conclusion: The Search for the Missing Link!**

Notwithstanding the conflicting nature of growth and equity as pointed out by scholars, efforts at rebuilding even a torn-society could be successful if there is a conceptual understanding of economic policies and the developmental model to be pursued according to time, requirements and demands of the people. First, it is to be understood that India is not a unique or the first example of 'growth without equality' as growth-generated inequality is found even among the developed countries. USA and West European countries both suffered social crisis and unrest during the period of industrialization and even after that. Massive retrenchment, unemployment and unrest were witnessed in western nations as recently as 2007 which continued for another five years following the global financial crisis. In fact, growth or no-growth, inequality has become a dominant factor in developing as well as developed countries. Scholars acknowledge the inevitability of growth-generated inequality in the process of a nation's forward movement. Today the need for rapid economic growth has been accepted by all countries, the only major issue being how this growth is to be achieved, whether through the state-driven or free-market economic system? As India has embraced globalization, it has to follow the free market system which allows for a greater role of the private sector and the state playing the role of an "honest regulator, facilitator and a service provider". The state would have to allow a greater role for the market and private capital while playing a positive role in social sectors and catering to social justice for the disadvantaged people. There can be no going back to the old socialism, nor would this be feasible when the whole world is increasingly integrating into a market-economy fold.

Though much criticized the role of the private capital and technology in bringing down extreme poverty and unemployment has been recognized by leading scholars like Jagdish Bhagwati and Arvind Panagariya. According to them, it is a fallacy to think that private capital and equity cannot go together on a misplaced notion that capital would always work at cross-purposes with state's affirmative policies or that capital would take a flight where demands of equity or social justice come in (Bhagawati and Panagariya 2013:304-390). In fact, as Bhagwati and Panagariya, through their seminal works have shown that the gains achieved from economic growth could significantly contribute to social justice and reduction in poverty given an honest and sincere implementation of redistributive policies (Bhagwati, 1993). While not totally disagreeing with Bhagwati, Amartya Sen and Jean Dreze too consider economic growth an imperative for the country. Both accept the need for reconciling equity and economic growth, both call for inclusive and harmonious development and both consider social stability as vital for economic growth. While demolishing the myth that equity and economic growth are contradictory, Sen, unlike Bhagwati and Pangariya however, suggest that the development of people's productive capacities and ensuring their basic freedoms through development should take place prior to economic reforms (Sen, 1999:366).

It would be false to attribute all the miseries arising out of economic reforms to the market and capital, totally disregarding the inept attitude and the role of the state and its agencies. In spite of sufficient resources at its command, the state has faltered in delivering results as is manifested by almost forty long years of socialism in the post-independence period. The growing prosperity in some States—Maharashtra, Gujarat, Goa, Haryana, Tamil Nadu—proves that the state has been active both in social and economic sectors due to which these states are much better off than States like Bihar, Odisha, U.P., Jharkhand, Chhattisgarh and West Bengal where basic social indicators like health, education, sanitation, maternal and infant mortality rates etc. have been abysmally low, much lower than the national average. Naturally, the issues of social justice, equity and growth have been relegated to the backbenches of development. However, it is encouraging to see the traditional BIMARU states doing better as compared to the past (Gupta, 2012)[1]. What ails India's growth story, however, despite a spectacular growth in the last many years is that a justified redistribution of the gains accrued has not taken place. The poor and the marginalized have not been benefitted by economic reforms. In fact, their condition has worsened in many ways after the reforms began. This is demonstrated by the fact that the much-needed poverty alleviation programmes have not yielded the desired results. In fact, as data demonstrates, the condition of the peasants and vulnerable sections have worsened in many respects. The skill development and capacity-building of the marginalized people has not taken place which could have gainfully ushered them in the job market. Rather, the unorganized sector largely employing the unskilled, untrained and unprepared population has grown over the years by leaps and bounds. The surplus population in agriculture and allied sector has not found a way out in non-agriculture job market. Only a marginal improvement in the poverty level can never bring about substantial development in a nation's status. The adoption of globalization or neo-liberal policies have not worked to India's social and human development as these policies produce positive results only with trained or skilled manpower and *vice-versa* would produce negative results in a weak or under-developed society. While economic reforms were adopted for faster economic growth in the post-1990 period, the fall-out of globalization on human security was not taken care of by the state. The state remained a mere by-stander allowing non-state actors to play their individual roles without bothering to protect the masses from the exploitative market forces. The scores of scams and scandals besides the virtual institutionalization of corruption resulting in the siphoning of precious resources from the economy and its concentration in few privileged hands, however, proves that the state indeed has become weak or an accomplice in exploiting its own citizens. The increased inequality and disparity in the face of heightened economic prosperity indicates that there is something vital amiss in our developmental model. The much-desired link between economic growth and equitable redistribution, between growth and social justice is missing.

Notwithstanding the contention of critics who argue that globalization is bound to unleash negative forces on the vulnerable people and a weak state remaining incapable to deal with this situation, many states in India have proved that a willing state can improve social security and provide social justice to people amidst economic growth. Policy-makers are sufficiently aware of the leakages and drawbacks of the system that has crept in as a result of irresponsible implementation of socio-economic policies.

The search for the elusive missing link between growth and justice, therefore, has to be in the form of not only attending to the corruption menace, but also ensuring that the welfare schemes for the vulnerable classes reach them in the right earnest, failing which market would manifest in its ugly form and economic growth would boil down to the growth of some privileged sections.

Any talk of economic growth and human development would be meaningful only when there is a rich stock of skilled and trained human resources at the nation's command living as we are in an age of globalization characterized by massive growth in information and communication technology. The search for the missing link demands that economic reforms need to be tailored according to the people's needs, aspirations and the environment we are living in. Only the skilled and the trained human resources will get greater opportunities to progress. India's booming service and IT sectors which contributed impressively to India's GDP (although only 1% to GDP) bears testimony to this fact. There is a complimentary relationship between the masses and the market, in as much as, markets being tailored to generate employment for the working population and masses being trained to meet the standards of the markets. Only when this two-way relationship is conveıted into policy framework, can there be a better harmony between the market and the masses leading to a just, fair and balanced growth.

Instead of developing harmony between the markets and masses, India today contrarily is witnessing an intense competition between the markets and the masses. Infact, the situation has become market *vs*. the masses, as both are pitted against each other, where the former is looked upon as an exploitative agency and a tool of western imperialism working in India for extracting the precious national wealth and destroying the livelihood, culture and wealth of the people. The critical balance between the markets and the masses has thus become the missing link. The role of the state becomes critical as with a rolled-back or a weak state, the balance between the masses and the markets and between economic growth and an inclusive society cannot be achieved.

India is a huge country with immense opportunities as well as challenges. In an age of globalization and intense competition, while economic growth aided by impressive growth in manufacturing and service sectors is to be expedited, the challenge of providing social justice and social security to the deprived masses through affirmative state actions assumes even a bigger challenge. It is a well-understood and acknowledged fact that India needs rapid economic growth which apart from generating the much needed employment would also give a boost to critical social sectors and contribute to poverty reduction which is the main objective of economic reforms. Therefore, enhanced economic and industrial activities and better performance on foreign trade and commerce fronts are a must for accelerating growth rate and initiating a meaningful change in the human security levels of the weaker population.

The search for the elusive missing link has thus to be in the form of a more responsive and a sensitized handling of the issues confronting weaker sections and an administration equally wedded to accountability and other norms of good governance. It is to be noted that social justice and economic growth are not strange bed-fellows but inherently intertwined. Without giving a fillip to economic growth, no amount of social upliftment policies or programmes can be successful for want of resources as Bhagwati and Panagariya have persistently tried to prove it. Social justice programmes can never fructify in the absence of improved economic growth. Foreign investments and entrepreneurship can play a vital role in expediting and expanding the country's economic potential.

India is gradually, but surely and steadily, moving in the direction of building a humane society and inclusive democracy where both growth and equity; justice and prosperity would co-exist. Time, energy and resources are the factors that would ultimately determine the achievement of this goal.

## Note

1. According to a 2012 Planning Commission survey of the newly created states of Uttarakhand, Jharkhand and Chhattisgarh, these states have performed much better than their parent states, improving poverty reduction, literacy rate, industrial growth and per capita income. http://www.indiaspend.com/states/jharkhand-uttarakhand-the-post-split-growth-story.

## References

Aiyar, Swaminathan, S. Anklesaria (2008): "Escape from the Benevolent Zookeepers", *Times of India*, 2008.

Banik, Dan (2007): "*Starvation and India's Democracy*" (Routledge Publishers), p. 246.

Bhagwati, Jagdish (1993): "*India in Transition: Freeing the Economy*" (Clarendon Press).

Bhagwati, Jagdish and Panagariya, Arvind (2013), "Why Growth Matters: How Economic Growth in India Reduced Poverty and the Lessons for Other Developing Countries" (London: MacMillan Publishers).

Bhagwati, Jagdish and T.N. Srinivasan (1975): "*Foreign Trade Regimes and Economic Development: India*" (New York: National Bureau of Economic Research).

Bhargava, Yuthika: "India has second fastest growing services sector", *The Hindu*, 23rd February, 2015.

Census of India (2011): "Ranking of states and union territories by literacy rate, Ministry of Home Affairs, Government of India.

Census of India (2011): "*Rural-Urban Distribution of Population*", Ministry of Home Affairs, New Delhi.

Das, Asit (2011): "Displacement: The Indian State's War on its Own People", 3 October, http://sanhati.com/uncategorized/4191/.

Das, Gurcharan (2000): "*India Unbound: A Personal Account of a Social and Economic Revolution*" (New York: Knopf).

Das, Gurcharan (2006): "The India Model: An Economy Unshackled", *Foreign Affairs*, July/August issue.

Desai, Ashok (1999) "The Economics and Politics of Transition to an Open Market Economy: India," *OECD Working Papers*, Volume VII, No. 100, 1999.

Dhar, Aarti (2012): "42 per cent of Indian children are underweight", *The Hindu*, 1 January.

Dreze, Jean and Sen, Amartya (2011): "Putting growth in its place", *Outlook*, 14 November.

Dreze, John and Sen Amartya (1996): "*India: Economic Development and Social Opportunity*", (Oxford University Press: New Delhi).

Dube, M.P. (1989): "Jawaharlal Nehru: A Profile", in M.P. Dube (ed.) *Jawaharlal Nehru: Legacy and Legend* (Kumaon University Publication).

"Economic Survey of India (2007): Policy Brief", *OECD*.

*Economic Times* (2013): "Agriculture's share in GDP declines to 13.7 per cent in 2012-13," 30 August.

Forbes Magazine (2014): "India home to 54 of world's largest, most powerful public companies", 8th May, 2014.

Gandhi, P. Jegadish (2008): "*Inclusive Growth in Globalized India: Challenges and Options*", (New Delhi: Deep and Deep Publications).

Goldman Sachs (2007): "India's Rising Growth Potential."

Gruère, G. and Sengupta, D. (2011), Bt cotton and farmer suicides in India: An evidence-based assessment, *Journal of Development Studies*, 47(2).

Gupta, Dhritiman (2012): "Jharkhand, Uttarakhand and Chhattisgarh: The Post-Split Growth Story", *Hindustan Times*, July 5.

*Hindustan Times* (2013): "53 per cent of Indian households defecate in open: World Bank", 19 November.

*Indian Express* (2014): "India ranks 102 out of 132 nations on social development index", 4 April.

Jain, Sachin Kumar: "Economic inequality in today's India" 6 August 2015. http://www.millenniumpost.in/NewsContent.aspx?NID=144349.

James Astill (2008): "A special report on India: An elephant, not a tiger", *The Economist*, 11 December.

Joshi, Vijay and Little I.M.D. (1994) "India: Macro-economics and Political Economy, 1964-1991" (New Delhi: Oxford University Press), p. 105. http://shodhganga.inflibnet.ac.in/bitstream/10603/27125/14/14_chapter%205.pdf.

Maddison, Angus (2001): *The World Economy: A Millennial Perspective*, OECD Publishers, Paris.

Meher, Rajkishor (2009): "India Agriculture Dependent Poor People: The Case of Mineral-based Industries", *Journal of Developing Societies* (Sage Publication).

Mishra, Asit Ranjan: "India's external economic profile improves significantly", *Hindustan Times*, 1 July 2015.

Mohapatra, Gadadhara (2012): "Globalization and Changing India", 3 August 2012. http://www.countercurrents.org mohapatra030812.htm.

Nagaraj, R. (ed.) (2012): "Growth, Inequality, and Social Development in India: Is Inclusive Growth Possible?" (New York: Palgrave MacMillan, 2012).

NASSCOM, "Indian IT services exports saw growing 12-14 per cent in the year ahead" 11 February, 2015. http://www.livemint.com/Industry/bCLOgyaLGiIi6TuhmN0S7J/Indian-IT-services-exports-seen-growing-1214-in-year-ahead.html.

NSSO 66th Nation-wide Survey (2015a): "Indian Economy: Share of different sectors in Indian GDP" Planning Commission Government of India, 3rd June (2015b): "Indian Economy" Share of different sectors in Indian GDP.

Panagariya, Arvind (2004): "India in the 1980s and 1990s: A Triumph of Reforms", IMF Working Paper, WP/04/43.

Patnaik, Prabhat (2010): "State must re-engage with peasantry", *The Hindu*, 6th February.

Planning Commission, Govt. of India (2006): "Towards Faster and More Inclusive Growth: An Approach to the Eleventh Five Year Plan" http://planningcommission.nic.in/plans/planrel/app11_16jan.pdf.

Planning Commission, Govt. of India, "Eleventh Five Year Plan". http://planningcommission.nic.in/plans/planrel/fiveyr/11th/11_v1/11th_vol1.pdf.

Planning Commission, Govt. of India," Twelfth Five Year Plan (2012-2017)". http://planningcommission.gov.in/plans/planrel/12thplan/pdf/12fyp_vol3.pdf.

Pursell, Garry (1992): "*Trade Policy in India*," in Dominick Salvatore, (ed.) "*National Trade Policies*" (New York: Greenwood Press), pp. 423-458.

Raju, Dr. Yerram, Dr. M. Sitarama Murty and Dr. Subbiah Singala (2015): "India's Growth Resurgence Sectoral Issues and Governance Risks", BS Publications, p. 315.

Ramadoss, Dr. Abhinandan S., "Medical and Healthcare Facility Plagued". http://drabhinandan.blogspot.in/2008/05/medical-and-healthcare-facility-plagued.html.

Reserve Bank of India Report: India's Balance of Payments 1948-49 to 1988-89 and Reserve Bank of India Bulletin" http://shodhganga.inflibnet.ac.in/bitstream/10603/27125/14/14_chapter%205.pdf.

Rieff, David (2009): "India's Malnutrition Dilemma", *The New York Times*, 11th October.

"Retail Industry in India: Sectoral Report," August 2015. http://www.ibef.org/industry/retail-india.aspx.

Robinson, Simon (2008): "India's Medical Emergency", *Time U.S.*, 1st May.

Sainath, P. (2014): "Have India's farm suicides really declined?" *BBC News*, July 14.

Sambandhan, V.S. (2015): "Poverty *Vs* Growth: Bhagwati, Sen and India's fight against poverty". 21 January. http://www.academia.edu/10267101/Bhagwati_Sen_and_Indias_fight_against_poverty.

Sen, Amartya (1999): "*Development as Freedom*" (New York: Oxford University Press).

Shah, Mihir (2015): "Tribal alienation in an unequal India", 4 July, http://www.thehindu.com/opinion/lead/mihir-shah-writes-on-tribal-alienation-and-need-for-inclusive-growth/article7383721.ece?ref=relatedNews.

Sharma, Suresh (2008), "Childhood Mortality and Health in India", Institute of Economic Growth University of Delhi, Working Paper Series No. E/292/.

Shashi Tharoor (2014): "Nehru's last stand?", June 17, http://blogs.reuters.com/india-expertzone/2014/06/17/nehrus-last-stand/.

Sheriff, Andrew M. (1998): "Oil and the Middle East— An Investigation of the Arab Oil Weapon", *Political and Economic Review* (University of Limerick).

Shiva, Vandana and Jalees, Kunwar (2009): "*Farmers Suicides in India*", Report of the Research Foundation for Science, Technology and Ecology, New Delhi, 28 July, pp. 51, at pp. 1-2.

Sikri, D.K. (2006): "Population Projections for India and States 2001-2026." Report on the Technical Group on Population Projections Constituted by the National Commission on Population, Office of the Registrar General and Census Commissioner, India.

Subramanian, K.: "When growth allows no trickling down", *The Hindu*, 1st November, 2012.

Sutherland, T; Bishai, D.M. (2008): "Cost-Effectiveness of Misoprostol and Prenatal Iron Supplementation as Maternal Mortality Interventions in Home Births in Rural India", "*International Journal of Gynecology and Obstetrics*", 12th December.

Swaminathan S. Anklesaria Aiyar (2009); "Socialism Kills: The Human Cost of Delayed Economic Reform in India", (CATO Institute: Washington, D.C.), Policy Briefing Paper, No. 4, 21 October.

*The Economist* (2003): "Economic Structure" 6th October, 2003.

_______ (2015): "India's malnourished infants", 2nd July.

_______(2004): "Indian manufacturers learn to compete", 12th February.

*Times of India* (2015): "India's forest reserves touch new record high", 9th May,

Transparency International India (2005): India Corruption Study 2005", 30th June, pp. 1-3. https://en.wikipedia.org/wiki Corruption_in_India.

Transparency International India, "India Corruption Study 2008". https://en.wikipedia.org/wiki/Corruption_in_India.

"Tribal People in India: Scheduled Tribes, Scheduled Areas and Tribal Self-Rule- Exclusion and Marginalization of Tribal People," 6th September, 2012. https://socialissuesindia.wordpress.com/2012/09/06/scheduled-areas-scheduled-tribes-and-tribal-self-rule/.

Varma, Pawan Kumar: "India's middle class awakes", *Times of India*, November 23, 2013.

Varma, Subodh (2015): "Land acquisition ignites mutinies: Study", 31st March http://economictimes.indiatimes.com/news/politics-and-nation/Land-acquisition-ignites-mutinies-Study/articleshow/46754871.cms.

Virmani, Arvind (1997): "Economic Development and Transition in India." Paper presented at the Tokyo Dialogue on Alternatives to the World Bank-IMF Approach to Reforms and Growth, Economic Planning Agency, Tokyo, Japan, November 7.

World Bank (2015), "A measured approach to ending poverty and boosting shared prosperity", *Policy Research Report*, Washington, D.C.

World Bank, "India Country Overview 2013". http://en.wikipedia.org/wiki/Economy_of_India.

World Health Organization Report (2014): "India: Green Growth—Overcoming Environment Challenges to Promote Development", 6th March, http://www.worldbank.org/en/news/feature/2014/03/06/green-growth-overcoming-india-environment-challenges-promote-development.

# 12

# Indian Agriculture and Livelihood Security of Small Farmers

## A Post-Reform Scenario

*Surendra Meher*

### Introduction

India lives in rural areas and agriculture happens to be the prime occupation for majority of population and therefore, their primary source of livelihood. If agriculture prospers, the prosperity of these people will increase through an increase in per capita income and eventually development process penetrates to other sectors of economy. The pace and pattern of agricultural development was, however, quite poor in India at the time of Independence. Even today such prosperity in agriculture has been far below potential except a few states and regions. Some of the important reasons behind poor agrarian growth were small size of holding, weak agrarian structure, lack of adequate formal credit, unscientific farm practices and so on. The early phase of India's agricultural development could be well understood in Schultz's (1964) seminal work "Transforming Traditional Agriculture" in which it was emphasised that countries that depend upon traditional agriculture have no or little incentive to save and invest in order to increase the stock of reproducible capital farmers are employing and are miserably poor. Therefore, according to Schultz's prescriptions in the context of Indian agriculture, there was a need of transformation from traditional agriculture into a modern one that requires a huge investment on a continuous basis both in physical capital as well as human capital. According to Bhaduri, (1973) economic backwardness in agriculture persists due to some institutional factors such as; intensive non-legalized sharecropping, perpetual indebtedness of the small tenants and overwhelming presence of usury specially in the rural sector, which has been conceptualised as 'semi feudal' mode of production. In this mode of production, there appears to be perpetual indebtedness of small tenants and consequently, it does not allow cultivators to undertake capital investment in agriculture for raising their productivity. As consequences of the above states of Indian agriculture in early phase of economic development, there was stagnancy in its growth leading to a massive shortage of foodgrain to feed the growing population.

A technological breakthrough popularly called 'Green Revolution', witnessed during mid-sixties, nevertheless, brought significant changes in the food economy of India. One of the important aspects of the change relates to the adoption of modern agricultural technology. Outdated and unscientific methods of production were replaced by modern farm equipment, improved seeds, irrigation, fertilisers and other scientific methods of production. It ushered in a reasonable agricultural growth that made the country "reasonably self-sufficient" in foodgrains production. The advent of Green Revolution also witnessed the expansion of credit facilities which helped to increase the use of modern inputs. Concerted steps were taken to improve the food management of the economy through the establishment of Agricultural Price Commission and Food Corporation of India. The 1980s remained the milestone of India's agricultural development. During this period, the country achieved maximum agricultural growth ever. One of the important reason was that Green Revolution extended to almost all parts of the country and that increase in agricultural production took place due to increase in productivity growth.

Today we are in a regime of globalization and liberalization, even agricultural sector is under the ambit of such regime. Efficiency and competitiveness in production hold the key. India being a labour surplus economy has always had a comparative advantage in primary products and expect that the agricultural sector would benefit in the free trade regime. Further, due to commitment of reduction in domestic support and export subsidy by member countries especially the developed one, terms of trade in agriculture was expected to move in favour of agriculture. But contrary to expectation, there was a dismal performance of agricultural sector and the country faced influx of imports of primary products in the post-liberalization phase especially after mid-1990s (Chand *et al.*, 2007, Bhalla and Singh 2009). However, growth performances of the economy as a whole continued to get better with the process of globalization and liberalization, in which service sector played a dominant role. On the other hand, contribution of agricultural sector to the Gross Domestic Product has declined sharply, but the proportion of population depending on agriculture did not decline as steeply as its contribution to GDP. Growth in GDP was not accompanied by significant growth in employment, meaning thereby that surplus labour could not get absorb in non-farm sector. Most of the workforce absorbed in low skilled and less gainful unorganized sector making the lives of millions of workers miserable.

The issue of livelihood strategies for small and marginal farmers and landless labourer is, therefore, of great significance in the wake of declining employment opportunities, especially outside the farm sector. It may be noted that majority of these small and marginal farmers are not adequately literate to find a job in the present global economic regime. The per capita income of workers engaged in the service sector is a number of times higher than the workers engaged in agriculture and industrial sector (Mazumdar and Sarkar 2009). Consequently, inequality overtime has increased, and sections of the population depending entirely on agriculture; majority being small and marginal farmers are most vulnerable, as they are not able to get out of the abject of poverty. Food inflation is another form of economic distress hitting hard to net buyers of foodgrain specially the poorer sections of the country including agricultural labourers and industrial workers. Such unwanted outcome of food inflation has reduced their real income and so their general well-being.

The declining average per capita land holding leading to increasing marginalisation of land holding is another area of major concern. With the process of economic development, trends of urbanisation and industrialization are on the increase resulting additional pressure on land for the purpose of cultivation. Consequently, there has been a decline in average per capita land holding that threatens the prospects for food security, increasing poverty among marginal and landless farmers. The problem could be more severe for the socially and economically deprived segments of society including Scheduled Castes and Scheduled Tribes, as their sole source of livelihood is agriculture either as an agricultural labourer or a small farmer.

With poor agrarian structure including inequality of land holding, lack of adequate institutional credit, lack of adequate agricultural infrastructure *viz.*, irrigation, power, input supply and a relatively larger concentration of workforce albeit less gainful in real sense of the term do not permit to realise the true growth potential of agricultural sector. Further, high food price, employment casualization, growing economic inequality across regions, sectors and individuals are some of the important outcomes during the last two decades that are losing the very essence of economic democracy. With this background, the chapter aims at studying the historical context and the present scenario of agrarian structure in India. The chapter further analyses the production performance in Indian agriculture with particular emphasis on the post-reform period. Further, it discusses some issues and concerns over food and livelihood security and identifies some policy options to make the lives of the majority of population who are either directly or indirectly depended upon agriculture.

The plan of the chapter is as follows. Section I briefly analyses historical background and the present agrarian structure in India. Section II discusses the trend of agricultural production in the country. Section III discusses some of the reasons of poor performance in agriculture, especially in post-reform period. Section IV deals with the issues of food and livelihood security and Section IV presents concluding remarks.

## Agrarian Structure in India

India during British period was characterised by repeated famine, drought and consequent food shortages leading to loss of human lives. Agriculture was in line with needs of British industries and primarily regulated by the Britishers. They brought a profound change in the land revenue system, of which the permanent settlement act 1793 was an important landmark. The motive behind that was that the newly created class of *Zamindars* would continue farm practices and regenerate agricultural development to pocket maximum land revenue from the farmers. Further, these newly created *Zamindars* would be utilised as intermediaries for political purposes and help to support the continuance of British government. The system proved to be exploitative and the hereditary and traditional rights of the tenants were made entirely defunct. Nevertheless, several legislations were passed by Congress government that came to power in many provinces and then committed to implementing radical land reforms after independence. During the mid-fifties, the agrarian reform legislation was passed with an aim of removing all structural impediments that were inherited from the past with broad objectives of social and economic justice within the agricultural system. The government launched the process of economic planning in the context of a mixed economy. During the first five-year plan, agriculture was given due importance and building up of agricultural infrastructure including irrigations, research for agriculture, agricultural credit were given top priority.

After Independence, the policy makers were committed to implement land reforms in the country. Most of the states passed land reform legislation during mid-fifties with the objectives of

**Table 12.1:** Percentage Distribution of Leased-in Area by Terms of lease for Major States (Rural 2002-03)

| *States* | *Fixed money* | *Fixed produce* | *Share of produce* | *From relatives (no terms)* | *Others* | *All terms* |
|---|---|---|---|---|---|---|
| Andhra Pradesh | 31.6 | 37.9 | 24.0 | 2.1 | 4.4 | 100 |
| Assam | 15.8 | 3.6 | 55.0 | 0.0 | 25.6 | 100 |
| Bihar (including Jharkhand) | 12.2 | 17.5 | 67.0 | 0.5 | 3.0 | 100 |
| Gujarat | 10.7 | 46.3 | 37.9 | 3.5 | 1.6 | 100 |
| Haryana | 71.2 | 9.8 | 15.8 | 0.1 | 3.1 | 100 |
| Karnataka | 32.4 | 41.1 | 24.8 | 0.0 | 1.7 | 100 |
| Kerala | 39.9 | 7.5 | 12.0 | 33.0 | 7.8 | 100 |
| Madhya Pradesh (including Chhattishgarh) | 18.3 | 32.5 | 39.0 | 1.6 | 8.6 | 100 |
| Maharashtra | 26.2 | 9.0 | 37.5 | 15.7 | 11.6 | 100 |
| Odisha | 11.1 | 7.8 | 73.0 | 3.5 | 4.6 | 100 |
| Punjab | 79.2 | 1.5 | 15.3 | 3.1 | 0.9 | 100 |
| Rajasthan | 35.0 | 17.7 | 39.3 | 1.1 | 6.9 | 100 |
| Tamil Nadu | 32.0 | 30.0 | 22.9 | 7.3 | 7.8 | 100 |
| Uttar Pradesh | 23.8 | 12.9 | 52.9 | 5.0 | 5.4 | 100 |
| West Bengal | 23.7 | 28.5 | 34.9 | 4.1 | 8.8 | 100 |
| **All India** | **29.5** | **20.3** | **40.3** | **4.0** | **5.9** | **100** |

*Source*: NSS Reports No. 492, Some Aspects of Operational Holdings in India, 2002-03.

removing obstacles to agricultural development that was inherited from the past and to ensure social and economic justice within the agrarian system. The main components of land reform legislations were (a) abolition of intermediary, (b) tenancy reforms, (c) ceiling on land holding, (d) consolidation of land holding, and (e) compilation and updating of land records. It has been claimed that the land reforms legislation has been relatively successful as far as the abolition of intermediaries is concerned. Considerable areas of cultivable waste land and private forests came under the management of the government. However, in many parts of the country, landlords with their political nexus were able to resume land through self-cultivation tactics by ejecting a large number of tenants. Some scholars argue that many of the beneficiaries of the abolition of intermediaries are now among those who are politically visible, large landowners who bitterly oppose ceiling on land holding (Ray 1996).

Another aspect of agrarian reform is tenancy reform with two-fold objectives, one; providing security of tenure to the tenants and two; regulation of rent payable by tenants. The primary aim of security of tenure is that ejectments do not take place except in accordance with the provision of law and that land may be resumed by the owner, if at all for 'personal cultivation' only. But despite the stricter regulation on the security of tenant, the landlords were able to make use of their clout to evict the poor tenants. Further, the fixation of the rate of rent was far from adequately enforced. The social and economic condition of the peasant was so poor to seek the protection of the law in the event of any wrongdoing by the landlords. Even today informal tenancy exists in many parts of the countryside and the rate of rent varies within a region which depends entirely on the basis of agreed-upon terms and conditions.

However, with existing inequalities in landholding and lack of gainful employment in the country tenancy could be desirable when it takes a commercial form, if it serves the very purpose of both tenants and landowners. In the event of inequalities in land holding, and large farmers' inability and unwillingness to carry out farm operations, it is always desirable that the marginal farmers and the landless agricultural labours take up the land on lease and contribute to agricultural production. The fact that small farmers are more efficient in terms of higher production per acre has been realised since 1960s (Sen 1962, 1964, Saini 1969, Rao 1966), though in later periods especially after Green Revolution, the inverse relationship ceased to exist (Rudra 1968, Chadha 1978). However, some scholars even in post-reform period concluded that the small farmers are more efficient in terms of production per acre compared to their large counterparts (Sharma and Sharma 2000, Chand 2011). Thus, if the process of land leasing bears a commercial nature, it could promote higher agricultural production and benefit marginal farmers and the landless labourers. But many times the tenancy arrangement takes semi-feudal characteristics, in which the poor social and economic conditions of the tenants do not allow them to get rid of debt bondage.

Table 12.1 makes clear that share of produce as terms of the lease is still mostly concentrated in the country. The poorer regions such as Bihar and Odisha, the percentage distribution of leased-in-area by 'share of produce' constituted 67 per cent and 70 per cent respectively. Whereas, in relatively developed states such as Punjab, Haryana and Kerala 'fixed money' constituted a higher percentage indicating that tenancy more or less bears a commercial nature in these regions.

Such a possibility of agrarian structure in these regions could be due to balanced economic development. With existing agricultural prosperity, one would perceive that availability of employment opportunities outside the farm sector would be better. In other words, agricultural developments have led to the process of industrialization and other scope of economic expansion. Therefore, tenancy may not be a force arrangement in developed regions of the country. On the other hand, in relatively less developed states such tenancy arrangement is due to social and economic compulsion and poor tenants are at the receiving end to all sorts of terms and conditions that do not generally favours them.

Imposition of ceiling and distribution of surplus land among the landless labourers happen to be the most important aspect of agrarian reform measures. Ceiling refers to fixation of maximum size of holding that an absolute cultivator may hold. The National Commission on Agriculture observed fixation of ceiling and distribution of surplus land is desirable because of acute pressure of population on land and there is a meagre prospect of shifting labour from agriculture to the non-agricultural sector. Other prominent reasons for ceiling on land holdings are: firstly, it would help to bridge inequality in distribution of land, secondly, enlarge the sphere of self-employment in agriculture, thirdly, it fulfils the desire to hold a piece of land and finally, it may help to bring a socialistic and democratic set-up of production within the agricultural society. However, fixation of ceiling on holding and redistribution of surplus land met with a very little success in its implementation. Since, the period when ceiling has been reinforced, land distribution is estimated to constitute only less than two per cent of the total operated area (Ray 1996). There were several lacunas in the legislation of land ceiling; most importantly; the lack of political will of the policy makers. The loopholes in the process of legislation allowed landlords to retain over land holding through 'Benami transfer'. There was also a lack of updated land records that was a major constraint in implementations.

**Table 12.2:** Share of Ownership Holding by Size Category: Rural India 1971-72 to 2003

| Category of Holding | Share of ownership holding by size category | | | |
|---|---|---|---|---|
| | 1971-72 (26th Round) | 1982 (37th Round) | 1992 (48th Round) | 2003 (59th Round) |
| Marginal (1.00 ha or less) | 62.62 | 66.64 | 71.88 | 79.60 |
| Small (1.001-2.00 ha) | 15.49 | 14.70 | 13.42 | 10.80 |
| Semi-medium (2.001-4.00 ha) | 11.94 | 10.78 | 9.28 | 6.00 |
| Medium (4.001-10.000 ha) | 7.83 | 6.45 | 4.54 | 3.00 |
| Large (above 10.000 ha) | 2.12 | 1.42 | 0.88 | 0.60 |

*Source:* NSS 59th Round, Report No. 491, p. 19.

As a consequence, despite legislation, the distribution of land has remained more or less skewed. In this respect, we lag far behind East Asian Countries and China, who were more or less successful in implementing thorough land reform programme. Nevertheless, imposition of ceiling on land holding has prevented further expansion of large holding. Table 12.2 above clearly reveals that the share of marginal holding and small holding has been increasing over the different NSS Rounds. In latest round, i.e., as on 2002-03, they constituted more than 90 per cent of total holding. The increase in the proportion of large holding could also be attributed to increasing pressure of population on land.

Consolidation of land holding has been initiated to consolidate fragmented holding over a long distance that confers numerous advantages to the cultivator. Since, cultivable land of a single owner is scattered in pieces in different areas, consolidation makes the size of holding viable. Other advantages of consolidation of holding are proper supervision of crops by the cultivators and make the size of holding feasible. However, in respect of this measure as well, only a little progress has been achieved. The updating of land records is probably the most significant steps in the direction of land reforms programme. A centrally sponsored scheme namely 'Computerisation of Land Records' has been initiated during 1988-89. In this system, efforts have been made to update land records electronically to make accessible to people, planners and policy-makers. The objective has also been to ensure accuracy, transparency and speedy resolution of the dispute.

A better agrarian structure would have a positive impact on economic growth and development. It ensures efficiency and maximisation of agricultural production. Further, if the landless are provided a certain piece of land, it would promote self-employment in agriculture. The poor and landless would engage efficiently as the job prospect in the non-farm sector is declining. Above all, it would ensure social justice. However, the possibility of surplus land distribution and other relevant measures of agrarian reform measures do not seem to be an important agenda. In the age of globalization and liberalization, we stress little on these aspects of land reform implementation. In fact, the entire agricultural sector was neglected in post-reform period. As a result, production performances were severely hit. This has a very miserable consequence on the lives of farming community including agricultural labourer.

## Trends of Agricultural Production

Achieving self-reliance and increase in production and employment of the country have been the basic objective of planning policy. It has been realised that above objective could be met only when agricultural sector is made to prosper. In those directions, significant attempts were made to rebuild the agricultural sector through several rounds of institutional and infrastructural reforms immediately after Independence. Apart from correcting the agrarian structure through land reforms programme, several other steps have also been initiated which include; programmes for developing irrigation facilities; both major and minor, investment in science and technology, community development programmes, research and development etc. But despite all these measures, the country still depended on import of food and raw materials to feed the rising population and the raw materials for running machinery. A package programmes namely; Intensive Agricultural District Programme was launched in 1961. The programme encompassed several packages to improve agricultural productivity such as improved inputs and machinery, price incentives for the participating cultivators, education and farm management training to cultivators and credit supply among others. The programme was subsequently extended to other parts of country. Agricultural Price Commission (APC) was set-up to advice the government in the fixation of Minimum Support Price for various agricultural crops. Indian Council of Agricultural Research was reconstituted in 1965. Several agricultural universities were set-up keeping in view the need for education, research and extension. Several other infrastructural facilities including an extension of credit facilities, power and irrigations, roads and communications were also developed to promote agricultural sector so as to give a boost to agricultural production.

As a result of above initiatives, there was a spectacular increase in foodgrain production. For instance, during 1950-51, total foodgrain production in the country was 50.8 million tonnes which rose to 108.4 million tonnes in 1970-71 (*Economic Survey* 2013). Table 12.3 makes clear that agriculture grew at the rate of 2.54 per cent per annum from the period 1951-52 to 1967-68 and later in the Green-Revolution period it grew at the rate of 2.44 per cent. It may, therefore, be observed that despite the introduction of new technology during mid-sixties, the

**Table 12.3:** Growth Performance of Agriculture in India

| *Period* | *Total Economy* | *Agriculture and Allied Services* |
|---|---|---|
| Pre-Green Revolution 1951-52 to 1967-68 | 3.69 | 2.54 |
| Green Revolution Period 1968-69 to 1980-81 | 3.52 | 2.44 |
| Post-Green Revolution Period i.e. Wider technology dissemination period 1981-82 to 1990-91 | 5.40 | 3.52 |
| Early Reform Period 1991-92 to 1996-97 | 5.69 | 3.66 |
| Ninth Plan 1997-98 to 2001-02 | 5.52 | 2.50 |
| Tenth Plan Period 2002-03 to 2006-07 | 7.77 | 2.47 |
| Eleventh Plan Period 2007-2012 | 8.2 | 3.2 |

*Source*: Planning Commission (GoI), 2013.

growth in agriculture and allied activities during the Green Revolution Period was lower than in the pre-Green Revolution period. This was because the Green Revolution was limited only in few selected areas notably in Punjab, Haryana and Western Uttar Pradesh. Further, during this period, the country witnessed a couple of severe droughts resulting in the decline in agricultural production. Similarly, oil crisis and crisis of war during this period led to a reduction in foreign exchange and foreign aid resulting in a decline in public investment in agriculture. However, one of the significant positive impacts of introduction of new technology was that it taught the farming community the use of modern seed-fertilizer technology which brought about a phenomenal growth in production and productivity of food crops, though it was restricted to a few pockets and few and selected crops only. The post-Green Revolution phase (1980-81 to 1990-91) nevertheless, witnessed a remarkable achievement in the performances of agricultural sector. It grew at the rate of 3.52 per cent per annum during this period. The reason being that Green Revolution reached to almost all parts of the country. A notable feature during this period was that the growth was not only confined to wheat and rice but also extended to other commercial crops as well such as: Cotton, Sugarcane and Oilseeds. The primary source of growth during this period was yield growth rather than growth in area (Bhalla 2009). Therefore, the country achieved self-sufficiency in foodgrain production only during the 1980s when Green Revolution reached to almost all parts of country especially to eastern regions.

The period after 1991 is called the period of economic reform. Several policy measures were initiated during this period broadly known as: globalization, liberalization and privatization. There were significant reductions in trade barriers to facilitate trade and commerce across countries. Licence Raj was done away with except a few industries and large scale disinvestment measures have been carried out. Agricultural sector came under the purview of world trade during 1995. There was lots of expectation from the agricultural sector as far as benefits from trade are concerned. India being a labour intensive and producer of primary commodities and having a comparative advantage in those commodity groups, one would certainly expect it to do better in the regime of globalization. But there has been the sluggish performance of the agricultural sector in the era of economic liberalization and globalization. Table 12.3 shows that the growth rate in agricultural sector was 2.50 per cent during Ninth Five Year Plan

(1997-98 to 2001-02), and it further declined to 2.47 per cent during Tenth Plan period (2002-03 to 2006-07). Studies in recent past also came to the conclusion that agricultural sector has performed very poorly in the post-reform period (Binswanger 2013, Chand *et al.*, 2007, Bhalla and Singh (2009). Chand (2007) concluded that while growth rate of GDP in the agricultural sector registered well in the early period of reforms, there was significant deceleration in the growth rate in the later period especially in the front of foodgrain production.

In recent years, however, some improvement has been made in the performance of agricultural sector especially after the emphasis laid on inclusive growth in Eleventh Five Year Plan. During Eleventh Five-Year Plan period, growth rate of agriculture was quite impressive, i.e. it grew at the rate of 3.2 per cent per annum.

In front of foodgrain production as well, it had touched a new peak of 241 million tonnes in 2010-11. This has come about because Planning strategies of inclusive growth have envisaged a substantial increase in public sector outlay on agriculture through massive expenditure on rural development. Some of these programmes are Rashtriya Krishi Vikas Yojana (RKVY), Mahatma Gandhi National Rural Employment Guarantee Act (MNREGA), Backward Region Grant Fund (BRGF) and rural infrastructure under Bharat Nirman, which are expected to develop rural infrastructure and help to accelerate agricultural production. The rural employment programme such as MNREGA helped to boost agricultural growth through building rural infrastructure in the country. Construction of water bodies' at large scale in such programme can contribute to improving irrigation facilities. Similarly, linking rural roads, one of the major components of the programme may help agriculture marketing and facilitate input delivery. One of the objectives of RKVY during Eleventh Five Year Plan was to incentivizing states to increase expenditure on agriculture and allied activities.

However, there are many concerns and challenges that still remain, more importantly, achieving four per cent growth in agriculture on a sustainable basis to achieve inclusiveness. The inclusiveness would be faster when targets are set for the poorer and other vulnerable sections of population are achieved in the process of growth and development. Those include persons depending on agriculture and allied activities either as cultivators or agricultural labourers who constitute bulk of the total population. In other words, inclusiveness would be expected to be sounded more when growth in agriculture sustained with adequate employment opportunities for landless labour, marginal farmers and other socially and economically poorer sections. Other principal concern is inter-regional disparities with respect to agricultural development. It is too worrying to note that inter-regional disparities concerning agricultural development still persist today. While Northern regions including Punjab and Haryana have continued to maintain the growth in agriculture and a high level of productivity, states belonging to eastern regions, the performance of agriculture has been quite dismal. Table 12.4 clearly depicts that agricultural productivity in developed states is many times higher than the poorer states. Agricultural productivity measured by yield per hectare in Odisha, Madhya Pradesh, Chhattisgarh and Bihar is quite small compared to states such as Punjab, Haryana. In respect of irrigation infrastructure, which happen to be a prime variable of agricultural growth, the richer states have an upper hand. Consequently, there appears to be a significant gap in agricultural productivity across regions.

**Table 12.4:** Interstate Variations in Foodgrain Productions

| *States* | *Area (Million Hectates)* | *% to All India* | *Production (Million Tonnes)* | *% to All India* | *Yield (Kg/ Hectare)* | *Area under Irrigation* |
|---|---|---|---|---|---|---|
| Uttar Pradesh | 19.8 | 15.62 | 47.25 | 19.30 | 2386 | 75.8 |
| Punjab | 6.51 | 5.14 | 27.87 | 11.39 | 4281 | 98.4 |
| Madhya Pradesh | 12.86 | 10.14 | 14.95 | 6.11 | 1163 | 45.9 |
| Rajasthan | 15.08 | 11.90 | 18.83 | 7.69 | 1249 | 25.9 |
| Andhra Pradesh | 8.03 | 6.33 | 20.32 | 8.30 | 2531 | 57.3 |
| Haryana | 4.72 | 3.72 | 16.63 | 6.79 | 3523 | 89.0 |
| West Bengal | 5.56 | 4.39 | 14.47 | 5.91 | 2603 | 49.3 |
| Bihar | 6.24 | 4.92 | 9.22 | 3.77 | 1478 | 64.2 |
| Maharashtra | 13.03 | 10.28 | 15.42 | 6.30 | 1183 | 17.1 |
| Karnataka | 8.24 | 6.50 | 13.88 | 5.67 | 1684 | 27.3 |
| Tamil Nadu | 3.17 | 2.50 | 7.59 | 3.10 | 2394 | 62.4 |
| Gujarat | 4.53 | 3.57 | 8.34 | 3.41 | 1841 | 41.5 |
| Chhattisgarh | 4.96 | 3.91 | 7.06 | 2.88 | 1423 | 27.2 |
| Odisha | 5.32 | 4.20 | 7.62 | 3.11 | 1432 | 33.6 |
| Jharkhand | 1.49 | 1.18 | 1.88 | 0.77 | 1262 | 5.9 |
| Assam | 2.77 | 2.19 | 4.88 | 1.99 | 1762 | 6.6 |
| Uttarakhand | 0.99 | 0.78 | 1.82 | 0.74 | — | 44.4 |
| Others | 3.47 | 2.74 | 6.75 | 2.76 | — | — |
| **All India** | **126.67** | **100.00** | **244.49** | **100.00** | **1930** | **47.8** |

*Source:* Directorate of Economics and Statistics, Department of Agriculture and Cooperation, Government of India.

In an estimate by Bhalla (2009), growth rate of crop output decelerated from 3.61 per cent from 1980-83 to 1990-93 to merely 1.00 per cent from 1990-93 to 2003-06 in Eastern Region, and Odisha registering a negative growth rate (–0.67% per annum). In an earlier estimate by Chand (2007), the net state domestic product in agriculture in the State of Odisha grew at the rate of 0.11 per cent in the State during the period 1995-96 to 2004-05. The author noted a deceleration in the growth of area irrigated and consumption of electricity in the state during same period. Level of agricultural productivity in the state is quite lower compared to the other states and at the all India level. Stagnant cropping pattern, poor quality and quantity of input use led to reduced income earning capabilities of farmers. Since, agriculture remains the mainstay of economy and sustenance of life of people in relatively less developed states, poor performance of agriculture could have severe implication on food and livelihood security of people in these states.

The Situation Assessment Survey of the National Sample Survey Organization (2003) also reveals a very interesting finding on the distress of farming community and their poor access to agricultural technology and other inputs. It shows that television, radio, newspaper, input dealers and other progressive farmers happen to be the major source of accessing modern agricultural technology. Nearly 60 per cent farmers did not access any information on modern technology from any source. More than 50 per cent farmers do not use improved seeds in their agriculture. And, only 20 to 30 per cent farmers use veterinary services. It is quite surprising to know that at the all India level, 52 per cent of the farming households reported the use of animal for ploughing. In States such as Jharkhand and Assam, proportion of household using animal for ploughing stood out to be 98 per cent and 97 per cent respectively. The Situation Assessment Survey further finds that 40 per cent farmers reported dissatisfaction with their profession. The percentage of the farmers who are unaware of institutions like WTO and Minimum Support Price are 92 per cent and 70 per cent respectively. 57 per cent farmers are unaware of crop insurance. SAS also brings out the fact that farmer households in most States of India have reported lower consumption expenditure compared to all rural households. Consequently, the incidence of poverty among farmer households is higher than that of all rural households. The Situation Assessment Survey, thus clearly brought out a very poor state of Indian agriculture and the serious concerns that the agricultural sector is facing today.

## Reasons of Poor Performances in Agriculture

There may be several reasons for such poor performances in agriculture in India, especially in the post-reform period. One of the principal reasons is the decline in public investment in agriculture particularly in irrigation and other rural infrastructures such as: power, rural roads, formal credit, soil and water conservation, research and extension etc. The Eleventh Five Year Plan also identified public investment in agriculture as one of the important factors determining agricultural growth in India. Consequently, the Plan laid specific emphasis on public investment in agriculture. The interregional inequalities with respect to agricultural development could, therefore, be attributed to the difference in the public expenditure for their agriculture. Further, agricultural growth has remained always less than targeted growth because of several other reasons such as lack of irrigation, unavailability of adequate formal credit, lack of access to technology, inadequate research and extension services etc. Some of the aspects of declining public investment and farmers' lack of access to formal credit has been analysed below.

## Declining Public Investment in Agriculture

There is no difference of opinion among scholars that public investment in agriculture is essential for promoting private investment and enhancing agricultural output (Rath 1989, Rao 1994, Alagh 1994, Chand and Kumar 2004). But there has been an apparent decline in public investment in agriculture after 1980s (Pattanaik 1987, Rath 1989, Alagh 1994, Gandhi 1996, Rao 1994, Krishnamurty 1985, Shetty 1990). Therefore, it has been concluded that decline in public investment in agriculture would have an adverse impact on agricultural growth. The conclusions above are mostly based on the data revealed by the National Accounts Statistics of the Central Statistical Organization, which is the organized source of information on public capital formation in the agricultural sector. The trend of public investment in agriculture revealed by National Accounts Statistics depicted in Table 12.5 and it suggests that Gross Capital Formation (GCF) in agriculture as a per cent of total gross capital formation increased steadily from 1960-61 to 1980-81, and thereafter it showed a continuous decline except a marginal recovery in the recent period i.e. in 2009-10. The main reason for the decrease in aggregate investment in agriculture has been the downward trend of investment from public accounts during the 1980s. The proportion of public sector capital formation as a per cent of total capital formation in agriculture fell from 51.5 per cent in 1980-81 to 29.6 per cent in 1990-91 and further to 17.7 per cent in 2009-10. The percentage of Gross Capital Formation in agriculture to total GDP during 1960-61 stood out to be 2.4 per cent which increased to 3.3 per cent in 1980-81, but declined further to 2.1 per cent in 1990-91 and again showed an improvement during 2009-10 (2.9%). Total capital formation as the per cent of total GDP has been increasing steadily and stood out to be 38.5 per cent during 2009-10.

**Table 12.5:** Gross Domestic Product and Gross Capital Formation in Agriculture (at Constant Prices)

| *Year* | *Pub Sec. CF as % of Total CF in Agr* | *Pvt Sec. CF as % of Tot CF in Agr* | *GCF in Agr as % of Total GCF* | *GCF in Agr as % of Total GDP* | *GDP in Agr as % of Total GDP* | *Total GCF as % of Total GDP* |
|---|---|---|---|---|---|---|
| 1960-61 | 46.4 | 53.6 | 12.2 | 2.4 | 47.2 | 19.5 |
| 1970-71 | 37.2 | 62.7 | 13.5 | 2.7 | 40.9 | 20.3 |
| 1980-81 | 51.5 | 48.4 | 14.6 | 3.3 | 35.7 | 22.9 |
| 1990-91 | 29.6 | 70.3 | 8.9 | 2.1 | 29.5 | 23.9 |
| 2004-05 | 21.3 | 78.7 | 7.5 | 2.5 | 19.0 | 34.0 |
| 2009-10 | 17.7 | 82.3 | 7.7 | 2.9 | 14.6 | 38.5 |

*Source*: National Accounts Statistics, CSO, Various Issues.

*Note*: Data up to 1990-91 is based on 1993-94 prices and 2004-05 onwards at 2004-05 prices.

The available trend, therefore, suggests that public sector capital formation in agriculture has declined since 1980-81. Capital formation in agriculture as a percentage of GDP has also declined but recovered marginally during 2009-10. The increased dose of public investment in the recent years is an attempt in the direction of achieving inclusive growth in the economy and a welcome step, but that need to be maintained with due emphasis to poorer and lagged regions.

Several other studies also indicated that investment in rural infrastructure directly or indirectly meant for agricultural sector has an important role to play in enhancing agricultural investment and output. Binswanger *et al.*, (1993) with the help of district level time series data found that education infrastructure and rural banks play an overwhelming role in determining investment, input and output decisions. Thc cxpansion of commercial banks into rural areas had a large effect on fertilizer consumption and fixed private farm investment. Fan *et al.*, (1999) with the help of state-level data in India showed that government spending on agricultural research and development, irrigation, rural infrastructures including road and electricity have all contributed to the growth of agricultural productivity and reduction in rural poverty. "There is always a trade-off between allocating money through subsidies or by increasing investments. The investment option is much better than subsidies for sustaining long-term growth in agricultural production and also to reduce poverty" (Chand and Kumar 2004). Roy and Pal (2002) in a state-wise analysis of agricultural investment and productivity concluded that agricultural productivity is Central to rural poverty alleviation and infrastructural and technological changes, in turn, play a crucial role in determining productivity.

The need of the hour, therefore, is to enhance plan expenditure on agriculture and allied sector especially in less developed states such as Odisha, Bihar, Jharkhand, Chhattisgarh, etc., with increasing support from the Centre. There is also greater potential for enhancing agricultural productivity in the rain-fed areas, where the land productivity is lower. The targeted growth should be realised through adequate public investment in the areas of irrigations and water management, soil conservation, rural infrastructures, livestock and fisheries, etc. The Twelfth Five Year Plan rightly pointed out that there is a need to shift from subsidies to public investment aimed at increasing land productivity on the grounds that this would produce better agricultural outcomes and would be more inclusive.

## Inadequate Formal Credit for Agriculture

Credits are necessary fuels for running farm business. It is especially true when farmers do not have adequate saving for further investment, particularly in backwards regions where the agrarian economy is characterised by low productivity and dominance of marginal and small farmers. These farming communities have a little marketable surplus and are in greater need of funds for investment in their agriculture. Since, Independence, the government has made several efforts to increase the flow of agricultural credit. The government has followed a multi-agency approach comprising co-operative banks, scheduled commercial banks and RRBs to provide credit to agricultural sector.

The concept of priority sector was introduced in 1969 to underscore the need for financing agricultural sector. National Bank for Agriculture and Rural Development (NABARD) was set-up in 1982 to provide refinance facilities to rural financial institutions to augment their resource base. The NABARD also administers Rural Infrastructure Development Fund (RIDF), which was established in 1995-96 and playing a significant role in the areas of rural markets, soil conservation, rural health and education and other related rural infrastructure. Further with the onset of structural adjustment programme under economic reforms, there have been significant changes in the policies and directions in the area of rural credit. The financial sector reforms turned out to be an important component of structural reforms initiated in the early 1990s, which included a number of measured in the area of agricultural credit (Mohan 2004). The micro-finance and Kisan Credit Card Schemes have also emerged as the major policy initiatives to meet the credit requirements of the farmers.

However, despite all these efforts, farming community in the country are still falling short of credit requirements to undertake their farm operations. Small and marginal farmers are the most deprived sections of all farming community in so far as access to formal credit and technology is concerned. The farmers seem to borrow more short term and consumption credit rather than on long-term credit to make sufficient investment in their agriculture. The flow of investment credit to agriculture is constrained by number of factors such as high transaction costs, structural deficiencies in the rural credit delivery system, lack of credit worthiness and lack of collaterals in view of small asset base of farmers (Golait 2007).

We could see from Table 12.6 that proportion of non-institutional credit of the total farm credit constituted 38.9 per cent during 2002. During 1971, it constituted 68.3 per cent of the total credit and declined sharply to 30.6 per cent in 1991. But surprisingly, it has taken an increasing trend during 2002 which is a cause of concern. The role of the commercial bank as a supplier of credit to the farm sector seems to have declined recently. There is, therefore, a need for revamping of the entire credit structure to improve the credit delivery in rural areas. The small farmers require special attentions. There is a need of exploring innovation in the fields of product design, improving the efficiency of credit delivery for raising economic viability of these farming communities.

**Table 12.6:** Sources of Farm Credit 1971 to 2002

| *Sources of Credit* | *1971* | *1981* | *1991* | *2002* |
|---|---|---|---|---|
| Non-Institutional of which | 68.3 | 36.8 | 30.6 | 38.9 |
| Moneylenders | 36.1 | 16.1 | 17.5 | 26.8 |
| Institutional of which | 31.7 | 63.2 | 66.3 | 61.1 |
| Cooperative societies/Banks | 22.0 | 29.8 | 23.6 | 30.2 |
| Commercial Banks | 2.4 | 28.8 | 35.2 | 26.3 |
| Unspecified | — | — | 3.1 | — |
| **Total** | **100** | **100** | **100** | **100** |

*Source*: All India Debt and Investment Survey and NSSO (Various Issues).

The creation of adequate job and skill training with market and technical support in rural sector is quite important. Public investment on those lines is greatly needed. Planning target of four per cent growth thus requires a sufficient and timely supply of institutional credit apart from suitable agricultural infrastructure. Beside this, there are other areas of concerns which require immediate attention for achieving the targeted growth which include; improving irrigation facilities mainly minor irrigation programme, watershed development, soil testing, research and extension services and more importantly improving the input delivery mechanism to benefit the small and marginal farmers.

## The Concern Over Food and Livelihood Security

It is true that the percentage of people depending on their employment and livelihood on agriculture has been declining over the years, but their contribution to Gross Domestic Product has been falling rather at a faster rate. In the recent year, agriculture contributes only 14 per cent to the GDP. The reason for such imbalance has been due to slower growth of agricultural sector than the growth in the non-agricultural sector specially in service sector. It has also been due to the failure of the non-agricultural sector to generate enough jobs so as to shift the workforce away from agriculture (Papola 2012). This also means that gap between rural and urban income has widened sharply as there has been an imbalance in the growth of farm and non-farm sector in the post-reform period. To say it, in other words, the recent growth experience of the Indian economy has been attributed to the growth in the service sector and the large influx of foreign investment. Mostly the non-commodity sector, i.e., the service sector has grown at a faster rate and therefore, its contribution to GDP has been quite substantial. On the other hand, the commodity sector such as agriculture and industry were grossly neglected. What has been witnessed in the post-reform period is a case of jobless growth; where, growth in output was not accompanied by growth in employment. The growing labour force took shelter in informal sector without much improvement in the quality of employment.

Since, these two sectors *viz.*, agriculture and industry are main providers of jobs and livelihood, the poor and marginal sections of society are left out in the growth process leading to an enormous gap in the income earning opportunities and capabilities of people (Mazumdar and Sarkar 2009). Such outcome during the post-reform period have denied the possibilities of achieving economic democracy that threatened the livelihood security of majority of population, of them, the small and marginal farmers; agricultural labourers are the most vulnerable.

The above discussion on the issue of sectoral growth and employment outcome in post-reform period raises several questions on the aspects of food and livelihood security. The lack of gainful employment opportunities and livelihood threats of marginal and small farmers coupled with rising food prices make the lives of these sections of society more vulnerable. Today, nearly one-third of India's population is poor of which marginal farmers and landless labourers constituted the majority. Food security implies all should have easy and equal access to food including the food quality and the aspect of hygiene. Food prices and the supply of foodgrains play a vital role ensuring food security in the country. The Government of India since the mid-1960s have taken adequate steps to address the issue of food security. The establishment of Agricultural Price Commission, Food Corporation of India was a couple of attempt in those directions. Nevertheless, the marginal and small farmers are not able to take adequate benefits of such price and input support programme.

The concern of food security naturally comes from two important indicators; one, the trends of agricultural growth and two; the purchasing power of the poor and vulnerable sections of the society. Agricultural growth, especially with respect to foodgrain production, is an important indicator of the state of food supply in the country. However, there may be several other factors that may affect food prices which includes shock in supply, international trade, global prices, food management speculative activities and demand (Chand 2010:10-13). Therefore, India needs to have adequate food management strategies to deal with the above factors. Agricultural growth in the past few years has been quite good, as we saw earlier, because of several policies implemented towards this end. There are several other factors that may influence agricultural growth most importantly the emphasis given to the sector in terms of resources flow to improve infrastructures such as irrigation, power, institutional credit, research and extension, road, transport and communication, price and input incentives etc. But still the growth is far from satisfactory to feed the entire population and time and again poor and other vulnerable groups are hard hit due to escalating food prices especially for pulses, vegetables, oil, etc.

Increase in food price hurt the poor in several ways; one cutting down on expenditure on essential food items that affect their health and nutrition. As the poorer are required working hard for a reasonable living, the nutritional deficiency further aggravates their problems of health and nutrition. Deaton (2009) rightly pointed out that the combination of rising price, falling employment and income in primary sector have impoverished a substantial section of population. Food price is, therefore, an important determinant of the purchasing power of the poor, which, if shown a rising trend for longer period, may deprived them their basic needs.

Secondly, an increase in the proportion of food expenditure by poor class, if at all, caused by food inflation would reduce their real income and may lead to significant cutting down of expenditure on non-food items. As the poor and unemployed constituted a large proportion of population, hike in food price may halt industrial progress through the deficiency in demand from rural sector and high cost of production in the industrial sector. Wage goods prices also influence wages and employment in other sectors of the economy, and thus have an impact on the urban poor as well (Pinstrup-Andersen, 1985). Therefore, food security through adequate foodgrain production and their equitable distribution hold the key to the balanced development of the economy. Nevertheless, targeting of the beneficiaries and leakages in the programmes must be taken care of. The real income of the poor and vulnerable groups could be protected with adequate gainful employment opportunities through employment generation programme. The programmes such as MNREGA and other self-employment programmes could play very crucial role in this regard.

## Conclusion

The chapter attempted to study the performance of India's agriculture sector with due emphasis to post-reform period. It also discusses some concerns on the issues of food and livelihood security of the poor and other vulnerable sections of society including small and marginal farmers. It has been seen that Green Revolution was the significant milestone of India's agricultural development and achieving self-sufficiency in foodgrain production though only in 1980s it could reach to almost all parts of the country. The notable feature during this period was that growth was not only confined to wheat and rice but also extended to other commercial crops as well such as; cotton, sugarcane, oilseeds among others. With well-equipped food stock and management system, India could avert the problem of food scarcity. Thereafter, it come to the regime of economic reforms. There were significant reductions in trade barriers to facilitate trade and commerce across countries. The agricultural sector was not an exception. India being a labour intensive and producer of primary commodities and having a comparative advantage in those commodity groups, there were lots of expectation from agriculture to do better in the regime of globalization. But, contrary to this, agriculture sector did not perform well in the post-globalization period especially after 1995. However, during Eleventh Five-year Plan period, the growth rate of agriculture was quite impressive i.e. it grew at the rate of 3.2 per cent per annum. This was the period in which the process of inclusive growth was initiated with due emphasis on agriculture and other rural development programmes.

Nevertheless, there are number of concerns and challenges still remain. Achieving four per cent growth in agriculture on a sustainable basis to achieve inclusiveness has been a challenging task. The interregional inequalities with respect to agricultural development persist today. The level of agricultural productivity in developed states is number of times higher than the poorer States such as Odisha, Bihar, Jharkhand and Chhattisgarh. The Situation Assessment Survey (SAS) of the National Sample Survey Organization further reveals a very discouraging picture on the distress of the farming community and their poor access to agricultural technology and other inputs. SAS also brings out the fact that farmer households in most States of India have reported lower consumption expenditure compared to all rural households. Consequently, incidence of poverty among farmer households is higher than that in all rural households. It thus presents a very poor state of Indian agriculture and the serious concerns that the agricultural sector is facing today, which need to be reversed in any case to achieve inclusiveness in growth process. The primary reasons of such a poor state of Indian agriculture and farmers distress in the post-reform period are, inadequacy in public investment in agriculture, inadequate formal credit to farmers, lack of irrigation facilities, lack of access to many other inputs and lack of several other rural infrastructure which are important for agricultural growth and development.

The chapter also raised some issues and concerns of food and livelihood security in India especially for the small and marginal farmers and agricultural labourers and for workers working in informal sector. The concerns of food and livelihood security arises from these sections of population because the contribution of agriculture to Gross Domestic Product has been declining quite sharply, but the dependence of population on it has not been declining at such faster rate. The possibility of gainful employment outside farm sector is meagre in the post-reform period. Most of labour force took shelter in informal sector without any social security and much improvement in quality of employment. Further, increase in food price has significantly reduced the real income and well-being of these sections of the population. Such outcome during post-reform period have denied the possibilities of achieving economic democracy and threatened the food and livelihood security of majority of population, of them, the small and marginal farmers, agricultural labourers are the most vulnerable.

A real economic democracy could be achieved when livelihood security of majority of population who are depending on agriculture could be ensured. Therefore, adequate attention on agriculture has to be given. Agricultural diversification has to be promoted with value addition in agricultural production. In the changed scenario, strong and viable agricultural, financial institutions are needed to cater to the requirements of finance for farming community. There is a need of exploring new innovation in areas of product design, improving the efficiency of credit delivery for raising economic viability of these farming communities.

The need of the hour is to enhance plan expenditure on agriculture and allied sector especially in less developed states such as: Odisha, Bihar, Jharkhand, Chhattisgarh, etc., with increasing support from the Centre. There is also greater potential for enhancing agricultural productivity in rain-fed areas, where land productivity is low. Therefore, there is a vast scope for achieving the growth target through adequate public investment in areas of irrigations and water management, soil conservation, rural infrastructure development, and providing appropriate incentives for livestock and fisheries and other allied activities for a diversified agriculture. Besides, provision of quality inputs with developing efficient delivery mechanism is essential to enhance farm productivity and income in those regions. The Twelfth Five Year Plan rightly suggested a shift from subsidies to public investment in Indian agriculture to improve productivity as public investment could produce better agricultural outcomes than subsidies. The proposed move can also help achieving inclusive growth. The long-term challenges of food and livelihood security, increasing scarcity of land and water, food inflation have to be met in the country through an adequate dose of public investment in agriculture and other rural infrastructure.

## References

Alagh, Yoginder K. (1994): "Macro-Policies for Indian Agriculture", in G.S. Bhalla (ed.) *Economic Liberalisation and Indian Agriculture*, (New Delhi: Institute for Studies in Industrial Development).

Binswanger, P. Hans and Shahidur, R., Khandker (1993): "How Infrastructure and Financial Institutions Affect Agricultural Output and Investment in India", *Journal of Development Economics*, 41(2): 337-366.

Binswanger, Hans P. Mkhize (2013): "The Stunted Structural Transformation of the Indian Economy—Agriculture, Manufacturing and the Rural Non-Farm Sector", *Economic and Political Weekly*, XLVIII, (26 and 27): 5-21.

Bhalla, G.S. and Singh Gurmail (2009): "Economic Liberalisation and Indian Agriculture: A State-wise Analysis", *Economic and Political Weekly*, December 26.

Bhaduri, Amit (1973): "A Study in Agricultural Backwardness under Semi-Feudalism", *Economic Journal*, 83(329):120-37.

Chand, Ramesh (2010): "Understanding the Nature and Causes of Food Inflation", *Economic and Political Weekly*, Vol. XLV (9): 10-13.

Chadha, G.K. (1978): "Farm Size Productivity Re-visited: Some notes from Recent Experiences from Punjab", *Economic and Political Weekly*, 13 (9): A-87-A-96.

Chand Ramesh (2011): "Farm Size and Productivity: Understanding the Strengths of Small Holders and Improving Their Livelihoods", *Economic and Political Weekly*, Vol. XLVI (Nos. 26 and 27): 5-11.

Chand Ramesh, Raju S.S. and Pandey L.M. (2007): "Growth Crisis in Agriculture: Severity and Options at National and State Levels", *Economic and Political Weekly*, 2528-2533.

Chand, Ramesh and Kumar, Parmod (2004): "Determinants of Capital Formation and Agriculture Growth, Some new exploration", *Economic and Political Weekly*, December 25, pp. 5611-5616.

Deaton, Angus and Jean Dreze (2009): "Food and Nutrition in India, Facts and Interpretation", *Economic and Political Weekly*, 44 (7): 42-64.

Fan Shenggen, Hazell Peter and Thorat, Sukhadeo (1999): "Linkages between Government Spending, Growth and Poverty in Rural India", *International Food Policy Research Institute*, Washington D.C., Research Report No. 110.

Gandhi, V.P. (1996): "Investment Behaviour in Indian Agriculture", *Indian Journal of Agricultural Economics*, 51 (4): 543-559.

Golait Ramesh (2007): "Current Issues in Agriculture Credit in India: An Assessment", *Reserve Bank of India Occasional Papers*, 28(1):79-99.

Krishnamurty, K. (1985): "Inflation and Growth, a Model for India" in K. Krishnamurty and V.N. Pandit (eds.) *Macro Economic Modelling of the Indian Economy*, Studies in Inflation and Growth, (Delhi: Hindusthan Publishing Corporation).

Mazumdar Dipak and Sandip Sarkar (2009): "The Employment Problem in India and the Phenomenon of the 'Missing Middle", *Indian Journal of Labour Economics*, 52(1): 43-55.

Mohan Rakesh (2004): "Agricultural Credit in India: Status, Issues and Future Agenda", *Reserve Bank of India Bulletin*, November pp. 993-1007.

Papola, T.S. (2012): "Employment Growth in the Post Reform Period, Keynote Paper on the Theme Employment in the Post-Reform India",

*54th Annual Conference of the Indian Society of Labour Economics,* 20-22nd December, Varanasi.

Patnaik, Prabhat (1987): "Recent Growth Experience of The Indian Economy some comments", *Economic and Political Weekly,* 22(19-21).

Pinstrup-Andersen, Per (1985): "Food Prices and the Poor in Developing Countries", *European Review of Agricultural Economics*, 12, (1/2): 69-85.

Rao, C.H. Hanumanta (1994): '*Agricultural Growth, Rural Poverty and Environmental Degradations in India'* (Delhi: Oxford University Press).

Rath, Nilakanth (1989): "Agricultural Growth and Investment in India", *Journal of Indian School of Political Economy,* 1(1), January-June.

Ray, S.K. (1996): "Land System and its Reform in India", *Indian Journal of Agricultural Economics*, 51 (1&2), pp. 220-237.

Roy, B.C., and Pal, Suresh (2002): "Investment, Agricultural Productivity and Rural Poverty in India", *Indian Journal of Agricultural Economics,* 57 (4), October-December.

Rao, C.H. Hanumantha (1966): "Alternative Explanation of Inverse Relationship Between Farm Size and Output Per Acre in India". *Indian Economic Review*, 1(2): 1-12.

Rudra, Ashok (1968): "Farm Size and Yield per Acre", *Economic and Political Weekly*, 3 (43):1041-1044.

Sharma H.R., Sharma, R.K. (2000): "Farm Size-Productivity Relationship: Empirical Evidence from an Agriculturally Developed Region of Himachal Pradesh", *Indian Journal of Agricultural Economics, 55* (4): 605-515.

Shetty, S.L. (1990): "Investment in Agriculture, A Brief Review of Recent Trends", *Economic and Political Weekly*, February 17-24.

Saini, G R (1969): "Farm Size, Productivity and Return to Scale", *Economic and Political Weekly*, 4(26): A119-A122.

Sen, A.K. (1962): "An Aspect of Indian Agriculture", *The Economic and Political Weekly*, Vol. 24 (Nos. 4, 5, and 6): pp. 243-266.

______ (1964): "Size of Holding and Productivity", *The Economic and Political Weekly*, Vol. 16 (Nos. 5, 6 and 7):323-326.

Schultz, T.W. (1964): *Transforming Traditional Agriculture* (New Haven, Yale University Press).

# 13

# Corporate-Politician Nexus in Contemporary India

## A Political Economy Perspective

*Amit Kumar Singh*

*The India Shining (also sounds as incredible India) things irritate people like us. You have to go to the rural villages and see whether India is Shinning, and you look into a Child's face and see whether India is Shinning. India is shinning okay for the glossy magazines, but if you just go outside Banglore, you will proposition that everything about India Shining is refuted. Thomas L. Friedman, "The World is Flat"* (New Delhi: Penguin Books India) p. 241.

**Thomas Friedman** *in The World is Flat.*[1]

## Introduction

Twenty-three years of economic reforms in India have been a great paradigm shift in post-Independence India. Constitutionally, India has declared itself a socialistic country, in the Preamble of its Constitution. But, after adopting the policy of economic reforms in India, the fundamental character of Indian state has changed, and its role has also somewhat declined. It has failed to serve and deliver. The Indian State is working like a multinational company (Singh 2013:6). It only visualizes, considers and understands different issues in the binary conclusion of economic profit or loss. Dalits, Adivasis, women, and minority groups, are still on the margins and not yet feel empowered. It poses serious threats and dangers as it leads to a sense of despair and alienation among them. It has created many problems before Indian state as it is seriously indulged in a crisis of conflict and violence (Kothari 2003:76). Identity politics in the name of caste, religion and region have once again emerged (*ibid.*). A problem like Naxalism has getting new language and voice in this post-globalized India. It seems an unholy nexus between the corporate world and political elite has emerged (Roy 2012:12-34). The Indian state is now of the rich, by the rich, for the rich. Some scholar defined it as Corporate Loot;[2] others defined it as Corporate Globalization (Alam 2007:137-148). All this has led to protest and anger and a new phase of Public movements have started but at present our political leadership is least bothered to address such serious democratic issues and concerns. Surprisingly, the state is using repressive measures to suppress these movements in which Dalit, Adivasi, farmers and common masses are the major stakeholders. Against this backdrop and perspective, the objectives of this proposed study are as follows:

1. To examine the democratic nature and character of Indian democracy after adopting the new liberal policy.
2. To review the nexus between the political elite and corporate sector.
3. To understand the basic notions of public anger and frustration and to analyze the action taken by the Indian state in dealing and addressing such concerns.

## Decision Making and Corporate-Sentiment

Democracy is not just a form of government. It has many meaning and concerns. Particularly in the Indian context, democracy is a tool and instrument of empowerment of a large section of the marginalized and deprived section of the society. India, where 25 lakh Dalits and *Adivasis* live together democracy is a ray of hope for them. Dr. Ambedkar had rightly pointed out that without establishing social and economic democracy, the basic goal and purpose of political democracy will not that. In modern context, Amartya Sen also talks about enlargement of choices through democracy (HDR 1991)[3]. After Independence, Indian state was sensitive towards goals of the establishment of social and economic democracy and series of provisions were made in the Constitution to realize this objective. However, after adopting new liberal policies, the basic character of state has changed completely.

Indian state seems apathetic towards the plight of marginalized groups including Dalits, Adivasis, women and minority groups. It completely ignores thirty-five crore poor, ten crores unemployed, forty per cent illiterate, five crore child labour, and sixteen crores physically challenged people. It is serving the basic interests of Bourgeoisie class only. The Indian state, which used to stand above classes before the neoliberal era has decisively shifted towards the big capital to the detriment of other classes. In other words, the Indian state is abdicating it's primary Constitutional responsibilities and drifting away from the Democratic sensitivity and concerns. The state has failed in its endeavour to fulfil the burgeoning demands and expectations of the ordinary populace leading to present mess. Old glory and power of the state has dwindled, and Common Masses that relied on the state have greatly disappointed. They feel that state is no longer capable of addressing their problems (Kothari 2003:76). On the other hand, the market is occupying the space vacated by the state. Many examples prove this submission and preposition.

In 1993, Enron operation in India offered a classic example of the crisis of nation-sate and its complete surrender in front of the MNC's (Roy 2006:8). In 1993, the Maharashtra state Electricity Board (MSEB) and the Indian subsidiary of Enron Corporation, the Dabhol Power Corporation (DPC) Signed a contract for the supply of 695 megawatts of electricity. The terms of purchase of power from Enron were very high; despite that Congress Party-led government in the state signed the contract. The opposition BJP-Shiv Sena opposed this deal. This deal was a very hot issue in the state of Maharashtra hence when BJP-Shiv Sena came to power, they cancelled the contract. But, there was heavy pressure by Enron company and American Government, therefore, the State Government of Maharashtra renegotiated the deal with Enron without any changes from the previous contract and increased the value of the contract by three times. It was surprising because this total money was equal to sixty per cent total budget of rural development (Bharadwaj 2003:314). However, surprisingly Indian Government offered counter-guarantees to DPC in case the State Government failed to honour its commitments. When in may 1996, the 13-day minority government of NDA came to power they ratified the counter-guarantee agreement with Enron, just hours before resigning after its defeat in Parliament.[4]

In due course of time, DPC threatened to drag the Indian Government to the court of law. This was not the end of the story.

The Enron Corporation also started appealing directly to the people of India through an advertisement in the leading national daily. If you believe in the metaphor of power to the people, we urge you to think if the current imbroglio is in your interest (Sethi 2006:42). However, we all know that Enron declared itself bankrupt, and a heavy amount of public money was wasted.

This example illustrates many observations regarding working of MNC's in post-globalized India.

(a) MNC's operating in India, are so powerful that they are easily creating the crisis of democracy deficit in India.
(b) Whichever political party is ruling at centre and state, they have surrendered in front of global market forces.
(c) The process of democratization is so week in India that this surrender of state does not come out in the public domain.

This example of 1995-1996 shows how the forces of MNC's are creating crisis before Indian nation-state, and it seems incapable of taking strong decisions for the benefits of ordinary people of India.

Issue of pesticides in the product of Coca-Cola in India could be another example to show domination of MNC's over Indian state. In 2006, the Centre for Environment and Science (CES) disclosed that the Coca-Cola is full of pesticides in its scientific research. There was very hue and cry in the political gallery of India. In public pressure, Central Government banned the products of Coca-Cola in the canteen of Parliament of India. But later on, the ruling government refused to accept the study of Centre of Environment and Science and set-up a joint committee of parliament to set a standard for Coca-Cola. Before this, Coca-Cola argued that the water of India is poisonous and, product of Coca-Cola is not responsible for pesticides in its product.[5]

The then agriculture minister Sharad Pawar instead of taking any action compared it with mother's milk and said that is also contaminated nowadays. There may be truth to it, but this does not exonerate the Coca-Cola from its responsibility and cannot be given a clean chit to play with the lives and health of the people. Finally, this issue was taken up with American Government and American undersecretary of Commerce, argued with the Indian Government that any further reactions on Coca-Cola would affect American investment in India. Although, the report of Joint Parliament

Committee under the chairmanship of Sharad Pawar had acknowledged the availability of pesticides in the products of cola-cola and also suggested active measures in this regard, but as it happens its recommendations are lying in the cold storage. Hence, the story of Enron and Coca-Cola shows the complete surrender of India state before MNC's. In the post-globalization period, many Indian MNC's have also emerged and have their business interest across the world. However during this time, we could also see the nexus between ruling political elite and different capitalist groups in India. The above-mentioned examples are sufficient in throwing light on this unholy and unethical alliance.

The latest example is concerned with Indo-US Nuclear Deal. India signed a historic nuclear deal with The US in 2006. Manmohan Singh was Prime Minister then, led by Congress dominated UPA coalition. BJP, as a principle opposition party, opposed nuclear deal due for two reasons. First, it argued that the international liability norms concerning suppliers were unacceptable, that in the event of an incident like Fukushima, suppliers would escape both civil and criminal liability.[6] Secondly, BJP raised question against the need of such costly energy.

However, once in power, BJP Government, backed out of its earlier stance. Prime Minister Modi and American President Barak Obama agreed on earlier statement regarding nuclear-deal. Although, Section 46 and Section 17(b) of liability acts, still remains unsettled and unconvinced. Section 46 of the 2010 Act states that, "the provision of the Act shall be in addition to, and not in derogation of, any other law for the time being in force, and nothing contained herein shall exempt the operator from any proceeding which might, apart from this Act be instituted against such operator." Whereas Section 17(b) entitled the operator to the right of recourse against the supplier or his employee, *inter alia*, for a nuclear incident, for patent or latent defects, sub-standard supplies, services, equipment or material.[7]

The BJP led Government did not try to convince opposition party and Indian people. Modi proposed a nuclear risk pool with the help of Indian taxpayer money. This nuclear risk pool will have five govt. owned insurance companies providing half the capacity for the 1,500 crore pool, the rest will come from the Central Government[8]. This event shows that how elected Indian Government is not focusing on the concerns of their people. On the contrary, the American Government is just trying to benefit the American companies. It is interesting fact that Nuclear power is on the decline. It is generating less than 11 per cent of the world's electricity production. Germany is planning to phase out nuclear power by 2022[9] whereas Indian Government is giving preference to costly and dangerous electricity production of nuclear energy.

The pattern of decision-making process is such that it is showing indifferent attitude towards its people. It is focusing more on primary interests of Business group. This tendency induces unholy practices. It gives birth to unholy-nexus and unethical-alliance. This is reflected in different reports of CAG, a Constitutional body. It discusses the negative implications of this unholy alliance in post-globalized India. It observes that big cases of corruption happened only after the beginning of Economic reforms in India.

In the post-globalized India, the nature and pattern of corruption have changed somewhat. For example, the elected Central and State Governments provided benefits to business groups in various ways. In this process, adequate compensation is not provided to the ordinary people, and land is granted to private companies at very cheap rate. Also, the allocation of natural resources to Multinational Companies to do mining operations in tribal's inhabited areas without taking into consideration their needs and aspiration has also caused immense hardship to them and many of them are taking recourse to violence as they have lost hope in democracy and democratic process.

A study of Rochester Institute of U.S.A. has proved the co-relation between liberalization and corruption.[10] It states that in those countries, where democracy came before the process of liberalization, it caused corruption. The co-relation between corruption and liberalization is quite clear. The process of liberalization invites unrestricted flow of unholy money, supported by Government policies and programmers. The weak democratically elected government cannot regulate the market forces, which always try to maximize their profit by making an unholy alliance between corrupt bureaucracy and weak elected governments. This is clearly visible in case of India. RBI Governor Raghu Ram Rajan has mentioned this. He states that— "by killing transparency and competition, crony capitalism is harmful to free enterprise, opportunities, and economic growth." He further said that "one of the greatest dangers to growth of developing economies like India is the middle-income trap where crony capitalism creates oligarchies that slow down the growth."[11]

Different cases of Corruption in India in post-reform India could be supported by the following table: 13.1.

**Table 13.1:** Various Scams in Post-Liberalized India

| *Scams* | *Estimated amount* |
|---|---|
| Telgi Scam | Rs. 20,000 crore |
| Hawala Scam | Rs. 100 crore |
| Fodder Scam | Rs. 1000 crore |
| CWG Scam | Rs. 70,000 crore |
| Spectrum Allocation Scam (2G) | Rs. 1,76,000 crore |
| Coalgate Scam | Rs. 1,85,591 crore |

*Sources*: track.in|tags|business|2010|11|25|top-ten-corruption-scams-scandles-india.

Thus, we find that in the present democratic state of India, an unholy nexus between corrupt politicians and unethical private companies is prevailing. This is only one side of the story. The Indian Government is also supporting corporate in many other ways. Indian state should act, work and behave legally with different corporate companies, which are always guided by profit making. However, corporate sectors hardly adhere to laid down norms, rules, and regulations. Even then, Indian state seems sympathetic towards them.

In this connection, different studies regarding corporate sector show that their working is non-democratic, unethical and immoral. Some of these studies would throw some lights on this observation.

S.P. Shukla, a former bureaucrat and Member of the Planning Commission made the following observation regarding the global character of corporate sector and their relation with concerned government.[12]

**Table 13.2:** Revenue forgone to corporate sector under various tax schemes over the years

| *Items* | *2005-2006* | *2006-2007* | *2007-2008* | *2008-2009* | *2009-2010* | *2010-2011* | *Total revenue foregone 2005-06 to 2010-11* | *% Increase 2010-11 over 2005-06* |
|---|---|---|---|---|---|---|---|---|
| Corporate Income tax | 34,618 | 50,075 | 62,199 | 66,901 | 72,881 | 88,263 | 3,74,937 | 155.00 |
| Excise Duty | 66,760 | 99,690 | 87,468 | 12,893 | 1,69,121 | 1,98,291 | 7,49,623 | 197.00 |
| Custom Duty | 1,27,730 | 1,23,682 | 1,53,593 | 2,25,752 | 1,95,288 | 1,74,418 | 1,00,463 | 36.60 |
| **Grand Total** | **2,29,108** | **2,73,447** | **3,03,260** | **42,946** | **4,37,290** | **4,60,972** | **21,25,023** | **101.20** |

*Source*: *The Hindu*, 07 March, 2011, p. 08.

(a) The underlying reason for the steady increase in corruption in the globalized regime is due to the involvement of corporate world into government activities.
(b) Corporate houses have started deciding policies and prices of government transactions.
(c) Corporate houses are not influencing the individual bureaucrats and politicians but the system as a whole.

How Indian Government is supporting corporate houses is best represented by following data:

This table 13.3 is enough to prove that how duly elected democratic governments in India are working in the interest of corporate houses. The above table 13.2 also reveals that from 2005-2006 to 2010-2011, the Government of India has written off Rs. 21,25,023 crores. under the various tax scheme such as corporate income tax, excise and customs duty in the midst of the global economic slowdown. Surprisingly and interestingly, this amount is 12 times more than 2G spectrum scam.[13]

It raises various questions, and a very significant one is that despite having free press guaranteed by our Constitution why it mostly went underreported in media. Its answer lays in the character of media groups itself, which are at present working in India. Most of the media groups are managed and owned by big corporate houses. They always show their democratic concerns by highlighting corrupt practices of politicians and bureaucrats and raise the question about their credibility but remain silent on their corrupt practices. They always work to enhance their circulation and mostly guided by the profit motive.

It is quite evident that big corporate houses also get the benefit

**Table 13.3:** Effective corporate tax paid by corporate over the years

*(In Rs. Crore)*

| *Years* | *Tax Paid* | *Profit Before Tax* | *Effective Tax%* | *Taxable Income* |
|---|---|---|---|---|
| 2005-2006 | 78,669 | 4,08,444 | 19.26 | 2,48,758 |
| 2006-2007 | 1,14,316 | 5,56,190 | 20.55 | 3,41,606 |
| 2007-2008 | 1,58,225 | 7,11,557 | 22.24 | 4,79,898 |
| 2008-2009 | 1,52,280 | 6,68,581 | 22.78 | 4,49,085 |
| 2009-2010 | 1,93,869 | 8,23,937 | 23.53 | 5,39,408 |

*Source: The Hindu, Business Line*, 03 March, 2011, p. 4.

of tax payment. Very often, their taxable income is enormous but they pay fewer amounts of taxes. Surprisingly, effective tax percentage varies from 19-25 per cent only. The following data will substantiate my argument:

It is observed that the profit before tax is Rs. 8,23,937 crore, but declared taxable income is Rs. 5,39,408 after availing various tax breaks and exemption benefits.[14] The trend of an exemption to different corporate houses has been regular features of each and every Central Government of India. After ten years of UPA Government, NDA came to power, with the full majority to BJP in Lok Sabha elections of 2014. Mr. Narendra Modi became Prime-Minister. During first hundred days of Modi Government, one Lakh forty-five thousand seven hundred fifty-three crores have been given as tax exemption to richest one per cent business houses (Sainath 2015).

Benefits in the form of tax exemption to the corporate sector could be always observed, but corporate sector also tries to influence the government's decisions-making process in many other ways. Lobbying for their personal benefit by corporate companies is becoming very popular in the present political scenario in India which mostly used to be the trend in Europe and America. During UPA II, FDI in the retail sector was a hotly debated issue. When a bill regarding this was passed in Parliament, a sensational fact regarding Wall Mart appeared as breaking news in Indian media, through a report of American Congress on lobbying. In 2012, as part of a routine disclosure under US law, Walmart revealed it had spent 25 million Dollar since 2008 on lobbying to enhance market access for investment in India.[15] An example of Wall Mart in India does not mean that only foreign companies are indulged in lobbying in India. Indian multinational companies and their corporate bosses also try to influence the decision-making process.

In this regard, many questions cropped up, and voices were raised against nexus between politicians and corporate sector. Tapes of Nira Radia disclosed that half of media groups were directly trying to influence the decision-making process.[16]

Many other cases of corporate sector's involvement in the decision-making process can be observed. During 2012, Jaipal Reddy was removed as Petroleum Minister and was given a very insignificant Ministry.[17] According to media reports he had not supported Mukesh Ambani in K.G. basin issue.[18] So, he was punished although he had done enough work in closing the Ministries doors to corporate influence. Therefore, corporate influence in governance is like a contagious disease and is not only confined to Central Government even State Governments are also profoundly affected by it.

## Marginalization of Common People

Marginalization of ordinary people in India is also the by-products of the present crisis of Indian democracy. This hypothesis has supporters like Rajani Kothari[19] who believes that marginalization is an essential characteristic of the globalization process. This hypothesis completely applies to Indian democracy that is already explained earlier as how Indian democracy is tilting towards corporate interests. It obviously affects the Constitutional duty of an elected government. Kothari is highly critical of this and alleges that Indian Government is not fulfilling its Constitutional obligations.

On the other hand, big Multinational Companies are exploiting natural resources that have been defined by some scholars as Corporate Loot because loot of natural resources has been a common feature of this liberalization process. Natural resources, like mineral, land or water are being used by MNC's as they are getting a green signal from respective governments for its cruel exploitation for the profit motive. For instance, illegal mining in Odisha, Goa, and Karnataka is prohibited by Supreme Court's which means that mining operation was going on without following the basic norms and regulation of laws. Many cases of corruption have also proved this. A recent example is Coalgate Scam.

Displacement of *Dalits and Adivasis* in the name of so-called development is another outcome of this process. It has uprooted them, although this trend could be also seen in the pre-globalized era as well. For instance, after 1950, 2.13 million people have been displaced out of which only 25 per cent population has been rehabilitated (Roy and Day 2012). Even, the figure of displacement of the tribal population appears more cruel and pathetic. The percentage of displaced tribal population in total displaced population is 40.9 per cent. This scenario of development-induced displacement seems very horrible, but it is still going on.

Another trend of this marginalization process is also directly linked with the naxal problem in India. It is a by-product of long and continuous neglect by the state and its agencies which has resulted in giving birth to a sense of despair and hopelessness among tribal people. In the post-globalized era, it has gained new salience. Social scientist

Manorjan Mohanty supports this hypothesis (Mohanty 2006:3163). The Naxal problem has engulfed mainly those areas that are inhabited by tribal and *Dalit* people. For instance, in Bihar *Dalits* are the backbones of this problem. In her study, Bela Bhatia had tried to understand the voices of anger, frustration and violence of *Dalits*. She insists that this is a common feeling among *Dalits* in Bihar that Naxalites are more sympathetic and sensitive towards their problems. (Bhatia 2002:317) She admits that labourers and *Dalits* have been empowered in Central Bihar by Naxalite. Similarly, in Andhra Pradesh, the rural poor are the social base of Naxalites (Kishor 2006:10). In Odisha, 22 per cent population is tribal, which is associated with Naxal activities (Sundar 2006:3138). In Chhattisgarh, Bastar, Kanker, and Dantewada are the worst affected areas (Bhunsh, 2005:16). The areas are mostly inhabited by the tribals. In Maharashtra, Adivasis are the main sufferer in an operation against Naxals. Again, in Jharkhand *Adivasis* are the backbone of Naxalism. Much of the region is rich in mineral wealth and being opened up for industrialization (Ramakrishna 2005:4). Apparently, *Adivasis* in these areas feels the pattern of development and industrialization process as an attack on their old pattern of life and livelihood. In Eastern U.P., *Dalits* are mainly Naxals, who are mostly poor and Landless. Due to the globalization process, the policy of SEZ are supported, accepted and acknowledged. Obviously, it might be essential for development purposes, but land acquisition process, rehabilitation of *Adivasis* are not being handled properly by governments. Thus, frustration leads to a large number of deprived *Adivasis* raising anti-government slogans and extends support to Naxalites. The story of landless *Dalits* is also similar as they feel that government is insensitive towards their genuine problem while it continually encourages big corporate houses. This ignorance attracts them towards Naxalites.

In a nutshell, the process of globalization in India has failed to fulfil the genuine expectations and aspirations of marginalized section of the society, who constitute the support base of the Naxal movement. Naxal-dominated areas are among the poorest in the country. It is no coincidence at all that the tribal areas of Andhra Pradesh, Odisha, Chhattisgarh and Jharkhand, where the Maoist are most active, are also among the areas in the country that have the lowest development indicators (Pandey and Singh). Pandey and Singh have studied the naxal problem in India. They conclude, "State is more tilted towards corporatization. This is an immediate manifestation of frustration that may be seen in from of movement against the corporatisation of agricultural land hence Naxalism is gaining a new support and acceptance in the era of globalization. The Prime Minister, as well as the Union Home Minister, has also declared it as the biggest internal security threat to the Country (Roy 2012:12-34). But, nothing concrete has been done so far by respective Union Governments.

Post-globalized India has also created inequality among common masses. The great divide between rich and poor has increased with alarming proportion. For instance, India's 100 richest people own assets equivalent to one-fourth to the GDP. According to the facts presented by global wealth intelligence firm in India, the richest, 8200 people have wealth of 472.50 billion which is equal to 70 per cent of whole Indian economy.[20] On the other hand, the poorest, hungry and malnourished people of the world also live in India. It is a great paradox that numbers of billionaires are increasing very rapidly in India and also across the world[21], but surprisingly, a large number of people are still not getting basic facilities. This clearly reflects that fruits of development are being cornered by a tiny segment of the population.

This contradictory trend of new globalized India could be concluded in words of Arundhati Roy, "In India, the 300 million of us who belong to the new, post-IMF "reforms" middle-class—the market-live side-by-side with spirits of the nether world, the poltergeists of dead rivers, dry wells, bald mount and denuded forces; the ghost of 2,50,000 debt-ridden farmers who have killed themselves, and of the 800 million who have been impoverished and dispossessed to make way for us. And who survive on less than twenty rupees a day" (Roy 2012).

## Repressive Measures against Common People

Theoretically speaking, votaries of globalization always emphasize upon its trickle-down effects across the globe (Stiglitz 2002:17). But trickle-down effect appears only self-justifying prophecy of its ideologue. Its successes story remains unsatisfying in most of the countries of the world (*ibid.*). No wonder, Indian experience remains the same. The corporatization of Indian democracy, marginalization of ordinary people and invisible corporate loot in the name of development have completely changed the traditional face and character of Indian ruling elite, which always propound a popular slogan in the name of common people.

Democracy does not mean only electoral politics. It always deals with common man inspiration and aspiration. Hence, it should always try to fulfil its socio-economic commitment towards ordinary people, which in case of India is mentioned in our Preamble and Directive Principals. Surprisingly, the Indian Government does not appear serious, sensitive and honest about their Constitutional commitment in post-liberalized era. This trend indicates that democratic regimes do not tolerate dissents, anger, agitation and frustration of common people through peaceful means. In most of the cases of democratic movements, the state uses coercive measure against them. Elected governments always try to curb these movements.

Kavaljit Singh, in his book "*Questioning Globalization*" discusses many repressive measures adopted by the states. He says, "There have been several instances (e.g.: Shell in Nigeria and mass protest against structural adjustment programmes in Mexico, Argentina, Venezuela and Indonesia) where the governments took repressive measures against their people in order to protect the interests of transnational capital (Singh 2005:169).

India is no longer, an exception to this repressive character of the state. Across the nation, the farmers, *Dalits, Adivasis,* poor and common people are protesting against governments, elected by them, as they work for the benefit of corporate sectors and ordinary people remain deprived. At both levels, Central as well as State, repressive measures are used against these apolitical and self-motivated local and ground level movements. Protest against SEZ could be seen in many States of India like West Bengal, Rajasthan, Uttar Pradesh, Haryana, Chhattisgarh, Jharkhand, Kerala, Punjab, Delhi, Maharashtra, Karnataka, Andhra Pradesh, etc.

This long list of democratic dissents and anger raise serious question regarding the democratic viability of democratically elected government and also raises the question regarding suitability and relevance of democracy. In other words, whether something is wrong with democracy itself or is it the application of brute force in the name of safeguarding democracy that needs to be condemned is a question that needs to be addressed.

## Hope for Future

It is quite clear that change of character of Indian democracy appears a hard fact in Indian politics. This trend among democratically elected governments could be visible across the globe. It does not mean that there is no way out to address this grave challenge. Indian experience and circumstances appear entirely different as it has a long tradition of democratic culture. Hence, democratization of politics could be parallel solution to the corporatization of Indian democracy in many ways:

(i) Unholy nexus between the political elite and corporate players are primarily responsible for series of corruption cases. Public vigilantism can check this trend of Indian politics. In recent years, after series of movements by civil society groups, particularly active protest by Anna Hazare and Swami Ramdev, issues of corruption has occupied an important place in the public domain and discourse. Obviously, if this momentum continues, it has the potential to check this unholy alliance of corporate sector and political elite by mobilizing public opinion.

(ii) New political players have emerged on the political horizon of India, who make corruption as the focal point in their political agenda. For instance, Aam Adami Party has added a new dimension to discourse on democracy in India. They forced established political parties to bring alteration in their style of functioning and change their attitude from being master of the people to be the servant of the people. How much change they would be able to bring about is difficult to predict at this juncture? Similarly, how much political mileage they would gain, is a matter of conjecture, but at least they have introduced an alternative discourse in Indian politics.

(iii) Local and ground level public movements appear very active nowadays. Water *satyagraha* of Khandwa in Madhya Pradesh and protest by the villagers near Kudankulam Nuclear plant in Tamil Nadu[22] has exhibited the power of the people at the ground level. March by landless farmers has also drawn the attention of Central Government. An estimated one lakh poor, landless poor people from across India marched from Gwalior in Madhya Pradesh to the capital New Delhi.[23] There are many such movements going on at present at different places that hardly find space in national dailies or electronic media because of their localized nature. Such self-governed movements would help in deepening as well as consolidating democracy and spread awareness among common masses.

(iv) In India, even though media is owned by big business houses and have their agendas but comparatively speaking, media in India is largely free. Debate and discussion that is aired is watched by the people at both urban and rural areas, and it largely helps them in shaping their opinion. Apart from that, print media is also playing a constructive role in this regard along with vernacular newspapers as it helps in the dissemination of information and helps in bringing about political awareness among people. However, it is yet to be quantifiably established as how the better-informed citizens exercise their right to bring pressure on the political dispensation to bring about substantial change and helps in making the government people-centric.

(v) The emergence of new middle class appears a positive and healthy trend in Indian politics. This middle class in India is vast. Their democratic aspiration is tilted in favour of Good governance and development. Many results of State legislative elections like Gujarat, Delhi, Bihar, M.P., Haryana have proved that the middle-class understanding of future Indian, politics is becoming more progressive.

(vi) Social media is also playing an important role in raising public awareness.[24]At the same time, it also connects people across the world. As we know India has the largest number of the youth population in the world. This youth population is the largest beneficiary of social media. In India, total numbers of Internet users are around 13.7 crores.[25] Along with this, a total number of Facebook account and Twitter I.D. are 6.8 crores and 1.8 crores respectively (Nayak 2013). Maybe, this involvement of youth would develop a new language and grammar of Indian politics. A large number of youth's appearance and protest in the rape case against Damini in Delhi shows a new hope for future, which would march toward better and effective politics.

(vii) Indian Judiciary seems somber about this process of corporatization of our politics. In many decision, the judiciary has taken firm steps against different corporate companies and given decisions in favour of common people. For instance, Supreme Court of India ordered Sahara group to return Rs. 24,000 crore to its investors. Supreme Court also rejected 122 licenses of private companies in connection with allotment of 2G spectrum.[26] This was a very bold step of Supreme Court against prevailing nexus between the corporate sector and ruling political elite.

(viii) The issue of corporate social responsibility is gaining more and more salience as civil society is also raising this issue. Private companies have started allocating money to philanthropic activities. They too are working for the causes of education, health and rural development. Azeem Premji of Wipro may be a good example of it. He has contributed eight thousand crores for educational development.[27]

(ix) RTI movement is also playing an important role in this regard. Different RTI activists have exposed private sectors supported by government.[28] Obviously, such type of stories published in media directly and indirectly influences public opinion against such corrupt practices.

Therefore, it can be concluded that present scenario of democratic deficit and governance failure has not been a permanent feature of Indian democracy. In future, the further democratization of Indian politics would help in establishing a more transparent, accountable and responsive democracy. As LAO-TZU has said, "*If a country is governed wisely, its inhabitant will be content*" (Lao-Tzu 1996:68).

## Notes

1. Thomas L. Friedman, *The World is Flat* (New Delhi: Penguin Books India), p. 241.
2. As Cited in Stephan Gill (1997): "Globalization, Democratization and the Politics of Indifferences," in James H. Mittelman, (ed.) *Globalization— Critical Reflections* (London:Lynne Rienner), p. 121.
3. *Quoted from Human Development Report,* 1991, p. 37.
4. "Proven Innocent Declared Guilty," An advertisement issued by Dhabhol Power Corporation, *The Times of India*, August 13, 2001, p. 3.
5. oneindia.com/2006/08/05/pawar-refuses-to-comments-of-ban-on-soft-drinks-1154928310.html accessed on March 15, 2015.
6. "Fact and Fission: The Indian Express." 20 August, 2015 <http://indianexpress.com/article/opinion/columns/fact-and-fission.

7. indianexpress.com/article/opinion/columns/fact-and-fission/accessed on February 17, 2015.
8. www.business-standard.com/article/current-affairinsurers-to-offer-rs-750-cr-capcity-for-nuclear-pool-rest-from-govt-115012500521-1.html, accessed on February 17, 2015.
9. www.bbc-com/news/world-asia-india-30978152.
10. https://www.researchgate.net/signup.sign.up.html, accessed on April 15, 2015.
11. www.thehindu.com/business/Economy/Crony-capitalism-hampers-economic growth/article6305270.ece accessed on March 20, 2015.
12. Cited in Rajkumar, Gandhian Philosophy of Trusteeship to overcome governance Deficit in a Globalized Regime, *Holistic Thought*, July-December, 2010, p. 26.
13. *Ibid.*
14. *The Hindu*, Business Line, 03 March, 2011, p. 4.
15. P. Sainath: 100 days of Narendra Modi—youtube, accessed on April 15, 2015.
16. www.nbs.edu/faculty/pages/item.aspx ?num, accessed on March 13, 2015.
17. http://www.bbc.co.uk/hindi/2012/10/121029-row-on-jaipal-ready-an.thml.
18. Is this it? *Business standard*, 30 October, 2012, p. 09.
19. http://businesstoday.in/story/reliance-industries-share-gain-following-cabinet-reshuffle/1/189448.html.
20. With 122 Billionaires India Fifth on rich list, *The Times of India,* March 19, 2013, p. 13.
21. articles.economictimes.indiatimes.com/2014-09-17/news/54024735-1-billionarie-wealth-combined-wealth-x-accessed on March 13, 2015.
22. *A Report published in Hindustan*, 03 October, 2012.
23. www.theguardian.comglobal-development/2012/1oct/02/india-handless-march-justice-in-pictures, accesseed on March 3, 2015.
24. Internet and Mobile Association of India, June 2012.
25. Kunal Pradhan, Election @2014, *India Today,* 20 February, 2013, p. 20.
26. www.thehindu.com/business/industry/sc-ticks-off-sahara-for-not-refunding-rs-24000-crore/article 4924200.ece, accessed on March 3, 2015.
27. timesofindia-indiantimes.com/india/azim-premji-tops-philanthropy-list-with-donation-of-rs. 8000-crore, accessed on December 27, 2014.
28. www.livemint.com/opinion/11QEOXAd/EOXadocvobsklv40MLo/Towards-a-transparent-state.html, accessed on March 24, 2015.

**References**

Alam, Javed (2007): *Loktantra Ke Talabgar*, (New Delhi:Vani Prakashan), pp. 137-148.

Bharadwaj, Atul (2003): Understanding the Globalization Mind Game, *Strategic Analysis*, Vol. 27, No. 3, July-September, p. 314.

Bhatia, Bhatia (2002): Naxalvadi Bante Dalit, Abhay Kumar Dubey, (eds.) *Adhunikta Ke Anine Me Dalit*, (New Delhi:Vani Prakashan), p. 317.

Bhunsh, Dioni (2005): Gurrila Zone, *Frontline,* October 21, p. 16.

Kishor, Amrinder (2006): Salva Judum Se Uljhi Naxalwad ki Guthi, *Hindustan,* 4 November, p. 10.

Kothari, Rajani (2003): "Janta Se Darte abhijan aur Kamjor hata rastra-rajya," in Abhay Kumar Dubey, (ed.) *Bharat Ka Bhoomandalikaran* (New Delhi: Vani Prakashan), p. 76.

Lao-Tzu (1996): *Tao Te Ching*, Kyle Cathie, London, p. 68.

Mohanty, Manoranjan (2006): Challenges of Revolutionary Violence, *Economic and Political Weekly,* July 22, p. 3163.

Nayak, Mahesh (2013): Kai Raston Ka Sahara, *India Today,* 13th March, pp. 8-9.

Ramakrishan, Venktesh (2005): The Naxalite Challenge, *Frontline,* October 21, p. 4.

Roy, Aruna and Nikhil Dey (2012): Antim Vikalp ho Vishthapan, *Danik Jagaran*, 10 June, p. 21.

Roy, Arundhati (2012): Capitalism: A Ghost Story, *Outlook*, New Delhi, 26 March, pp. 12-34.

——(2006) Do Turkeys enjoys thanks giving, *The Hindu*, 18 January, p. 8.

Sethi, Amit (2006): Colas Cornord, *Frontune*, 25 August, p. 42.

Singh, Amit Kumar (2013): Arthik Sudharon Ki Siyasat, *Kashmir Times,* 3 November, p. 6.

Singh, Kawaljit (2005): Questioning Globalization (London: Zed Books) p. 169.

Stiglitaz, Joseph (2002): *Globalization and It's Discontents* (New Delhi: Penguin Books), p. 17.

Sundar, Nandini (2006): Bastar, Maoism and Salwa Judum, *Economic and Political Weekly,* July 22, p. 3138.

# Index